T0271415

ROUTLEDGE LIBRARY EDITIONS:
AGRIBUSINESS AND LAND USE

Volume 15

AGRICULTURE AND ECONOMIC GROWTH IN ENGLAND 1650–1815

AGRICULTURE AND ECONOMIC GROWTH IN ENGLAND 1650–1815

Edited with an Introduction by
E. L. JONES

Routledge
Taylor & Francis Group

LONDON AND NEW YORK

First published in English in 1967 by Methuen & Co. Ltd

This edition first published in 2024
by Routledge
4 Park Square, Milton Park, Abingdon, Oxon OX14 4RN

and by Routledge
605 Third Avenue, New York, NY 10158

Routledge is an imprint of the Taylor & Francis Group, an informa business

British Library Cataloguing in Publication Data
A catalogue record for this book is available from the British Library

ISBN: 978-1-032-48321-4 (Set)
ISBN: 978-1-032-47087-0 (Volume 15) (hbk)
ISBN: 978-1-032-47903-3 (Volume 15) (pbk)
ISBN: 978-1-003-38642-1 (Volume 15) (ebk)

DOI: 10.4324/9781003386421

Publisher's Note
The publisher has gone to great lengths to ensure the quality of this reprint but points out that some imperfections in the original copies may be apparent.

Disclaimer
The publisher has made every effort to trace copyright holders and would welcome correspondence from those they have been unable to trace.

Agriculture and Economic Growth in England 1650–1815

edited with an introduction by
E. L. JONES

METHUEN & CO LTD
11 NEW FETTER LANE LONDON EC4

First published 1967 by Methuen & Co Ltd
Introduction © 1967 by E. L. Jones
Printed in Great Britain by
Richard Clay (The Chaucer Press), Ltd,
Bungay, Suffolk

Distributed in the U.S.A.
by Barnes & Noble Inc.

Contents

vi   *Contents*

Preface

The present series, of which this is the inaugural volume, will seek to fill a widening gap in the teaching of economic history. Its object is to bring to a larger audience the results of recent research on important topics which have first appeared in the academic journals. The original articles will be published *in extenso*, with their footnotes, a bibliography, and an editorial introduction which will define the main issues in each theme and relate the selected articles to their context in the argument. There is unlikely to be a consensus of opinion at any one time, of course, which the introduction and the body of articles will doubtless reflect. There will clearly be a continuing change in perspective as new research focuses upon new problems and changes the emphasis in the bids to resolve old ones. All subjects with life still in them (which means research) are in this position. However, the pace of change in economic history has recently been becoming more rapid, while its range has been widening. One of the characteristics of a rapid rate of growth in research tends to be that the journals grow in importance relative to books as vehicles for bringing new ideas into the debate. Increasingly, books take on a secondary role (with some important exceptions) of consolidating positions first staked out in the journals; and by the time the books have reached the shelves the frontier of research has often moved on. When the frontier is moving very rapidly indeed, then new work may never get consolidated in book form at all (which has been the case for the past fifteen years in the historiography of population change in Britain). It thus becomes progressively more dangerous in economic history, as in the sciences, to rely upon elderly textbooks for one's generalizations, even where they have grown old gracefully.

With periodical literature becoming a key medium for plotting new trends in a subject, the complexities of keeping up to date have become much increased. Apart from the great rise in the volume of work being published, recent decades have seen an explosion in the range of periodicals. Economic history has always been an eclectic subject, sustained by the infusion of new ideas and new work from scholars based originally in neighbouring social sciences, such as sociology, demography, geography, anthropology, (even medicine), as well as the heartlands of history and economics. In particular, the surge of research since 1945 upon the problems of economic growth – the biggest groundswell ever to have sustained the social sciences – has carried economic history forward with a wholly new momentum. The 'journal explosion' has come in the wake of this. Although *The Economic History Review* in England, the *Journal of Economic History* in the United States, and *Annales* in France remain the three main vehicles for new work, all the main journals in history and economic theory across the globe now carry much research in economic history. Their numbers also continue to increase. Among the many new specialized periodicals which have widened the range of sources so much – to cite just one or two of those in English founded in the last twenty years – there are the *Agricultural History Review*, *Business History*, *Comparative Studies in Society and History*, *Economy and History*, *Economic Development and Cultural Change*, *Explorations in Entrepreneurial History* (with its phoenix EEH/II), the *International Review of Social History* and the *Journal of Transport History*. At the same time, in Britain the economic historians have led an invasion into that twilight world of the county archaeological and antiquarian society journals, once full of flints and fossils.

Such a growing diversity of journals – the annual review of periodical literature published in *The Economic History Review* shows the extent of it – raises the premium on professional guidance through the maze. The operational problem of communication is now, *pace* Lord Snow, not so much between scientists and non-scientists, but between the practitioners and students of the six styles of physics or the five varieties of history. Economic history has also been expanding as a teaching subject in universities, colleges, and schools. Papers now appear at A-level and O-level examinations. Membership figures and print numbers of its journals continue to rise. This widening market, matched with the growing gap between the frontiers of research and the student, calls for new intermediary communication, new teaching media.

It is always said that presentations of selected reprinted material are dangerous: the more predigested and the more highly selective then the greater the dangers. Agreed. But selectivity and generalization are demanded increasingly by the logic of the situation so that the only operational choice lies in doing it well or doing it badly. The present series will attempt to guard against the worst evils. The introductions will be full and critical, and as in the present instance important contributions to scholarship in their own right. They will plan to explain and establish guide lines, rather than necessarily to resolve by arbitrary assertions the range of debate in the topics. An extensive bibliography leads on from the selected articles. The articles themselves will be printed with their original footnotes, which contain the references, qualifications, and guerrilla warfare supporting the main campaign waged in the text.

The British case history of economic growth and industrialization is of prime interest to economic historians and students of economic growth across the world. The first publications in this series will, therefore, concentrate upon different aspects of this wide theme. From this base it is hoped to move outwards in time and area and topic. In eighteenth-century England, which saw the effective stimuli leading into the first industrialization of any economy in the world, no subject is of greater relevance than the relationships between rural society and agriculture and the process of growth. In our own day many countries are finding to their cost that the success of industry in their five-year plans is all too dependent upon the farmer, the peasant, and the landlord. Important revaluations have also come to traditional interpretations in this field. It is therefore, on both counts, a suitable theme to begin the series, and no editor is better qualified to undertake it than Dr E. L. Jones of Nuffield College, Oxford.

PETER MATHIAS

Acknowledgements

The editor and publishers wish to thank the following for permission to reproduce the articles listed below:

Professor J. D. Chambers for 'Enclosure and Labour Supply in the Industrial Revolution' (*The Economic History Review*, 2nd series, Vol. V, 1953); M. A. Havinden for 'Agricultural Progress in Open-field Oxfordshire' (*Agricultural History Review*, Vol. IX, 1961); Hutchinson & Co Ltd for Lord Ernle's 'Obstacles to Progress' (Chapter III of *The Land and its People*, London, 1925); Professor A. H. John for 'Agricultural Productivity and Economic Growth in England, 1700–1760' (*Journal of Economic History*, Vol. XXV, 1965, with a postscript added March 1967); Dr E. L. Jones for 'Agriculture and Economic Growth in England, 1660–1750: Agricultural Change' (*Journal of Economic History*, Vol. XXV, 1965); J. M. Martin for 'The Cost of Parliamentary Enclosure in Warwickshire' (*University of Birmingham Historical Journal*, Vol. IX, 1964); Peter Mathias for 'Agriculture and the Brewing and Distilling Industries in the Eighteenth Century' (*The Economic History Review*, 2nd series, Vol. V, 1952).

Acknowledgements

The editor and publishers wish to thank the following for permission to reproduce the articles included below:

Editor's Introduction

THE BACKGROUND

By any measure of resources used or value of output agriculture was still much the largest sector of the economy at the end of the period which this volume surveys. Figures for 1811 and 1812 indicate that one-third of the total occupied population of Britain was engaged in farming, forestry, and fishing; that the value of land plus farm capital comprised almost two-thirds of the national capital stock; and that over one-third of the total national income was produced by agriculture.[1] Since the middle of the seventeenth century the country had made remarkable headway as measured by real income per head of the population, had seen forceful developments in several manufacturing industries and considerable expansion and sophistication in many other branches of technology and economic life. No matter if the changes to come in the nineteenth and twentieth centuries were to dwarf those of the preceding period: England had already achieved a higher level of economic development than the more backward countries in the world today. Our problem is to isolate the contribution which her agricultural sector made to this advance.

The web of rural activities was so vast and formed the setting for so many of the other productive enterprises of the time that it naturally clamours for attention from students of the entire process of economic growth. Accordingly, while studies of changes within agriculture continue to appear, any discussion of the development of the national economy is virtually certain to touch on agriculture's role. For a time this wider sphere was greatly taken up by analysis of the possible short-run influences on the size of harvest. Then, following the publication in 1962 of Deane and Cole's *British Economic Growth 1688–1959*, with its aftermath of erudite review

[1] Phyllis Deane and W. A. Cole, *British Economic Growth 1688–1959* (Cambridge, 1962), pp. 142, 161, 271.

articles, attention switched to the longer-run involvement of agriculture and the remainder of the economy. This is strictly in accord with the current preoccupation with the less-developed countries of the modern world, where almost by definition agriculture bulks large.

Britain, it is often said, is the worst exemplar for the population-swamped, backward lands. Professor Kuznets has calculated that already in the seventeenth century as little as 60 per cent of its labour force was in farming, whereas even in the other advanced countries of Western Europe (with the probable exception of Holland) the agricultural proportion did not fall to this level before the first quarter of the nineteenth century.[1] Special circumstances operated in Britain's favour, as also in the other early developed countries in Western Europe and North America, with Japan and European Russia. All these were quite industrialized before the First World War and they have held their lead ever since. The identification of the advantages in any one of them may thus be of value to those other countries which still seem bereft of a good hand of cards. No one should expect the historical record, with all its gaps and uncertainties, to offer a precise programme for economic development, yet it may surely indicate priorities.

In the case of eighteenth-century England, however, such a range of suggestions about the relation of agriculture to economic advance is current that confusion reigns. At one extreme it has been claimed that agriculture's greatest contribution was to contract smoothly, shedding factors of production to industry *en route*, and at the other that agricultural development was an indispensable prerequisite of industrial progress.[2] Surprisingly few writers have set out to list the ways in which agriculture may have contributed to economic growth

[1] Simon Kuznets, 'Underdeveloped Countries and the Pre-industrial Phase in the Advanced Countries: an Attempt at Comparison', in A. N. Agarwala and S. P. Singh (eds.), *The Economics of Underdevelopment* (New York, 1963), p. 143. This measure may mislead unless the extent to which farm workers engaged in rural domestic manufacturing is also stated, but for present purposes it is a sufficient index.

[2] The latest fashions are to play down the possibility that agriculture was an 'engine of growth' or to persist in asserting that agricultural and industrial developments were contemporaneous. See, e.g., Phyllis Deane and H. J. Habakkuk, 'The Take-off in Britain', in W. W. Rostow (ed.), *The Economics of Take-off*

and gone on to provide any really informed historical appraisal of each transaction.[1] Much of the literature therefore contains *ad hoc* suggestions running well ahead of real empirical knowledge and scattered among broad surveys of eighteenth-century economic history. The whole debate is further confused by diverse opinion as to the respective chronologies of industrial and agricultural advance. The recent tendency has been to push the origins of industrial change well back into the eighteenth century while simultaneously bringing its main weight forward to the railway era in the nineteenth century.[2] Modern research has also spread developments within agriculture over a longer time-span, although it is still not generally conceded that techniques began to improve strikingly in the seventeenth century, far earlier than was once thought.[3]

It is therefore difficult to bring the developments in agriculture into relation with those elsewhere in the economy. Farming in particular is so diverse regionally and in the mix of its products (each evolving continuously but unevenly) that its advance almost defies summing up. In a short space there is nothing for it but to resort to somewhat heroic simplification. I shall of necessity take a rather simple-minded view of the contributions of agriculture to the growing English economy, dealing one by one with a number of exchanges which in the real world were inextricably entangled and sometimes pulled in

---

into Sustained Growth (London, 1963), p. 69; Phyllis Deane, *The First Industrial Revolution* (Cambridge, 1965), p. 50; and M. W. Flinn, *The Origins of the Industrial Revolution* (London, 1966), p. 96.

[1] Exceptions are M. M. Postan, 'Agricultural Problems of Underdeveloped Countries in the Light of European Agrarian History', *Communications*, Second International Conference of Economic History, Aix-en-Provence (1962); Deane, op. cit.; and H. J. Habakkuk, 'Historical Experience of Economic Development' in E. A. G. Robinson (ed.), *Problems in Economic Development* (London, 1965), esp. pp. 123–5.

[2] See the succinct survey by Deane and Habakkuk, in Rostow, op. cit.

[3] J. H. Plumb, 'Sir Robert Walpole and Norfolk Husbandry', *The Economic History Review*, 2nd series, v (1952), should have long since prompted sharper questioning of the conventional notion of an 'agricultural revolution' limited to the later eighteenth century. Since 1952 there has, of course, been further work pushing widespread innovation back to the mid-seventeenth century, but resistance to this conception remains strong. It is still asserted that early instances of the growing of 'new' crops like clover or turnips were highly localized and that agricultural investment and innovation were crippled by low farm product prices until the mid-eighteenth century.

4 Agriculture and Economic Growth 1650–1815

opposite directions. The whole field of study is experiencing
the familiar paradox of the early stages of any academic
inquiry, that is a 'query explosion'. The modern literature has
multiplied the number of problems of which we are aware
without keeping pace either in solving them or accumulating
relevant data. What is needed now is a more intensive drive to
assemble evidence: there are plenty of minds ready to build or
demolish economic models based on any historical material
which is to hand, but so far there is barely enough in this sphere
for their activities to be rewarding. The words of the nineteenth-century polymath, Charles Babbage, seem to apply:
'Political economists have been reproached with too small a use
of facts, and too large an employment of theory . . . the errors
which arise from the absence of facts are far more numerous
and durable than those which result from unsound reasoning
respecting true data.'[1]

On these counts, I shall try to describe what we now know of
the springs, form, and timing of productivity changes in agriculture, and then to treat sequentially the main flows of resources between agriculture and industry in the eighteenth
century. There is a grave danger of making probabilities and
possibilities much too categorical when coping with them in a
brief space, and it is certainly possible to give only illustrative
examples of tendencies and trends, but given the space constraint little more can be done than to note the danger. Professor Habakkuk pointed out in 1958 that the problem is two-
fold – to explain 'why the output of English agriculture was so
much more "responsive" in the eighteenth century than in the
sixteenth' and to decide in what manner a rise in agricultural
investment and incomes stimulated industrial investment.[2]
In my introduction I shall discuss both issues. I shall not use

[1] Quoted by Jeremy Bernstein, *The Analytical Engine* (London, 1965), p. 42.
Italics supplied. Of facts on some themes we do have a superabundance – it is
sobering to realize how little specialists in this field have failed to respond to
Professor Fisher's tilt, a generation ago, at their peculiar obsession with the 're-
condite niceties' of land tenure. ('The Development of the London Food Market,
1540–1640', *Econ. Hist. Rev.* v [1935]).

[2] H. J. Habakkuk, 'The Economic History of Modern Britain', *Journal of
Economic History*, XVIII (1958), esp. p. 500. Professor Habakkuk and Miss Deane
have since urged that 'earlier bursts of economic growth had been checked by the
production barriers in agriculture.' (In Rostow, op. cit., pp. 68–9.)

my space to paraphrase the articles reprinted in the body of the volume, though each will be mentioned in its place. The articles have been chosen to stand on their own feet,[1] and taken together to provide an overview of our changing perspective on the origins and phasing of agricultural progress and the ways in which this influenced other parts of the English economy.

THE SPRINGS OF AGRICULTURAL PRODUCTIVITY
General

> *Do you or I or anyone know*
> *How oats and beans and barley grow?*
> *First the farmer sows his seed,*
> *Then he stands and takes his ease,*
> *Stamps his feet and claps his hands,*
> *And turns around to view the land.*
> *Waiting for a partner,*
> *Waiting for a partner.*
> *Open the ring and take one in.*

This traditional children's singing game might almost be an allegory of the primitive state of farming until the middle of the seventeenth century. It is thoroughly fatalistic. Despite the beginnings of a literature exhorting farmers to improve their techniques,[2] there might as well have been no body of scientific knowledge about husbandry matters. Farmers are presumed to have exerted little or no control (through their cultivations or fertilizer inputs) over the growth or yield of their crops – ' 'Tis not the husbandman, but the good weather, that makes the corn grow,' wrote Thomas Fuller, whose *Worthies of England* was first published in 1662. As the song suggests, farmers were at the mercy of the elements. Agriculture might in effect have been waiting, as it had waited throughout history, for some agency to burst the age-old ring of inflexible organization, rudimentary methods, and insufficient capital.

---

[1] Professor A. H. John has taken the opportunity of replying to criticism of his article which has been voiced since it appeared.

[2] See the chapter reprinted in this volume from Lord Ernle's *The Land and its People*.

A partner was indeed about to unite with the farmer, when in the late seventeenth century England was the special beneficiary of a 'commercial revolution'. Much wealth was generated by the rapid expansion of the export and re-export trades and much of it was invested in land by the successful merchant class, so great has the social magnetism of a country estate always been to Englishmen. As Josiah Child remarked as early as 1668, 'if a merchant in England arrives at any considerable estate, he commonly withdraws his estate from trade before he comes near the confines of old age'.[1] The rich merchant bought a country seat. Agriculture could not but be the gainer from this transfusion of trading capital, allied as it was to new farming practices spreading among a more progress-minded rural community. Several strands thus wove into one in raising the productivity of agriculture. They may for convenience be divided into advances in husbandry technique and improvements in agrarian organization.

Advances in Husbandry Technique
> *'Dutch commodities are but trash and trumpery.'*

The old view of an 'agricultural revolution' firmly placed in the second half of the eighteenth century still persists despite mounting evidence that it was merely a phase, although an agitated one, of changes which stretched well before and far beyond that time. Its organizing conception was of the Norfolk four-course shift (wheat/turnips/barley/clover) spreading on land enclosed by Acts of Parliament, and accompanied by brand-new advances in stock-breeding. Between the 1760s and 1815 Arthur Young was propagandizing for the Norfolk rotation; the parliamentary enclosure movement was at its height (supposedly sweeping away the static, forage-scarce farming of the open fields);[2] and the renowned breeders like Robert Bakewell were selling their over-fat animals to hobby-farming aristocrats amidst a blaze of publicity. But the choice

---

[1] Quoted by H. J. Habakkuk, 'English Landownership, 1680–1740', *Econ. Hist. Rev.*, x (1939–40), p. 11.

[2] On this compare the views of Lord Ernle in his chapter reprinted below with those of Michael Havinden in his article, 'Agricultural Progress in Open-field Oxfordshire', also reprinted below.

of these indicators makes the notion of 'agricultural revolution' in that period a self-fulfilling prophecy.

A more up-to-date interpretation would expand the base of the relevant changes and extend their time-span appreciably. The middle of the seventeenth century seems the most appropriate starting-point for the infinitely expansible improvement of farming practice. Observers like Charles Davenant, John Aubrey, and John Houghton were certain it was then that new husbandry systems flowered. Houghton pointed out 'the great improvements made of lands since our inhuman civil wars, when our gentry, who before hardly knew what it was to think, then fell to such an industry and caused such an improvement, as England never knew before'.[1] Documentary sources bear this out. The crucial innovations pertained to the supply of fodder, partly the diffusion of the turnip as a field crop but much more important at that early date the first widespread cultivation of clover, sainfoin, and ryegrass, with the vigorous 'floating' of water meadows (i.e. the irrigation of stream-side pasture).[2] These crops and practices, with later additions like the swede (a much hardier root), went on spreading into new counties, new estates, new farms, and new fields throughout the period which this volume covers. What is especially important to note is that well before the middle of the eighteenth century they had already colonized sizeable chunks of the country: this is of the utmost significance to understanding the chronology of agricultural change and its consequences.

[1] R. Bradley (ed.), *Husbandry and Trade Improv'd:* [by] *John Houghton* (1727) p. 56. The authoritative new *Agrarian History of England and Wales*, Vol. IV, 1500–1640 (Cambridge, 1967), edited by Joan Thirsk, contains few references to the forage crops though it notes that they became prominent after the mid-seventeenth century. The stock of ideas about new farming systems, and the range of plant species available, grew during Tudor and early Stuart times and seems first to have been drawn on heavily under the Cromwellians, when Samuel Hartlib was granted a pension for publicizing various utilitarian plants, and garrisons as far afield as Kirkwall taught the locals how to grow cabbages. See Mea Allan, *The Tradescants* (London, 1964), p. 184, and Eric Linklater, *Orkney and Shetland* (London, 1965), p. 81.

[2] These innovations and their consequences are further discussed in my article, 'Agriculture and Economic Growth in England, 1660–1750: Agricultural Change', reprinted below.

What may have inspired this long movement was a probable swing in the ratio of cereal to livestock prices from approximately 1650 to 1750 in favour of expanding livestock production. Fodder crops which had lain almost dormant in England during Tudor and early Stuart times, when grain prices were high relative to those for stock, were therefore extended. They were rotated with cereals in new systems of mixed farming. They fed fattening stock, the dung from which raised the yields of the cereal courses. By the second half of the eighteenth century, when there was renewed pressure on cereal production, there was no danger of a recession of forage crops. Mixed farming had come to stay, since either its fatstock or its cereal enterprises offered reasonable returns under most market conditions. Often both paid well.

The mechanism by which new crops and methods were diffused was evidently less through the early didactic literature reviewed by Lord Ernle in his section reprinted below than by a combination of landlord endeavour and the entrepreneurship of the larger farmers.[1] Landowners themselves were not enormously active in promoting the new techniques in detail, except perhaps in 'underdeveloped' districts like the Yorkshire Wolds,[2] but they and their agents were by no means inert.[3] Their direct participation was probably most important in the seventeenth century, when many of them returned from an exile which had afforded ample leisure for inspecting the advanced practices of Flanders.

In considering the spread of cropping innovations it is simplest to envisage English agriculture as made up of three parts. Firstly, there is the rearing country of the Highland

---

[1] As one example, by the second half of the eighteenth century Thomas Johnson of Wild Court Farm, Hampstead Norris, Berkshire, was selling turnip and clover seed to other farmers from a wide area of Berkshire, Hampshire, and Oxfordshire. Journal, Berkshire Record Office, D/Ex 62/2, 1764–94.

[2] See G. E. Mingay, 'The Large Estate in Eighteenth-century England', *Contributions*, First International Conference of Economic History (Stockholm, 1960), p. 378.

[3] See for example Edward Wallwyn's instructions to his agent on introducing the swede to his Herefordshire tenantry in 1795. E. L. Jones, 'Agricultural Conditions and Changes in Herefordshire, 1660–1815', *Woolhope Transactions*, XXXVII (1961), pp. 41–2.

Zone, which may be left aside as it seems hardly to have been penetrated by the 'new' crops. Then alternating across the Lowland Zone are the light soils of the chalk, limestones, light loams and more fertile sands, and the heavy soils of the clay vales.[1] Left for centuries under sheep pasture, the light soils were now found to hold the advantages for mixed farming. They were free-draining, their working season was long, their traction costs were low. Unaided, they had been too infertile to sustain permanent cropping, but with the introduction of fodder crops – notably legumes which fix their own nitrogen – rotations of these and cereal courses could be maintained. The Norfolk four-course was only one rather limited variant of these light land rotations. Novel farming systems appeared early in many light-soiled localities besides the famous 'good sands' of West Norfolk. Everywhere these systems disturbed the existing dependence of the light lands on access to the better 'natural' (that is, unsown) pasture of the low vale country. For example, the steward of an estate at Croft wrote of the Lincolnshire Wolds about 1725 that 'of late, since the practice of improveing Lands with Turnops is set up, they take y^t [that] way of so improveing their own lands, & feeding ye sheep themselves . . . a great detriment of letting ye Marsh Lands so well as heretofore'.[2]

The ill-drained vales and heavy soils, for long one of the country's main 'granaries', could not take up the 'new' crops so readily. Such soils were especially unsuited for growing roots. Further, although there was no exact correspondence, many of the heavier soils in central England were farmed on the old common-field plan and within their communal system were sociological rigidities and a lack of capital to buy lean stock to fatten which impeded the adoption of fodder crops. Available case studies show only a sluggish uptake of the 'new' crops in heavy land localities. The rigidities were not as severe a

---

[1] The management advantages of light land and disadvantages of heavy land are described in E. John Russell, *The World of the Soil* (London, 1961), pp. 244–55. My discussion also leaves aside the infertile lowland heaths.

[2] G. Eland, *Shardeloes Papers of the 17th and 18th centuries* (O.U.P., 1947), p. 61.

constraint as was once believed,[1] but they were present. Had they not been, common fields might have survived to this day as more than rare museum pieces like Laxton and Yarnton.[2]

The large, privately occupied farms freshly taken into cultivation on the light-soiled uplands suffered no comparable disabilities. Their forage and grain courses were pinned together by the device of the sheepfold, which had made much of the southern chalkland fertile by Defoe's day. ' 'Tis more remarkable still,' he observed, 'how a great part of these downs comes by a new method of husbandry, to be not only made arable, which they never were in former days, but to bear excellent wheat, and great crops too . . . for by only folding the sheep upon the plow'd lands, those lands, which otherwise are barren, and where the plow goes within three or four inches of the solid rock of chalk, are made fruitful.'[3] The sheep were fed during daylight on the 'artificial' forage crops and folded at night to dung and tread the land sown to cereals. Higher crop yields were one result, though as has been mentioned the system was perhaps first brought into being by a desire to increase the output of livestock products. On the light lands the rise in total output beyond the previous return of scanty mutton and a wool clip was clear. On the heavy lands the small farmers were financially distressed because of the new competition from the light soils or because they could not adapt to market changes, but although they do not seem to have been able to amend their ways, neither – in a pre-industrial society – did they have much option but to keep on farming. The net effect was surely an expansion of output in agriculture as a whole. To take a single illustration, the situation in Gloucestershire was summed up by Thomas Rudge in 1803 as follows: 'The HILL district includes the Cotswolds . . .

---

[1] Compare once again the literary work by Lord Ernle with the investigation of the primary documents by Mr Havinden, but note that Havinden's examples of particularly flexible open-field systems come from light land on the edge of the Cotswolds. A new study of a common-field village in Buckinghamshire emphasizes how belatedly the fodder crops often came in. (A. C. Chibnall, *Sherington* [Cambridge, 1965].)

[2] Laxton in Nottinghamshire is properly preserved by the Ministry of Agriculture. Yarnton Lot Mead in Oxfordshire ought to be.

[3] Daniel Defoe, *A Tour through England and Wales*, Everyman edn, n.d., I, p. 187.

Within the last hundred years a total change has taken place
on these hills. Furze and some dry and scanty blades of grass
were all their produce, but now with few exceptions the downs
are converted into arable inclosed fields ... The VALE includes the whole tract of land, bounded by the Severn on the
west and the Cotswolds on the east ... The produce ... has
continued nearly the same for many centuries.'[1]

In addition to the better nutrition which new forage crops
ensured,[2] livestock were being more systematically bred. This
was not restricted to the hey-day of the market in pedigree
fatstock in the late eighteenth century but was under way long
before, although the earlier exchanges between breeders have
left few traces.[3] Few as they are, signs of an early and quite
widespread concern with the systematic breeding of both cattle
and sheep are to be found. Peter Mathias has suggested to me
that this interest may have been an outgrowth of the attention
which Restoration gentlemen lavished on breeding swifter fox
hounds and Arab horses. This is very plausible.

About 1670 John Franklin was already upgrading the cattle
and sheep of his enclosed farm at Cosgrove in Northamptonshire with an eye to the London market and the dealer who
came down by coach every autumn to purchase his fatstock.[4]
Franklin catches our gaze through the exceptional chance of
having a descendant who has written about his farming. There
must have been innumerable unsung agriculturists who about
the same time were mating picked sires and dams. Their choice
of pairs was guided still by intuition rather than performance
records, but at least they were making cattle and sheep more
docile and easier to fatten, by selection 'for frank mental
deficiency'.[5]

[1] *The History of the County of Gloucester* (Gloucester, 1803), I, pp. xviii–xix.
[2] By 1674 Anthony Wood reported that meat was now rarely spiced, probably
because meat from animals fed on the new forage crops was of better quality (and
being in greater supply was not stored so long) than formerly. David Ogg, *England in the Reign of Charles II* (Oxford, 1934), I, pp. 68–9.
[3] I was wrong to exclude systematic stock-breeding from the pre-1750 innovations discussed in my article below. Relative price movements probably favoured
attention to better breeding, while the growing number of enclosed pastures
assisted farmers to determine which animals mated.
[4] T. B. Franklin, *British Grasslands* (London, 1953), p. 90.
[5] P. B. Medawar, *The Future of Man* (London, 1960), p. 120.

Some other early selective breeders come more fully into view. Sir Thomas Gresley of Drakelow, Derbyshire, was recorded as owning a dairy of Longhorn cows all chosen for similarity in colour and conformity by 1720. He was followed by Webster of Canley, Warwickshire, who began with Drakelow stock. And to show that the eminent breeders of the late eighteenth century were not blazing an untrodden trail, Robert Bakewell himself then started with some Canley heifers, lineal descendants of one of which were still in his herd at his death.[1] Even more indicative of a sturdy trade in carefully bred animals, though it barely breaks the surface of the historical record, is an observation of the 1730s that 'of late years there have been improvements made in the breed of sheep by changing of rams and sowing of turnips and grass seeds, and now there is some large fine combing wool to be found in most counties in England'.[2]

Improvements in Agrarian Organization
These developments in the methods of farm production were a yeast trying to ferment a rather cold agrarian structure. They come first because they represent the most sharply changing element within agriculture and the one which contributed most obviously to rising production during our period. The matrix of tenurial arrangements, farm-size distribution and field lay-out within which they acted did alter consistently in favour of large-scale production for the market, but comparatively slowly. The organizational evolution formed a centuries-old continuum in England; so did technical advances, but as decisive an upturn as can ever be detected in the rate of agricultural change occurred in their case in the mid-seventeenth century. Novel systems of husbandry thus account much more for the new 'responsiveness' of agricultural supply than do improvements in agrarian organization. Only during the French wars at the end of the eighteenth century was struc-

[1] C. S. Orwin, 'Agriculture and Rural Life' in *Johnson's England* (Oxford, 1932), p. 277.
[2] Arnold Toynbee, *Lectures on the Industrial Revolution of the 18th Century in England* (New York, n.d.), pp. 41–5, quoting a *Pamphlet by a Woollen Manufacturer of Northampton* (1739). Cf. p. 174, n. 4, below.

tural change greatly accelerated. Further, while in the long run organizational improvements did make agriculture flexible – particularly compared with the Continent – they did not inevitably lead to increasing productivity. Often their impact was on the shares of the proceeds of agriculture which different social classes received. Better farming practices on the other hand led straightaway to rising productivity.

The most dramatic aspect of change in the agrarian framework was parliamentary enclosure, the chronology of which may be indicated as follows:

Numbers of Enclosure Bills, 1730–1819		Acres of common pasture and waste enclosed by Acts of parliament	
1730–1759	212	1727–1760	74,518
1760–1789	1,291	1761–1792	478,259
1790–1819	2,169	1793–1815	1,013,634

Source: Deane and Cole, op. cit., pp. 94 n. 3, 161 n. 1, 272 n. 1, drawing on State Papers, 1836, VII; Slater; and Gonner.

This conveys the impression that the reallocation of common fields and the reclamation of 'waste' (lightly grazed land) welled up late in the period. It throws the weight of change very heavily on the later years. This is partly an artefact of excluding enclosure by agreement and all reclamation on privately held land. Since these procedures were simpler and cheaper than those of parliament they were usually carried out early and legislation was resorted to only in more stubborn instances. The non-parliamentary evidence has never been codified – to attempt it for more than local areas would be a prodigious task, rendered incomplete in any case by gaps in the manuscript sources[1] – but if it could be included a different chronology would emerge. Parliamentary enclosure would appear as the culmination of a process of land reallotment, reclamation, and fencing into separate parcels stretching far back in time. Similarly, since parliamentary enclosure was strongly concentrated in central England, the inclusion of adequate data from the eastern and western flanks where piecemeal enclosure and reclamation had long preceded it would reinforce the account

[1] The most instructive effort is W. G. Hoskins, 'The Reclamation of the Waste in Devon, 1550–1800', *Econ. Hist. Rev.*, XIII (1943), esp. pp. 90–1.

of a steadier rate of structural change. The apparently rapid upswing represented by the parliamentary enclosures of the second half of the eighteenth century [1] would not be steam-rollered out of existence by the inclusion of other evidence, but it would be somewhat flattened.

Tenurial and managerial organization also gradually improved. The latest summary of work on the distinctively English landlord–tenant symbiosis refers to the pattern of land distribution as 'of great continuity and stability coupled with a definite but gradual growth of great estates'.[2] The great estates did expand between the end of the seventeenth century and 1790, but the mid-eighteenth century marks no upturn, while 'relative growth, it must be emphasized, was always very gradual'. The estates of the lesser gentry were also expanding and a class of absentees among the smaller landowners was emerging, but again only steadily. These developments were largely the outcome of social factors – 'prestige-maximization' on the part of England's well-to-do, to whom the social values of an estate made up for the lower monetary return than trade or industry.

Farming proper was something done by tenants. Landowners provided the capital-in-land. They threw farm units together in order to create more efficient holdings and they paid for the fixed capital on the farm. The growth of an estate system where the owners often possessed large extra-agricultural resources which they were willing to invest in the land was crucial in raising English agriculture from the rut of capital-starvation in which the continental peasantry remained stuck. Investment by landowners was helped by the appearance of the long-term mortgage about the middle of the seventeenth century, together with a fall in the rate of interest. This had usually been 10 per cent to landowners before 1625 but was seldom above 5 per cent after 1680.[3] At first land-

---

[1] Especially in the final war years. Since the procedures were increasingly costly this means that there was a rise then in this component of agricultural investment.

[2] F. M. L. Thompson, 'The Social Distribution of Landed Property in England since the Sixteenth Century', *Econ. Hist. Rev.*, 2nd series, XIX (1966), pp. 505–17.

[3] H. J. Habakkuk, 'The English Land Market in the Eighteenth Century' in J. S. Bromley and E. H. Kossman (eds.), *Britain and the Netherlands* (London, 1960), p. 160.

owners met barriers of inadequate working capital, ignorance, and lack of initiative among the farm community, so that in the early eighteenth century 'there was in fact a market in good tenants, and the inducements which competing landowners offered were improvements'.[1] Management and enterprise among farmers did, however, become more satisfactory.

Part of the increased managerial efficiency stemmed from the intervention of the landowners' stewards or agents: Thus in 1749 a tenant at Tong in Shropshire agreed that 'with respect to my Tillage, I am to be governed by his Grace's Steward, and to lay down each year so much in clover and Grass Seed as I shall be allowed to take up of Ley Ground'.[2] But much of it evidently came from the emergence of a more informed class of farmers, tenants many of them, especially on the new farms carved from the sheep downs of the light lands. One substantial Hampshire chalkland farmer repeatedly interspersed his accounts with the eager phrase 'Land for money and money for Land'.[3] Up on the Cotswolds the occupier of Bowldown Farm near Tetbury, a John Smith who arrived there in 1744, wrote down what he termed his 'system of farm management' (it was a six-course rotation which extended the four-course by keeping the seeds down for a second year and taking oats after wheat) and sent rules for the economical running of a farm business to a Major Ogilvie at Montrose. The occupier of a nearby farm at Didmarton recorded the annual produce from 1774, switched from a five-course rotation to John Smith's six-course about 1781, and left among his papers observations on the merits of threshing by hand or by machine, with calculations of the cost of almost every task on the farm.[4] And down on Romney Marsh it was reported in 1786 that the graziers

[1] Habakkuk, 1939–40, loc. cit., p. 14.
[2] G. E. Mingay, *English Landed Society in the Eighteenth Century* (London, 1963), p. 173. Cf. note 3 on p. 8 above.
[3] Farm Book of James Edwards, 1744–53, Hampshire Record Office, 2M37/338.
[4] J. C. Morton, 'A Lifetime on the Cotswolds', offprint from *Gardeners' Chronicle and Agricultural Gazette, c.* 1863, pp. 4–6. Subsequent occupiers at Didmarton were still continuing the annual production records when Morton wrote.

'keep a register of all their stock, noting down the number of the whole, and in what fields .... how many of each have died – what their skins sell for – when any are sold, the price they are sold for and to whom. The number of Bullocks they take in from the Farmers and at what charge per head per week – the price they sell their wool at and the number of Packs – their rent – their assessments and their other expenses, with every other particular relative to their businesses during the course of the whole year; and by casting up the Debtor and Creditor's side they know to a farthing the profit or loss of every year'.[1]

On all sides there was evidence of a constant advance in farm business methods.[2]

The units on which farmers operated were changing for the better, at least on the reasonable assumption that larger and better-equipped holdings were a benefit to agriculture. This was the result of the amalgamation of farms and their consolidation from intermixed open-field strips and scattered fields. Landowners were seeking more professional advice about these matters. They received recommendations like that offered by Nathaniel Kent when he was brought in to survey Lord Malden's extensive Herefordshire lands in 1786–87. He proposed exchanges so that certain parcels of land might be relet to neighbouring farms where land of that particular type was more needed, and pressed that some small farms might with advantage be 'melted down into the others'.[3] This was indeed already happening on Lord Malden's estate, and in fact widely. 'In general,' it has been concluded, 'eighteenth-century conditions encouraged a persistent bias towards larger farms occupied by tenants rather than freeholders', while 'there was a

[1] [Daniel Jones], 'Sheep Farming in Romney Marsh in the XVIII Century', *Wye College Occasional Publications*, 7 (1956), pp. 14–15.

[2] The keeping of farm records was not confined to an exceptional few. See E. L. Jones and E. J. T. Collins, 'The Collection and Analysis of Farm Record Books', *Journal of the Society of Archivists*, III (1965), pp. 86–9, and E. J. T. Collins, 'Historical Farm Records', *Archives*, VII (1966), pp. 143–9. The collection which Mr Collins assembled from private hands for the University of Reading in 1965–66 bears this out.

[3] See Jones, 1961, loc. cit., pp. 43–4.

long-term tendency towards larger and more efficient units
even in open-field villages, and enclosure merely tended to
hasten this process'.[1]

Nevertheless, the small farmer was neither swept away by
enclosure nor entirely bought out of existence by the bigger
landowners. The growth of population from the mid-
eighteenth century actually increased the demand for small
farms, which since quite high rents were offered it often paid
to satisfy. Very large and very small tenanted holdings may
have been increasing at the expense of the intermediate range.
At the upper end of the scale the amalgamation of farms into
larger units operated by a smaller number of more capable
tenants was not, however, always accompanied by the
thorough consolidation of their newly enclosed fields.
The process of building larger farm units and bringing them
within ring fences was being accomplished by the buying-out
of small freeholders, by private exchanges and by enclosure.
Since larger enclosed farms were more progressive technically the drift was advantageous. Yet it was slow. It has not
always reached its goals today.

The pattern of the countryside and the agrarian organization which evolved in England made production more flexible
and far more responsive to the market than a peasant system
could have been. However, structural improvement was a
sedate procession winding its way down the years, while
better husbandry practices made the real running. Technical
advance made a more conclusive contribution to rising agricultural productivity.

CONTRIBUTIONS TO ECONOMIC DEVELOPMENT
The Supply of Food and Raw Materials
The self-evident functions of an agriculture are, firstly, to
supply food and certain desirable beverages. Secondly, it
should afford industrial raw materials, notably for clothing and
footwear but also in our period for other goods like soap for
washing and tallow for candles so that the well-scrubbed

[1] Mingay, op. cit., pp. 89, 183.

results might be seen and admired. To these might be added, thirdly, the provision of fodder for the large number of horses which was vital to keep traffic moving by pulling wagons on the roads and barges along the waterways.

Napoleon's dictum that an army marches on its stomach applies *a fortiori* to a nation. Had agriculture failed in its primary task (given no overseas sources of supply), so that the population was regularly thinned by famine or alternatively growing equally fast as the supply of food, we need proceed no farther. The interest of agriculture would be restricted, as with any stagnant system, to understanding its built-in constraints. Society would have been so occupied in struggling to maintain output from the land that at best there would have been a minute surplus of income for spending on industrial goods: economic growth would have been checked by the inflexibility of agricultural supply. This was the fate of France through much of our period, just as it is the misery of mankind in many less-developed countries today. English agriculture was more vigorous. It shook off the dead hand of the 'crises of subsistence' which periodically afflicted wide areas of France.

English agriculture started well. Until the 1760s the country exported more and more grain. This was reversed during the third quarter of the eighteenth century. Plenty was again attained at the end of the seventies and in the eighties (when temporarily the tide of parliamentary enclosures and transport improvements ebbed), but shortages returned in the French wars with which one century ended and the next began. There were cases of starvation among the very poor in 1795–96 and 1800–1,[1] and presumably other deaths from hypothermia due to insufficient food and fuel. Even the rich suffered the shocking embarrassment of requiring a certificate to show that they were burdened with more than a brace of unmarried daughters before the girls could titivate themselves with hair-powder made from flour which their less fortunate neighbours might have been glad to eat.

[1] T. S. Ashton, *An Economic History of England: The 18th Century* (London, 1955), p. 235.

Taking the long view to which twentieth-century comfort conduces we can, however, see that these shortages did not last, but served to spur the heavy agricultural investment of the Napoleonic wars. After a bumper harvest in 1813, our period ended with ample food supplies. In any case, neither the export of cereals before 1750 nor much less the import subsequently was equivalent to more than a small fraction of home consumption. It is reasonable to conclude that agriculture more than adequately supplied the country's wants until the mid-eighteenth century (without fatally depressing farm-gate prices) and failed to do so afterwards only by the slenderest margin.

The expansion of output was helped by definite economies in the use of the materials produced. Striking illustrations of this increased efficiency are displayed by Mr Mathias in his article reprinted below. He shows how the waste grains from important agricultural processing plants – distilleries, breweries, and starch yards – were all absorbed in fattening large numbers of hogs for the metropolitan market. Later, many lean cattle were fattened too. This novel and sophisticated 'industrial agriculture' was based on several thrifty linkages. For instance, the waste grains became available in the cooler months, when the processes of brewing and distilling were carried out, precisely when feed for livestock was otherwise scarcest. Ordinary farmers might, of course, winter-feed barley to animals, but if the harvest were poor and barley dear they would buy fewer beasts to fatten and the price of store stock would fall. The distillers would then be well-placed since they had to buy barley come what may and were, of course, left with waste grains to dispose of – while animals to fatten were cheap. They could thus offset the costs of their main business by comparatively high returns from the sideline of stock fattening. The only weakness of the system was that manure from the city-fed animals was flushed away instead of being returned, as it would have been on the farm, to the soil. The dung was too bulky to collect from the London distilleries.

Otherwise, the eighteenth century saw a more economical interlocking of the harvest and the leavings of the drink trade with the production of fat hogs and cattle for the butcher, the tallow chandler, the soap boiler, and the leather currier. Like mixed farming, 'industrial agriculture' neatly re-used most of its by-products. At this most advanced end, the business of agriculture had become enormously complicated, with subtle changes in productive methods taking over from one another as the costs of different feedstuffs altered from season to season.[1]

English agriculture, then, was approximately successful, even when most strained by the inflation, population pressure, and glowering blockades of the Napoleonic wars. Valuable results flowed from this, beyond the fundamental go-ahead which it gave to the growth of population. Sufficient food supplies and raw materials helped to minimize the upward movement of industrial wages and input costs. Consumers found elbow room for the purchase of industrial goods. In addition, there was a small but useful contribution to the balance of payments. As Professor John argues in his article reprinted below, grain exports ensured command over foreign currency in the first half of the eighteenth century when European markets for British manufactures were dull. France paid 10·5 million *livres* for British cereals in 1748–50. A similar exchange was noted in 1739: 'there being at present a great scarcity of corn in many of the provinces of *France*, the duke of *Orleans* caused 2,000,000 of livres (near 100,000 *l.* sterling) to be expended in the purchase of corn from this country, to be distributed at a moderate price among the poor in those provinces where he had any interest'.[2] Even when the export of grain was converted into a net import at the end of the century, resulting in an outflow of bullion, there were occasional panics in the money market but the effects do not seem to have been serious.[3]

[1] The complex business history involved does not come out well in most agricultural histories, which tend to emphasize the supply side. They emerge best when the viewpoint is inverted and farming is looked at from the market side. Almost the only substantial attempts at this for our period are the sections on barley and hops in Peter Mathias, *The Brewing Industry in England 1700–1830* (Cambridge, 1959).

[2] *The British Chronologist*, ii (London, 1789), p. 228.

[3] T. S. Ashton, *Economic Fluctuations in England 1700–1800* (O.U.P., 1959), pp. 47–8.

All in all, the 'responsiveness' of English agriculture was a victory, an excellent underpinning for an economy which was growing in all directions – in population, average income per head, and capital stock. The advantages are perhaps seen most clearly when contrasted with the sour experience of that other early commercial and industrial nation, the Dutch, which in the freer years before the mid-eighteenth century had set its economy squarely on imported cereals. When the cost of these mounted and sources of supply were sometimes cut off by wars in the second half of the century, the Dutch burnt their fingers badly, suffering high costs for labour which damaged the competitiveness of their industry.[1] England escaped only a little singed and for all the frictions of growth retained an agriculture of great potential.

The Release of Factors of Production
I. LABOUR. For long the chief contribution of agricultural change to the development of industry was depicted as the 'institutional' creation of an urban proletariat. Enclosure was the supposed means. It was treated as if consciously contrived to dislodge countrymen from the land and herd them into the new factories. In this form of a concerted, disappropriating recruitment drive the view was never very coherent and it was thoroughly exploded by Professor Chambers in his article reprinted below. The conspiracy theory of parliamentary enclosure may linger in the doctrinaire wings of economic history but it is no longer a serious proposition that the enclosure commissioners were a kind of capitalist press-gang.

Professor Chambers more plausibly points out that the newer systems of husbandry (especially the labour-intensive root breaks), the reclamation of barren land, and the physical processes of enclosure and improvement (hedging, in-fencing, building farms, and laying out accommodation roads) all

[1] Charles Wilson, 'Taxation and the Decline of Empire', *Bijdragen en Mededelingen van het Historisch Genootschap, Utrecht*, LXXVII (1963), pp. 10–26; E. L. Jones, 'English and European Agricultural Development, 1650–1750', forthcoming in R. M. Hartwell (ed.), *Nuffield Studies in Economic History*.

C

demanded more labour, not less. Where forests, fens, and moors were enclosed and reclaimed totally new settlements were sometimes established. Apart from threshing machines, labour-saving machinery on the farm was unimportant before the middle of the nineteenth century. Far from the land giving forth its sons, between the first census in 1801 and that of 1851 the absolute numbers engaged in agriculture, forestry, and fishing never ceased to climb. They were 1·7 million in 1801 and 2·1 million in 1851.[1] This of course does not mean that productivity per man was not rising alongside productivity per acre.

Neither does it mean that enclosure did not influence the character of the rural workforce. Professor Chambers emphasizes the protection which the small owners of rights on the land usually received,[2] but he observes that the frequent appropriation of almost all the common grazing by the *legal* owners tore down the curtain, 'thin and squalid' though it may have been, which shielded men with only customary rights from utter proletarianization. And as Dr Martin shows in his article reprinted below, whatever the correctness with which the small owner was treated, the cost of enclosure lay disproportionately heavily on him. Many small owners sold out. They did not do so simply to grasping landowners but often to other relatively small operators, including numerous professional gentlemen who crowded to get farms at the height of the war boom.[3] Of those who sold, many doubtless quickly ran through the cash they had realized and sank into the ranks of common labourers. For example, at Broughton, Hampshire,

[1] Deane and Cole, op. cit., table 31, p. 143.

[2] Until at least 1851 the Crown itself possessed no machinery to throw open an *encroachment* on its land in the New Forest – 'an interesting reflection on an age which is usually blamed for "stealing the common from the goose" by means of enclosure Acts'. C. R. Tubbs and E. L. Jones, 'The Distribution of Gorse (*Ulex europaeus* L.) in the New Forest in relation to former Land Use', *Proc. Hants. Arch. Soc.*, XXIII (1964), p. 5.

[3] According to Henry Hunt, *Memoirs* (London, n.d.), II, p. 39, in 1801–2 'there was scarcely an attorney in the whole country that did not carry on the double trade of quill-driving and clod-hopping'. But much seems to have depended on the exact locality and period. See J. M. Martin, 'The Parliamentary Enclosure Movement and Rural Society in Warwickshire', *Agricultural History Review*, XV (1967), pp. 19–39.

the expenditure on poor rates was slashed by half for the one year 1791, following the enclosure award of 1790, but thereafter soared away up far into the years after the Napoleonic wars.[1] In the affected parishes, parliamentary enclosure brought fast changes in agrarian structure at the turn of the eighteenth and nineteenth centuries.

Whatever the fate of the small owner, the labourer who merely rented property to which common rights once attached, and the small tenant farmer whose holding might be amalgamated with others to form bigger units, were often converted into workers to be hired and fired at will. More impersonal labour relations in farming were here to stay. While common-field husbandry had seldom been so inflexible as Lord Ernle insisted, the new, brisk, businesslike agriculture was clearly more efficient in production.

Enclosure hurried the process whereby rural labour became wage-dependent, though Dr Mingay has made the telling point that the very old enclosed areas of Kent and Sussex suffered exceptionally grim rustic poverty.[2] There is a conflict of emphasis between Professor Chambers and Dr Mingay on one side and some other writers on the creation of a proletariat by enclosure.[3] Chambers and Mingay stress the alternative force of a blindly swelling rural population. Others wish still to stress the role of enclosure in destroying village culture and the quasi-independence afforded by common grazing,[4] but it is not clear how long they think that this 'thin and squalid' curtain could have stood between the burgeoning population and dire want. Social issues are, however, aside from our purpose. It is

[1] Broughton Poor Book 1791–1802, and annual series of sums spent since 1692, seen by courtesy of Rev. N. G. Powell.

[2] Op. cit., p. 185.

[3] See the long review of J. D. Chambers and G. E. Mingay, *The Agricultural Revolution 1750–1880* (London, 1966), in *The Times Literary Supplement* for 16 February 1967, and W. G. Hoskins, *The Midland Peasant* (London, 1957), pp. 267–72.

[4] From acquaintance with commoners in the New Forest and the Forest of Dean I entirely accept that common rights conduce to an independence of mind not found among hired farm hands. But it is a luxury made possible precisely by economic growth stemming from the replacement of communal farming by commercial agriculture over most of the country.

apparent that enclosure was not the creator of a labour force for industry.

Enclosure itself tended to mop up labour from the country-side. Rural labour resisted being sucked into the industrial sector. Much of it remained immobilized and poor in southern and eastern England long after our period. Switching freely from skilled land work to skilled work in industry was hardly possible. A nineteenth-century Wiltshire incumbent who saw both sides of the fence commented that, 'in-door and out-door habits, the loom and the plough, the shuttle and the sickle, the soft hand and the hard hand, cannot be interchanged at pleasure'. He noted that the Spitalfields silk weaver did not dare do her own housework since if she chapped her palms they would catch and spoil the threads, and that this applied, though less, even to woollens.[1] Dairying could be combined with industry but hard field work could not.

Industrialists could not therefore draw quickly on reserves of rural labour. The English were long accustomed to a work-ing holiday at harvest time, combining high earnings with a social occasion and permitting the women and children to glean the fallen ears for their winter flour. Joseph Veale re-ported from Exeter in August 1717 that 'our markett have advanced ocationed chifly by busy harvest times. when few goods are made', and William Willmott wrote from Sherborne in the 1770s of his workpeople that 'they rather chose to do very little of the short silk and get into the Fields a leasing as it is harvest time'. The Yorkshire woollen industry was inter-rupted by the dispersal of men, women, and children to hay-making and harvesting in the Vale of York, the East Riding, Lincolnshire, and Nottinghamshire. Equally, throughout the eighteenth century iron furnaces and forges were brought to a seasonal halt by the preference of their operatives to go harvesting.[2] These habits were frustrating to manufacturers

---

[1] J. Wilkinson, 'History of Broughton Gifford', *Wilts. Arch. Mag.*, vi (1860), p. 37.

[2] Delmé Radcliffe correspondence, 13A, 1706–85, Hertford C.R.O.; Maureen Weinstock, *Studies in Dorset History* (Dorchester, 1953), p. 91; H. Heaton, *The Yorkshire Woollen and Worsted Industries* (Oxford, 1920), p. 342; T. S. Ashton, *Iron & Steel in the Industrial Revolution* (Manchester, 1963 edn), p. 197.

striving to stockpile goods for sale immediately after harvest when the whole agricultural population was most flush with money.

In the Midlands and North during the late eighteenth century the demand for hands in the cotton industry became acute and the old system of part-time work on a putting-out basis could not stretch to meet it. The supply of such labour among the wives and daughters of small farmers and rural labourers was drained and this, it seems, provided a stimulus for mechanization in the industry during the 1770s.[1] It would be tendentious to praise agriculture because its inability to release enough labour prompted inventiveness, but it must be concluded that it was not usually an immediate source of labour for industry. Arthur Young's farming correspondents in Cheshire, Lancashire, and the West Riding in 1792 would not have agreed, but they were witnessing localized competition for workers between agriculture and industry.[2] In general, agriculture itself secured bigger absolute numbers of hands, and its ancient seasonal rhythms long continued to disturb the work flow in industry. Industry, in fact, had creamed off part of the surplus growth of the rural population for its own workforce. We must look to the deeper currents of demographic change for the source of the labour which fed all-round economic expansion.

2. CAPITAL AND ENTREPRENEURSHIP. The industrialization of a predominantly rural society will understandably draw where possible on agrarian resources of capital, entrepreneurial talent, and technical skill. If these do not originate in agriculture proper, they may well come from its penumbra of servicing and processing trades. Conceivably industry might be wholly financed and staffed from the mercantile enclave which even weakly developed economies usually possess, but this

---

[1] J. D. Chambers, 'The Rural Domestic Industries during the period of transition to the factory system, with special reference to the Midland Counties of England,' *Communications*, Second International Conference of Economic History, Aix-en-Provence (1962), p. 442.

[2] Arthur Young, 'Of Manufactures mixed with Agriculture', *Annals*, xxxii (1799), pp. 221.

was the English experience only in so far as capital originally
generated by foreign trade was often filtered into agriculture
through the buying of country estates, and out again through
the early industrial activities of landowners.

Landowners did play a noteworthy role in fostering industry.[1] Where their estates overlay deposits of coal or iron
and carried standing crops of timber for pit-props or charcoal-
burning they were well placed to do so. They were also active
in the fields of transport and urban housing: the aristocratic
nameplates of west London squares are a tribute to enterprise,
not gentility. Landowners were able to command finance for
such developments and could call readily on professional or
technical advice. Often their enterprises were no more than an
extension of the exploitation of the natural resources of their
land, but their willingness to engage in them at all gave the
English an edge over the more aloof European aristocracies.
Nevertheless, as the eighteenth century progressed and industry became firmer on its feet, English landowners with-
drew more and more from active participation in non-agricultural ventures, leasing off their mines and ironworks.[2]
Admittedly, there were always individual landowners who
opposed industrialization. In Nottinghamshire and Derbyshire
some of the magnates tried to exclude textile mills from access
to water power, though all they succeeded in doing was to
drive mill-owners to set up steam engines as a substitute. But
landed society by and large was tender to the manufacturer,
presumably because the sources of wealth in the English
economy had so long been very varied. The ironmasters, the
Foleys and the Knights, and the cotton spinners, the Arkwrights, were freely admitted to county society in that most
rural of shires, Hereford, while the Peels were greeted

---

[1] See Mingay, op. cit., Chapter VIII, 'The Landlords and Industrial Development'.

[2] See, e.g., R. L. Downes, 'The Stour Partnership, 1726–36: a note on Landed
Capital in the Iron Industry', *Econ. Hist. Rev.*, 2nd series, III (1950), pp. 90–6.
Occasional landowners whose family fortunes had originated outside agriculture
sometimes sold off their other assets to finance farm improvements. For example,
Sir Christopher Sykes sold his interests in stock and shipping in order to develop
the Yorkshire Wolds at the end of the eighteenth century. Mingay, op. cit.,
p. 165.

respectfully in Staffordshire, even though they set up cotton mills on their land.

Like the landowners, practising farmers also made early moves into industry. This was even more true of their sons, who shifted into the towns to become apprentices. On average during the eighteenth century about 50 per cent of the immigrant apprentices to the cultery trades of Hallamshire were the sons of men engaged in farming, but the proportion was falling over time; in 1720, 60 per cent of youths apprenticed in Leicester hosiery trades came from villages outside, though by 1780 the proportion had fallen to 45 per cent.[1] Those of their families who attained the status of minor gentry or clerics thus had an open line through which they could place their investments with relatives in manufacturing. Benjamin Franklin's English forebears were in this category. His family had lived for at least 300 years on a freehold at Ecton in Northamptonshire, but of his father's generation in the late seventeenth century all except the eldest brother, who inherited the land, moved away to become dyers in the textile trades.[2] The Crowley family rose from small farmers to the heights of the iron industry in three generations. Small farmers in northern England and the north Midlands had, of course, long engaged in part-time manufacturing, but the emphasis shifted until their agricultural connexions wore thin. More advanced processes of manufacture and more insistent demands for industrial goods became too absorbing for half a man's attention to remain occupied with crops and animals.[3] In remote parts of the Peak district, away from the purview of urban putting-out merchants, a handful of workshops on isolated farms

[1] D. L. Linton, *Sheffield and its Region* (Sheffield, 1956), p. 173; Hoskins, op. cit., pp. 257–9.

[2] Lewis Leary, *The Autobiography of Benjamin Franklin* (New York, 1962), p. 17. Similarly the major London brewer, Samuel Whitbread, was the son of a prosperous Bedfordshire yeoman and set up in business with his £2,000 patrimony. Peter Mathias, 'The Entrepreneur in Brewing, 1700–1830', published in a separate issue of *Explorations in Entrepreneurial History* (1957), p. 35.

[3] See Chambers, 'The Rural Domestic Industries', loc. cit., pp. 433, 436–7; S. D. Chapman, 'The Transition to the Factory System in the Midlands Cotton-Spinning Industry', *Econ. Hist. Rev.*, 2nd series, XVIII (1965), pp. 526–43; Ashton, 1963, op. cit., pp. 209–10.

evolved into full-blown cotton factories, but agriculture otherwise figured rarely among the original occupations of the principals of cotton firms established in the Midlands after 1769. There was already a big enough base in older textile industries to supply most of the founding personnel for cotton. The same was the case in the iron industry which drew most of its eighteenth-century entrepreneurs not from the yeomen, as Toynbee and Mantoux thought, but from a wide spectrum of secondary metal workers. Agriculture was a source of industrial entrepreneurs but it tended to be at a generation or so's remove.

From the case studies of the careers of industrialists, it is not immediately apparent whether agriculture gave more than it took away. The English pattern was for a small farmer, dealer, or craftsman to become a rich manufacturer and for him or his son to become a country gentleman. A nice example is Joseph Wilkes (1735–1805), Peel's partner, who came of a farm family, prospered by promoting transport improvements, became a cotton manufacturer and then a landowner in Staffordshire. Capital equipment in industry was naturally created in the course of such a progression, and something possibly added to technology, but a man's descendants commonly bled his factories to subsidize their life as country gentlemen and the improvement of their estates.[1]

There are innumerable instances of this outflow of capital from industrial undertakings into the financially less profitable business of landowning. The pattern is much complicated by regional questions – by the possibility that industrialists more readily quit the older industries of southern England and thus speeded their contraction. It was, for example, customary for

[1] See the summary in my 'Industrial Capital and Landed Investment: the Arkwrights in Herefordshire, 1809–43', in E. L. Jones and G. E. Mingay (eds.), *Land, Labour and Population in the Industrial Revolution* (in press). In 1809 a single cotton spinner, Richard Arkwright jun., may have spent on buying one of his estates a sum equivalent to 30 per cent of the total annual investment in the cotton industry. His father, Sir Richard, had, however, once probably pulled out of land for a few years to release capital for mill-building. The first generation of successful industrialists typically held off from land purchases until they were satisfied with the size of their fortunes, and only then plunged into estates in a big way. Cf. also Mathias, loc. cit., p. 37.

west country clothiers to buy estates and become 'Gentlemen Clothiers'.[1] In Gloucestershire the practice was said to have caused the failure of clothiers whose assets thus became too illiquid to tide over trade depressions. A Stroud banker stated that many had borrowed half the capital to buy estates at 5 per cent interest when the land yielded at most 3 per cent. Others were alleged to have become so enamoured of landed pleasures that they dissipated their fortunes in gambling, entertaining, and other forms of social display. In Berkshire the preference for buying land instead of reinvesting in the woollen industry has been put forward as the reason for the industry's decline, though this presupposes that returns from the trade were inadequate or that abnormal local rigidities prevented replacement investment by fresh personnel. The latter might just have been true of Gloucestershire if outgoing clothiers hung on too long to the strictly limited number of watermill sites. Although as in Nottinghamshire steam engines could have been substituted, and were slowly, it is a possibility that a prolonged and unfortunately timed withdrawal from industry into land may have persuaded 'free' capital that it was better meanwhile to set up new firms on the northern coalfields. Even this is not altogether likely, for Gloucestershire had access to Somerset coal. It is rather more probable that the movement of capital from the declining southern and eastern sections of the cloth trade into agriculture was not simply the universal prestige buying of landed estates but a recognition that local industrial investments were no longer very rewarding. There is some support for this in the case of Thomas Griggs (1701–60) in Essex, who transferred his surplus funds

[1] Lists of clothiers who bought estates are given by G. D. Ramsey, *The Wiltshire Woollen Industry in the Sixteenth and Seventeenth Centuries* (O.U.P., 1943), p. 127; R. Perry, 'The Gloucestershire Woollen Industry 1100–1690', *Trans. Bristol & Glos. Arch. Soc.*, 68 (1945), pp. 112–14; and J. de L. Mann, *Documents illustrating the Wiltshire Textile Trades in the Eighteenth Century*, Wilts. Arch. Soc. Records Branch, XIX (1964). See also R. F. Dell, 'The Decline of the Clothing Industry in Berkshire', *Trans. Newbury District Field Club*, X (1954), pp. 60–1; W. Hicks Beach, *A Cotswold Family* (London, 1909), pp. 38–9; E. A. L. Moir, 'The Gentlemen Clothiers' in H. P. R. Finberg (ed.), *Gloucestershire Studies* (Leicester, 1957), pp. 242–4; and K. H. Burley, 'An Essex Clothier of the Eighteenth Century', *Econ. Hist. Rev.*, 2nd series, XI (1958), p. 291.

from textile manufacturing into speculations in real estate, fattening livestock, and malting barley. Agriculture and agricultural processing had become the more productive outlet for funds in the south and east.

An assessment of agriculture's contribution of entrepreneurial and managerial skills, and capital, to industry must thus take special account of locality and date. Landowners and farmers promoted valuable industrial undertakings in the earlier part of the period. They were instrumental in getting many manufactures started, though later the industrial sector was able to produce the men it needed to continue expanding. While fortunes made in industry did leak into landownership, from the common-sense point of view it appears that since manufacturing did expand, the counter-attractions of rural life may have retarded but could not block industrialization. Indeed, the drying-up of the land market in the late eighteenth century may have been important in holding much industrial and mercantile money in the capital market. As Dr G. E. Mingay has concluded, 'the limited amount of land available for purchase meant that such newcomers [to estates] were less numerous than at any time in the two previous centuries'.[1]

There was no overall shortage of capital in the economy. A pool of funds existed in rural and market town society. Many small towns and villages were devastated by fire, with very high computed losses, but money was usually forthcoming to rebuild them promptly – for example, after the 110 fires which destroyed ten or more houses each (over 100 houses in five cases) in Berkshire, Dorset, Hampshire, and Wiltshire alone between 1650–1815.[2] Sir F. M. Eden, who was not accustomed to withhold information on poverty, maintained that some working-men, by dint of extreme parsimony, had hoarded considerable sums. He thought they should be persuaded to put these out at interest. In Gloucestershire he knew a village shoemaker with £300 and a barber with £800.[3] In addition, there are instances like that of the labourer at Eyns-

[1] Mingay, op. cit., p. 47.
[2] From my unpublished paper, 'The Effects and Eradication of Fire in Southern England, 1650–1850'.
[3] *The State of the Poor* (London, 1797), I, p. 496.

ham, Oxfordshire, who in 1773 lent £160 to a shoemaker in the village.[1] In the Midlands and north, as Professor John shows below, these local pools of capital were already being drawn on by industrialists in the early eighteenth century. What was needed was a means of mobilizing rural savings in the south and east for the use of manufacturers elsewhere.

Much has indeed been made of a chain of banking arrangements which siphoned the surplus profits of farmers in the arable areas of southern and eastern England to the expanding industries of the more northerly areas. With the stimulus which the 'new' forage crops had given to mixed farming on the light lands in the south and east – but not to the poorer environment of the north and west – there had occurred a separation between the zones of highest agricultural profits and highest demand for industrial investments. Country banks in the arable districts received deposits when the crops were threshed and sold in the months after harvest, remitted the cash to London clearing banks, which in turn lent to the manufacturers. Banks like Barnard's in Bedford sent an increasing flow of country money along this channel, to finance the cotton spinners of Lancashire and the metal workers of Birmingham.[2]

The proportionate significance of this flow until the very end of the period is, however, doubtful. The credit needs of arable farmers in the southern parts of England were high between the spring sowing and harvest, higher and longer-lasting than in the livestock districts of the north,[3] and at that time surely required a reverse flow of lending. This must have been inconvenient for manufacturers who also spent the summer trying to accumulate stocks of goods for post-harvest sale. Before harvest, supplies of working credit in the country as a whole must have been stretched to their limit. And since

[1] Bond of Hercules Humphreys, one of a collection of documents seen by courtesy of Mrs C. Bolton of Eynsham.
[2] T. S. Ashton, *The Industrial Revolution 1760–1830* (O.U.P., 1948), p. 106; L. S. Pressnell, 'Joseph Barnard: Westminster's Predecessor in Bedford', *Westminster Bank Review*, February 1960, p. 10.
[3] M. Marks, 'The Measurement of Agriculture's Seasonal Credit Requirement', *The Farm Economist*, IX (1960), pp. 449–56.

country banks were few before the late eighteenth century and only began to lend to farmers on any scale rather late in the Napoleonic wars, it may be wondered whether farmers had hitherto been willing to dispatch substantial sums even after harvest through the banking system to industry. May they not have preferred to hold their receipts against summer needs which the country banks did not yet meet? They may have had a high liquidity preference, simply hoarding cash as it came in, as for example in 1774 when one agriculturist near Canterbury noted his 'current silver in the iron chest' as '50 crown pieces, 80 half crown pieces, 520 shillings, 180 sixpences'.[1] I have examined a number of account books which seem to indicate that farmers became serious lenders, and then locally, only on the strength of their windfalls during the profit inflation of the French Revolutionary and Napoleonic wars.[2]

The direction in which agriculturists channelled their non-farming outlays may have been of more consequence than the volume. Landowners and farmers invested heavily in the infrastructure of the economy, that is in its communications network. With other rural residents like attorneys, merchants and parsons many of them were prominent shareholders and promoters of regional transport improvements. Only in the canal mania of the 1790s were non-local investors much drawn to these schemes. Admittedly, Dr Mingay has emphasized the suspicion with which landowners sometimes regarded improved communications. Although better routes would cheapen industrial inputs to agriculture (much of the interest was in securing coal to burn in making lime for the claylands and bricks for farm buildings), certain landowners opposed the schemes for fear that an easier flow of grain would glut the

---

[1] Lee Warley Disbursements Book, 1766–1825, Rothamsted Collection, now in the University of Reading archive of historical farm records.

[2] Tax on farm incomes rose from £18·87 million in 1803 to £26·7 million in 1814. P. K. O'Brien, 'British Incomes and Property in the Early Nineteenth Century', *Econ. Hist. Rev.*, 2nd series, XII (1959), p. 262; Hunt, op. cit., I, pp. 398, 477, 534–5; II, pp. 38–9, provides a contemporary description of high profits in Wiltshire but stresses how much farmers spent on conspicuous consumption; see also L. S. Pressnell, *Country Banking in the Industrial Revolution* (Oxford, 1956), pp. 346–7.

markets, depressing prices and rents. The sideline of carting in which their tenants engaged during slack seasons might also be damaged.[1] Yet such opposition was greatly outweighed by the involvement of the rural community as a whole in promoting better communications.[2]

Agriculturists were concerned for their own reasons. The majority did want to obtain cheaper industrial inputs and to dispatch their farm products more easily. For instance, the landed promoters of the canal from Andover, Hampshire, to Redbridge at the head of Southampton Water offered their hefty subscriptions in 1788 not to turn Andover into a second Birmingham but specifically to send out grain and bring in building materials, grass seeds, and woollen rags for manure.[3] Aims were closely similar and pressures even greater in the more isolated county of Hereford. There, in the late seventeenth century, schemes to improve the navigation of the River Wye were put forward. By the late eighteenth century local attention had shifted to canals on the grounds that further work along the Wye would merely speed up connexions with Bristol, whereas canals could link the county to the faster-growing food markets and sources of manufactured goods in the Midlands and north.[4]

These schemes did not always bring the anticipated profits. One half of agriculture was perhaps uninterested – the livestock producers still moved their animals about on the hoof, using the green lanes to avoid turnpike tolls and finding the canals both too slow and too little focused on the London market. Only the railways could work a great change in their mode of transport. But grain growers became better served. The opening, for example, of a turnpike to Wantage market and its hinterland of barley fields on the Berkshire Downs greatly increased the production of malt at Wallingford for shipment down the Thames to London. The average annual

[1] Mingay, op. cit., pp. 196–9, 201.
[2] Consideration of this should not be limited to canals and turnpikes, figures for which exaggerate late eighteenth-century developments. River improvements were well under way in the second half of the seventeenth century.
[3] E. L. Jones, 'An Agricultural Canal', *The Hampshire Farmer*, *14*, 1959, p. 2.
[4] Jones, 1961, loc. cit., pp. 33–6.

make of five years ending 1754 was 49,172 bushels, of five years ending 1774, 113,135 bushels.[1]

Even if efforts at improving transportation were directed at strengthening the rural economy, they had an obvious effect in permitting the wider diffusion of industrial goods. The narrow island of Britain was well placed for linking coastwise and inland water traffic, which was so much cheaper than overland carriage. A striking example of the results was to be seen at Reading during the Napoleonic wars. Once the Kennet and Avon canal connected with the Thames, with the Oxford canal a few miles up-river tapping the Midlands, Reading was able to import cheap coal, cheap hardware, and iron from Birmingham, pottery from Staffordshire, stone from Bath, and groceries from London or – when they came from the West Indies or Ireland – across from the west coast.[2]

Two major interactions of agricultural capital and the remainder of the economy remain to be considered. Firstly, it has been argued that high spending on enclosure and follow-up improvements caused a transfer of funds into agriculture during 1760–1815. 'It may very well be,' writes Professor Landes, 'that in the early decades of heavy enclosure, that is, the very years that also saw the birth of modern industry, British husbandry was taking as much capital as it was giving; while in the period from 1790–1814, when food prices rose to record levels, the net flow of resources was probably towards the land.'[3] His cited cost of £5–£25 per acre for enclosure plus subsequent improvement seems high for England compared with, say, the figures provided by Dr Martin for Warwick-

[1] Eden, op. cit., ii, p. 18.

[2] Charles Hadfield, *The Canals of Southern England* (London, 1955), pp. 164–5.

[3] David Landes, 'Technological Change and Industrial Development in Western Europe, 1750–1914', in H. J. Habakkuk and M. Postan (eds.), *The Cambridge Economic History of Europe* (Cambridge, 1965), vi, p. 307, and his 'Japan and Europe: Contrasts in Industrialization', in William W. Lockwood (ed.), *The State and Economic Enterprise in Japan* (Princeton, N.J., 1965), pp. 166–7. Professor Landes's figures of the costs of post-enclosure improvement come from A. Pell, 'The Making of the Land in England: a Retrospect', *Journal of the Royal Agricultural Society of England*, 2nd series, xxiii (1887), pp. 355–74, which is overweighted by the costs of reclaiming Wychwood Forest in the 1850s and by other high costs (especially for drainage) during the third quarter of the nineteenth century.

shire. It is a fair point that much enclosure did not pay at once, that there was no necessary improvement of agriculture immediately, and that the full force of the increased capacity was only felt at the end of the Napoleonic wars. Yet it is undesirable to isolate enclosure as if it were the sole occasion for moving capital between agriculture and industry. If agriculture was so long neutral and for the last twenty-five years of our period an actual drain on resources it is surprising that industry managed to grow. In fact, although the contribution of farming to the British national income increased in the war years, faster than that of industry, the agricultural share in the national capital did not increase.[1]

Against the enclosure-based view that farming was a drain on the country's capital during the wars can be set the contrary argument that it was agriculture which carried much of the burden of the state at war, through the yield of the land tax plus the relative ease with which Pitt's income tax could be collected from the agricultural community. From 1803-4 to 1814-15, whereas incomes assessed for tax in the trade and industry sector rose by less than 10 per cent, those of the land sector rose by almost 60 per cent. Miss Deane concludes that 'had the commerce and industry sectors paid their "fair share" of the mounting cost of the French wars it is likely that the industrial revolution . . . would have suffered a severe setback'.[2]

Aggregating the fragments of evidence on the exchanges of capital and entrepreneurship between agriculture and industry is hazardous. It does seem that agriculturists contributed handsomely to the earlier industrial enterprises. Later their entrepreneurial involvement with industry lessened, but they were contributing much by helping to construct the communications system. For all the serious rigidities of the capital market in the countryside, all the feedback of investment by industrialists keen to acquire the social colouring of landed society, and all the expense of enclosure, the balance of probabilities is that agriculture did make a net contribution to the

[1] Deane and Cole, op. cit., pp. 160-1, 271.
[2] Deane, op. cit., p. 50.

formation of industrial capital and did release entrepreneurs who played a significant role in industrialization. Agriculture paved the earliest paths to growth.

INCOME EFFECTS OF AGRICULTURAL CHANGE AND THE DEVELOPMENT OF A MARKET FOR INDUSTRIAL GOODS

Thus far we have been in territory where economic historians have erected a few signposts. The signs do not mark every route or always agree about directions, but at least someone has been there before. With the subject of demand for industrial goods we enter virtual *terra incognita*. This is a land full of uncharted levels of income for different regions and social and occupational classes. Many scholars have preferred to stress the role of export markets for British industrial production in the eighteenth century, for on this more figures survive – dangerous to play with, no doubt, but definite series bearing some relation to the output of major branches of industry.

More recently writers have begun to study the home market, which was clearly so very much larger than the export market.[1] In the present state of knowledge we can discuss this only generally; budgetary studies are urgently needed for further progress. However, the agricultural sector was certainly of great significance for incomes right through the period, accounting for one-third of the occupied population at its close quite apart from affecting the level of demand among all consumers of foodstuffs.

Firstly, there is an effect of agriculture on the development of the economy which has been largely overlooked.[2] The low cereal prices from the Restoration to about 1750 (low compared with long periods before and after) were damaging to the incomes of small farmers in northern districts and in the common-field parishes on the Midland clays, where advantage was not readily taken of the innovations of the time. These farmers were squeezed by the flow of grain from the newly cultivated light lands or could not expand production to offset

[1] Deane and Cole, op. cit., p. 42 and n. 1.
[2] I have advanced a similar case for several early developed countries in an unpublished paper, 'Agricultural Origins of Industry'.

poor prices. Regional differences in agricultural prosperity intensified as the south and east became increasingly superior at producing grain and fatstock. Agriculturally inferior districts in northern and western England and the Midlands (despite improvements to Midland river navigation) were edged into stock-rearing and fattening, dairying, and taking up domestic industries. A strong growth of domestic manufacturing in several industries can definitely be assigned to the late seventeenth and early eighteenth centuries. It was important as a supplement to inadequate farm incomes, or in cases like Midland hosiery a remedy for the loss of agricultural work among those dispossessed by the enclosure of parishes which were laid down to pasture. Northern graziers and men on the Midland clays attempted in the late seventeenth century to have the new fodder crops, which were shifting the agricultural advantage southwards, suppressed by legislation. These stultifying efforts failed and regional differentiation continued. Domestic industries like cloth making, hosiery, lace and leather work and nail-making thickened in the areas less favoured for farming long before the fortuitous presence of coal beneath many of them brought heavier manufactures based on the steam engine or coke-smelted iron.

In this early and gradual fission southern England became increasingly agricultural and its old industries withered. Northern and some Midland districts became more industrial precisely because the readier uptake of the 'new' crops on light land in the south had made them relatively poorer agriculturally. 'North' and 'South' thus evolved as complementary markets which it became worth linking by better communications. When food prices rose later in the eighteenth century part-time farmers in the 'North' might have been expected to revert to full-time agriculture, but by then the growth of industrial demand (including for export) was sufficient to sustain the manufacturing sector. And these areas were now able to realize a superior industrial technology based on advances in the use of coal.

Professor John's article, reprinted below, brings us more directly into contact with the agriculturally induced demand for

D

industrial goods. His case is that the cheap grain of the first half of the eighteenth century, especially 1730–50, raised the incomes of consumers of bread. This was particularly beneficial to the poorer groups in society, among whom an appreciable margin for spending on industrial wares may have been released for the first time. The high proportion of wage earners in England, compared with Europe, would benefit both from cheap food and more work during the run of good harvests. This was exactly what Malthus thought about these years. Professor John cites evidence for a greater consumption of the products of the woollen, metal goods, and pottery industries at this time, although some of the income freed by cheaper bread was doubtless spent on other food (meat), imported produce (tea and sugar), and on grain in a potent guise (gin).

It may be thought that gains for food consumers would be cancelled by falling farm incomes and rents, but apart from some short spells this was apparently not so. There was no general depression. Losses in the heavy land districts were probably offset by the gains of innovators on the light lands, a situation neatly summed up by John Aubrey in the 1680s:

> Great increase of sainfoine now, in most places fitt for itt; improvements of meadowes by watering; ploughing up of the King's forests and parkes &c. But as to all of these, as ten thousand pounds is gained in the hill barren countrey, so the vale does lose as much, which brings it to an equation.[1]

Total agricultural purchases from the industrial sector therefore held up. They may not have risen, but since purchases by the buyers of cheaper food did there was a net expansion of demand before 1750.[2]

Professor John's thesis has been critized by Dr M. W. Flinn on the grounds that the statistical evidence on wheat prices is too narrow and can be rearranged to suggest that there was not

[1] J. Britton (ed.), *John Aubrey: The Natural History of Wiltshire* (Oxford, 1847), p. 111.

[2] Professor A. W. Coats seems to accept this two-pronged argument in his inaugural lecture, 'Economic Growth: The Economic and Social Historian's Dilemma', University of Nottingham (1966), pp. 12–13.

a great fall.[1] In that case the price data might not be able to
bear the weight of the argument for an income-induced expansion of home demand for industrial goods which Professor
John has built on them. Admittedly, the decennial figures of
retained imports of industrial raw materials and production in
the few industries for which series have survived show little
rise before 1750, with another spurt after 1770 or more especially 1780,[2] and Professor John has had to piece together other
items which suggest a more favourable view of production
and consumption in the first half of the century.

Dr Flinn may be moving towards an alternative explanation
of similar phenomena. He refers to two recent articles (by
Tucker and Youngson) which indicate that the population
may have grown more steadily throughout the eighteenth
century than is usually thought.[3] If this is so, the demand for
industrial goods might have risen simply because there were
more people to buy them and the fall in grain exports from the
1750s might be explicable in terms of greater numbers of consumers – though the rise in population would surely have had
to be sharp to account for all the observed fall. Such an interpretation would need two further props. Firstly, the economy
would have had to possess some different thrust to maintain the
purchasing power of a growing population. This might have
come partly from the 'commercial revolution' of the late
seventeenth century and partly from early industrial and transport improvements which, instead of being the *result* of income released by greater agricultural productivity, contributed to it and raised the real incomes of some farmers even

[1] 'Agricultural Productivity and Economic Growth in England, 1700–1760:
A Comment', *Journ. Econ. Hist.*, xxvi (1966), pp. 93–8. See also his *The Origins of
the Industrial Revolution* (London, 1966), p. 66. Dr Flinn does not provide any new
series and rests part of his case on the irrelevant failure of wheat prices to fall in
Scotland, while the strongest construction he can put on the available English
price series still leaves them weak compared with, say, the first half of the
seventeenth century or the second half of the eighteenth century.
[2] Deane and Cole, op. cit., Table 15, p. 51; Table 18, p. 72. Habits of con-
suming boughten goods were first engrained in the mass of the populace by the
collapsing prices and soaring (retained) imports of tobacco, sugar, calicoes, tea,
coffee and porcelain in the late seventeenth century. See Ralph Davis, 'English
Foreign Trade, 1660–1700', in E. M. Carus Wilson (ed.), *Essays in Economic
History* (London, 1962), ii.
[3] Flinn, op. cit., pp. 24–5.

during the first half of the eighteenth century.[1] But this leaves the earlier industrial and transport developments inadequately explained. Secondly, it would still need to be shown why mixed farming should have developed through the vigorous extension of forage crops right from the mid-seventeenth century.[2] This is easiest to explain by accepting the customary view of slight population growth, with needs for bread more readily satisfied and the price of grain thus low relative to the prices of livestock products. A mild incentive to expand the animal enterprises would be favourable to the spread of the 'new' fodder crops. More and better-fed livestock would then have given more dung and thus boosted the rise in grain production.

More recently still, Dr D. E. C. Eversley has written an important paper which extends Professor John's thesis.[3] Dr Eversley considers that demand did not fall between 1750 and 1780 but went on deepening very largely because of the expansion of a middle-class market which was immune to erosion from such rise as occurred in food prices. Starting from Gregory King's social accounts he demonstrates the early existence of a sizeable middle class of consumers, and he attributes much of the increased demand for industrial goods between 1750 and 1780 to its further growth.[4]

A systematic connexion between food prices or agricultural incomes and the movements of industrial output is unclear. What may conceivably have happened is that transport improvements from the fifties were sufficient to narrow the gap between farm-gate prices and the price to the urban consumer, so that returns to agriculturists were reasonable while

[1] Something along these lines was suggested by A. J. Youngson, *Possibilities of Economic Progress* (Cambridge, 1959), p. 123, n. 1.

[2] I am indebted to a 40,000-word digest of manuscript and published material on improvements in fodder supplies between 1600 and 1800 prepared for me at Nuffield College by Mr E. J. T. Collins in 1965.

[3] D. E. C. Eversley, 'The Home Market and Economic Growth in England, 1750–1780', in E. L. Jones and G. E. Mingay (eds.), *Land, Labour, and Population in the Industrial Revolution* (in press).

[4] Flinn, op. cit., pp. 65, 67, illustrates the difficulties of the literature by revealing the different definitions and emphases attached by authors to labouring, middle, and upper income groups.

consumers were less pinched than they would have been by any previously comparable rise in the price of grain. The effect on the market for industrial wares of changes in the incomes of agricultural producers vis-à-vis changes in the incomes of food consumers are almost impossible to separate on present evidence. Since farmers were such important employers, the two were closely linked. At the end of the eighteenth century wages were high during boom years but poor rates were high during slumps.[1] Up to a point the social security of the poor law constantly shifted income between employers (including farmers) and labourers, so that total demand approximated more closely than it might have done to the curve of population growth.

Dr Eversley urges that expanding middle-class demand between 1750 and 1780 was backed by continued working-class demand on the grounds that the size of the labouring population did not much increase before the final quarter of the century, and meanwhile growing employment for industrial workers in many cities bolstered real wages. Labourers could therefore continue to buy 'decencies' (goods half-way between necessities and luxuries) in all but occasional years of high food prices. The rise in food prices was not drastic, he claims, until after 1780 and the bad weather which is often supposed to account for difficulties in agriculture from the 1750s has been exaggerated. Working-class income on this view was only reduced at brief intervals. This does not wholly agree with the Phelps Brown index of real wages and the Gilboy wage material, which show slight losses for labourers in the south of England in the 1750s and 1760s, while the gains in real wages in the north during the early part of the century were reduced (though not eliminated) during the middle decades.[2] Perhaps the economic development of the third quarter of the eighteenth century, which after all was not impressive compared with the final quarter, should be attributed more simply to a rise in middle-class income. An important component of this would have been the income of agricultural producers.

[1] Arthur Young, loc. cit., pp. 220–1.
[2] See the summary in Flinn, op. cit., p. 63.

Compared with the second quarter of the century, the third quarter was not a time of favourable weather. According to one of the most reliable contemporaries, the years from 1764 to 1774 were wet ones and there never was known 'a greater scarcity of all sorts of grain, considering the great improvements of modern husbandry. Such a run of wet seasons a century or two ago would, I am persuaded, have occasioned a famine.' [1] The 'corn vales' were drowned. But the centre of gravity of grain production was shifting to the drier, light-soiled uplands, and Dr Eversley is clearly right to point out that food supplies were successfully maintained in most seasons. By the late 1770s and again in the mid-1780s agriculture was more than adequately filling the markets, farm incomes fell and landlords found it difficult to collect their rents. [2]

Although, as John Aubrey put it, the losses among heavy land farmers in the 1650–1750 period may have been so offset by gains for the innovators on the light lands as to come to 'an equation', this need not mean that the rise in the incomes of agriculturists in the third quarter of the eighteenth century was unimportant. Some tentative suggestions may be made about the impact of regional swings in agricultural improvement on the incomes of producers. During the third quarter of the century the previous energetic reclamation of downs and floating of water meadows on the southern chalklands seems to have slackened. This is not too far out of line with Arthur Young's version of the periodicity of development on the 'good sands' of Norfolk: 'for 30 years from 1730–1760, the great improvements of the north western part of the county took place . . . For the next 30 years to about 1790 they nearly stood still; they *reposed upon their laurels*. [3] Possibly the explanation is that having already created a viable mixed husbandry where once only sheep had grazed, light land agriculturists found that

---

[1] Gilbert White, *The Natural History of Selborne* (Everyman edn, 1949), p. 169.
[2] See, e.g., Lincs. R.O. TYR iv/i/87 and iv/i/100, referring to 1778–79; Hertford C.R.O. DE 5003 referring to 1779; Clementina Black, *The Cumberland Letters 1771-1784* (London, 1912), p. 229, referring to 1779; and Oxford C.R.O. DIL I/C referring to 1786.
[3] *General View . . . Norfolk* (London, 1804), p. 31.

they could make satisfactory profits without additional expensive reclamation. Prices were moderately high; rotations could be improved without the heavy outlays necessary to bring new land into cultivation. Only the steep price rise at the end of the century was to spur renewed activity in every sector of agriculture. From 1750 it was the turn of the heavy land sector to try to catch up.

Here, notably in the clay triangle of central England, the heavy, ill-drained soils were overlapped by the zone of densest common-field husbandry. This sector was resistant to change. Professor John has argued that the failure of agriculture to respond swiftly to the demands of the 1750s and 1760s was important because it prompted legislation to admit Irish tallow, meat, and dairy produce, and because it diverted resources to industrial expansion.[1] The pertinent area of resistance would surely have been the heavy lands, especially where common-field farmers were numerous. It was overcome but only at high cost. In parts of the Midlands where the land had belonged to a few proprietors enclosure had come early, the 'new' crops had been sown and farmers specialized in fatstock breeding.[2] More usually the 'peasant' farming of the Midland clays defied any change except the pungent expedient of parliamentary enclosure. Professor Chambers states in the article reprinted below that of twenty-one Leicestershire villages enclosed by Act after 1790, ten were on clays too stiff for mixed husbandry based on the turnip. In others the communal system had maintained itself by partly adopting the new methods, but most small farmers in the Midlands lacked the capital to carry out thorough reform. Dr Martin's paper (below) shows that in Warwickshire, too, only the inflationary prices at the turn of the eighteenth and nineteenth centuries made it worth while to enclose and bring the advanced methods to parishes on cold, unproductive clay or where large numbers of small proprietors

[1] A. H. John, 'The Course of Agricultural Change, 1660–1760', in L. S. Pressnell (ed.), *Studies in the Industrial Revolution* (London, 1960), pp. 152–5. But as has been mentioned, the restricted land market of the second half of the eighteenth century may also have dissuaded as much capital from entering agriculture as would otherwise have been the case.

[2] See, e.g., Franklin, op. cit., p. 90.

meant that reallotment costs must be high. In a more recent
paper Dr Martin gives further details of the successive waves
of enclosure in Warwickshire, costing least before 1750, more
between 1750 and 1779, and more than ever after 1780.[1]

During the second half of the eighteenth century agriculture
thus ran into high cost barriers to the further expansion of output. It had jumped one fence by the eighties, when parliamentary enclosure slackened and the proceeds of farming
seem to have been low. The inflation of prices after 1790 then
overrode the highest obstacles of soil and sociology. Both
waves of enclosure were doubtless profitable, though not
necessarily very quickly. It seems therefore that in one region
or another gains were being made by agricultural producers
throughout the eighteenth century. Before 1750 the gains in
one area counterbalanced the losses in another (not counting
the gains of food consumers). After 1750 the gains tended more
than to balance any losses. The periods 1730–50, 1750–80, and
1790–1815 may approximately mark phases in the development
of tastes for industrial consumer goods among the farm community.[2]

The purchase of industry-made producer goods by farmers
lagged well behind. Chambers and Mingay comment that 'a
remarkable feature of the agricultural revolution was the slow
pace at which improved tools and machinery were brought
into use'. This is certainly true compared with some other
institutional or technical changes in agriculture. Winnowing,
chaff-cutting, and threshing machines were introduced mainly
during the Napoleonic wars. It was only at the close of the
eighteenth century that iron ploughs widely replaced wooden
ones. However, little is known in detail about the purchase of
producer goods by farmers and an analysis of the ledgers

[1] Martin, 1967, loc. cit., pp. 27–30. The development of the clays, where liming
was essential, may have given a special impetus to transport improvements from
1760 to 1800. Cf. Mingay, op. cit., p. 201.

[2] Types of goods bought, indicative of solid comfort for many farmers by the
late seventeenth century, may be seen from Mingay, op. cit., pp. 235–9. See also
Chambers and Mingay, op. cit., p. 69 and the detailed studies by G. H. Kenyon,
'Kirdford Inventories, 1611 to 1776', and 'Petworth Town and Trades', *Sussex
Arch. Colls.* XCIII–XCIX (1954–61).

relating to the Hedges family's four forges at Bucklebury, Berkshire, from 1736 to 1763, is accordingly of interest.[1] Ploughshares were pointed by this firm twenty or thirty times for every new one supplied. The plough beams, mouldboards and handles, and the frames of harrows, were all made of wood. While quantities of nails were sold, the preciousness of iron is illustrated by the constant return of nails and small bolts for repair, while it is clear that the forges relied heavily on scrap returned by customers.[2] 'Turnup pickers' were made, but only a single drill plough and a solitary winnowing fan were repaired. Only about 10 per cent of the ledger entries refer to household goods, but by 1750 there are signs that some agriculturists were buying such factory-made items as cast-iron bedsteads, mended but not made locally. Wealthier members of the rural community were already using consumer goods from distant factories, while relying much longer on local forges and blacksmiths for producer goods on the farm.

It is unlikely that higher food prices ever seriously eroded the expansion of the home market for consumer goods by eliminating the margin for such spending among the working population. Agriculture constantly demanded more labour. The 'golden age' of the labourer in the second quarter of the eighteenth century apparently engrained in him tastes for manufactured goods which he was willing to work harder thereafter to gratify. Old haphazard working habits and slackness when food and drink were plentiful may thus have gradually disappeared without much goading from real physical want. The marginal propensity to consume was seemingly high among the rural poor, whose purchases, though individually

[1] I am indebted for this analysis to Miss Felicity Palmer. Christopher Hill, *Reformation to Industrial Revolution* (London, 1967), p. 196, asserts that the high cost of iron tools was 'a bottleneck in agriculture', but unfortunately offers no authorities or evidence.

[2] According to *The Field Book* (London, 1833), p. 38, gun barrels were still extensively made from the iron of 'old horse-shoe nails, procured from country farriers, and from poor people who gain a subsistence by picking them up on the great roads leading to the metropolis'. The Woodstock steel jewelry industry relied exclusively on spent horse-shoe nails. Metallurgists are not unanimous as to whether or not these were merely convenient scrap or possessed special properties.

small, were large in aggregate. Gilbert White remarked in 1775 that 'little farmers use rushes much . . . but the very poor, who are always the worst economists, and therefore must continue very poor, buy an halfpenny candle every evening, which, in their blowing open rooms, does not burn much more than two hours. Thus have they only two hours' light for their money instead of eleven.'[1]

Even the final years of war probably failed to wipe out the demand for industrial goods among the poorest employed group, the farm hands, except in spells of extraordinarily high prices for food like 1795–96 and 1799–1801. During the wars the conjunction of a removal of workers into the armed forces and war trades with the need to produce more food in this country put pressure on the agricultural labour market. This helped to sustain real incomes just as it induced farmers to introduce threshing machines to save labour.[2] In any case, as far as the total consumption of industrial goods by the labouring population is concerned it must be recalled that whatever happened to their average income, their numbers grew fast in the last quarter of the eighteenth century. This was the period when the output of the mass production industries really rose. In so far as any conclusion is as yet possible on agriculture's contribution to the demand for industrial goods it is that living costs were held down remarkably well, freeing money to buy manufactures while the total income received by agricultural producers bore up before 1750 and rose afterwards. Agriculture played no small part in the expansion of the home market.

CONCLUSIONS

In terms of the balance sheet which has been presented the agricultural sector made a valuable net contribution to economic growth in the 1650–1815 period. The exact nature of the exchanges were not always those of the textbooks – in particular labour was not ejected into factory industry by the

[1] White, op. cit., p. 191.
[2] E. L. Jones, 'The Agricultural Labour Market in England, 1793–1872', *Econ. Hist. Rev.*, 2nd series, XVII (1964), pp. 323–5.

force of the parliamentary enclosure movement – nor was every contribution a positive one. It must be obvious how very much more sheer historical research remains to be done on items in the accounts. But of the overall picture there seems no reasonable doubt.

England was early in the field with a productive, expansible agriculture, which as the eighteenth century went by increasingly spread its influence by means of books, correspondence, and personal inspection to willing pupils in other countries. The tough resistance of mainland Europe's peasant agriculture, a much less flexible system than the landlord–tenant nexus in England, delayed the acceptance of new methods there. In our nearest and greatest rival, France, Arthur Young saw the rigidities of a society where 'you pass at once from beggary to profusion' and where men with money refrained from investing as freely as they would in England.[1] Our earlier commercial and industrial rival, the Netherlands, was not well suited to cereal growing and was in any event much embarrassed in the later eighteenth century by an excessive reliance on dearer and dearer imported grain. Landed society was much more cut off from economic enterprise in Europe than in England so that the diffusion of new techniques was slow. Nevertheless it continued. Even in southern Europe, where climatic considerations limited the effectiveness of the 'new' roots and grasses, and where an already dense population lacked reserves of land comparable with the open-field fallows and 'wastes' of northern Europe, efforts were made to copy England. For example, in backward Corsica General Pasquale di Paoli, who from 1755 to 1769 tried to free the island from Genoese rule and actually brought it briefly under George III's protection, was an agricultural propagandist of some success. Perceiving Corsica's shortage of farinaceous foods he was proud to become known as the 'Generale delle patates', the Potato General.[2]

English influence on American agriculture was greater than is usually thought and would have been greater still had America

---

[1] *Travels in France 1787–9*, quoted by Chambers and Mingay, op. cit., p. 204.
[2] Moray McLaren, *Corsica Boswell* (London, 1966), p. 148.

needed to intensify her farming instead of being able to spread
to untold fresh territory in the west. Links between well-to-
do and highly similar 'improving' circles spread English
methods to Virginia, Pennsylvania, New Jersey, and Massa-
chusetts in the second half of the eighteenth century. Some
Americans imported English seeds and above all improved
strains of livestock. Coke of Holkham remained pro-American
throughout the Revolution; his estate was visited by several
Americans. Others were made honorary members of the British
Board of Agriculture, while Arthur Young and Sir John
Sinclair corresponded with Washington at Mount Vernon and
Sinclair with Jefferson at Monticello.[1]

Agriculture had thus contributed in real, if complicated,
ways to the emergence of industrialism in England. In turn
in the nineteenth-century English industry communicated its
technology to the more receptive countries in Europe and to
the United States. Besides this, English agricultural methods
were taught directly to these other advanced lands. The development of progressive farming in England was thus vital
to growth over much wider areas than simply its home
ground. It was one of the leading forces of economic advance.

[1] See, e.g., R. C. Loehr, 'The Influence of English Agriculture on American
Agriculture, 1775–1825', *Agric. Hist.*, XI (1937), pp. 3–15; E. E. Edwards (ed.),
Washington, Jefferson, Lincoln and Agriculture (Washington, D.C. 1937), *passim*;
C. R. Woodward, *Ploughs and Politicks* (New Brunswick, Rutgers University
Press, 1941), *passim*; and C. and J. Bridenbaugh, *Rebels and Gentlemen* (New York,
1942), pp. 184, 191, 220.

1 Obstacles to Progress

LORD ERNLE

[This article was first published as Chapter III of *The Land and its People*, Hutchinson, 1925.]

Between the two great periods of enclosure – between, that is, the sixteenth century and the second half of the eighteenth century, the case for the enclosure of village farms was immensely strengthened by the accumulation of new resources of farming. Experience had demonstrated that the supply of bread-corn was rather increased than diminished by the consolidation of holdings in the hands of individuals. Discoveries had been made which could not be put in practice on village farms without drastic alterations in their organization. Adopted and tested on individual tenancies, they had proved their value in raising the productivity of the soil and keeping pace with the growing needs of urban populations. Agriculturally, village farms became obstacles to farming progress. Nor did the enthusiastic advocates of the new methods believe that their adoption would depopulate rural districts. They thought, and rightly thought, that arable farming on the improved lines would necessitate a larger demand for agricultural labour.

For the greater part of the period the new discoveries had been only enshrined in the pages of those strange compounds of wisdom and folly which compose our earlier agricultural literature. They appealed as little to individual occupiers as they did to partners in village farms. What was needed was proof of their efficiency. When that had been given, farmers were ready and eager to put them in practice. In the second quarter of the eighteenth century the new methods were tested by the enterprise of large landlords like Turnip Townshend and gentlemen farmers like Jethro Tull. The farming community were converted. They became enthusiasts. Thus, from 1760 onwards, village farms were faced by a new and formidable foe. The national demand for food was growing rapidly. It could be met by the adoption of new practices of recognized value which could not be introduced upon land cultivated on medieval principles.

The strength of this agricultural argument is multiplied, if we realize in detail how many of the methods, which between 1780 and 1870 made British agriculture famous, were anticipated and discussed a century and a half before they came into general use in this country. The struggle between practice and science was protracted, and in its course the story of Joseph and his brethren was daily re-enacted. The elder sons of Jacob were plain practical men, experienced in the traditional routine of stock-rearing and corn-growing, wearing the weather-stained garments of their industry. It is possible that their younger brother, with his dainty clothes and indoor airs, had spoken disrespectfully of their lives and methods. He was a theorist. They may have known that he could not milk a goat. The day came when they saw their chance. 'Behold this dreamer cometh!' So they stripped him of his variegated raiment, 'his gold spectacles, spats, and tall hat', and thrust him into a pit. But Joseph lived to save them from starvation and become their leader. Again and again in subsequent times, science has saved practical agriculturists from ruin.

Yet it must be admitted that farmers had good reason to distrust the pseudo-scientific advice of book-farmers. Before the end of the eighteenth century it was often indistinguisable from quackery, often false in its conclusions, often so mixed with folly as to be ridiculous, often based on hasty generalizations, often so extravagant in its promises as to arouse suspicion. To the theories of would-be teachers the practical man opposed his traditional routine of farm management. Its growth had been slow. It had been built up by protracted processes. Here and there some isolated agriculturist had, either by accident or experiment, chanced upon some new process or substance which increased the yield of his crops. Often the discovery would be ignored or forgotten, perhaps to be revived a century later. Sometimes it would be tried and confirmed by neighbours, spread over an ever-extending circle, and gradually incorporated in the general stock-in-trade of farmers. Tested experience of this kind is not easily disturbed. Why the given results follow may be unknown; it is enough that they are produced. Another process will not be adopted merely because it is new. Proof of better results is needed, and printed pages, especially when reading was a rare accomplishment, carry less weight than ocular demonstration. Seeing is believing. Sound sense often lies behind the conservatism of farmers. Mistakes in agriculture are costly, and sure returns are necessary where subsistence is at stake. The path of the industry is strewn with the wreckage of those who have tried to grow rich by short cuts.

When true science began to speak, it had to remove the mass of suspicion engendered by the quacks who professed to speak in her name. Agricultural chemistry dates from the discovery of the composition of air at the close of the eighteenth century. Before that time, the prejudices entertained by agriculturists against the unverified theories of book-farmers were often justified. They rested on a sure instinct. But rural ruts were so deep that they restricted the horizon. Old agricultural writers often recommended practices, now in universal use, a century before they were adopted. Their new-fangled notions might have enriched the great-grandfather instead of the great-grandson.

The history of agricultural literature printed in English begins with the sixteenth century. In 1520 a Dutch bookseller, named John Dorne, carried on his business at Oxford. His trade was especially brisk at the two great annual fairs in May and October. In his day-book for that year he enters his sales. He sold one copy of *Husbandry* at one penny, and three copies of *Medecens voer Hors* at twopence each. Both books have disappeared. They have been thumbed out of existence.

The true father of the English literature of the farm is John Fitzherbert. He was a Derbyshire man, whose *Boke of Husbondrye* was printed in 1523. He did not presume to write on farming till he had accumulated a practical experience of forty years. In this restraint he set a good example, which has not always been followed. A shrewd hard-headed man, he wrote a sensible book. Even in those days Derbyshire was famous as a horsebreeding county. Fitzherbert owned '60 mares or more'. He knew the trade. He had as little faith in a horse-dealer or a 'horse-leche' as in a 'potycarye'. 'It were harde,' he says, 'to truste the best of them.' His object in writing seems mainly to have been to demonstrate the superiority of an enclosed farm in separate occupation to a village farm cultivated on the prevalent system of a tenancy in common. The few improvements which he suggests, and the arguments by which they are enforced, strike us as antiquated. Both are now everywhere accepted: but it takes a heavy hammer and many blows to drive a nail through heart of oak. It was two centuries and a half before they were recognized in practice. He insists on the advantages of a farm in individual occupation, divided by hedges and ditches into separate enclosures. In the first instance, he admits, the expenditure would be considerable, but it would pay any farmer with a twenty years' lease to make the outlay. He would get his money back with interest by saving the charges to common herdsmen and shepherds and the expenses of hurdles and stakes, by enjoying the longer season on the grass which the enclosed land allowed, and by gaining a greater choice of the time for marketing his calves and lambs. Enclosed land was better for the stock and better for the corn.

Fitzherbert did not believe in the abandonment of tillage or the adoption of ranching. He advocates mixed husbandry. If a farmer is to prosper, stock and corn must go together. A man, he says, cannot thrive by corn unless he has livestock, and he who tries to keep stock without corn must either be 'a buyer, a borrower, or a beggar'. Though his resources were limited, though winter-keep remained an unsolved problem, and roots and artificial grasses were still unknown, he sees with a prophetic eye the verification of the maxim that 'a full bullock-yard and a full fold make a full stack-yard'. If his advice had been heeded in the years 1480–1640, England might have escaped some of the misery which was caused by the transformation of common arable farms into sheep-walks, and by the consequent loss of employment, rural depopulation, and destruction of houses and farm buildings.

Half a century later than Fitzherbert came Thomas Tusser, whose *Hundredth Good Pointes of Husbandrie* (1557), afterwards expanded into *Five Hundredth Pointes of Good Husbandrie* (1573), was written in doggerel verse. The book was so popular and so frequently republished that his name cannot be omitted. It is a valuable storehouse of information on existing practices, habits, and customs. Tusser was a recorder rather than an improver. He makes no new suggestions, and has no theories to expound. He is an eager champion of the superiority of land enclosed for individual occupation over land occupied in common by a number of occupiers. With Tusser begins the long line of agricultural writers, who failed in the business before they turned to literature, and thus strengthened the prejudice against book-farming. He was 'a musician, schoolmaster, serving-man, husbandman, grazier, poet – more skilful in all than thriving in his vocation'. He 'spread his bread with all sorts of butter but none would ever stick thereon', and he is said to have died in the debtors' prison of the Poultry Counter. Probably his best-remembered lines are:

> *At Christmas play and make good cheer,*
> *For Christmas comes but once a year.*

On one question, which from time to time is still disputed, both these old authors had made up their minds. Neither had any doubt that rooks were greater malefactors than benefactors. They charge them with preferring grain to grubs. Against pigeons, rooks, and crows, Fitzherbert proclaims a crusade. Tusser proposes to arm girls with slings and boys with bows and arrows, to drive away the marauders. Tudor England knew nothing of Board Schools.

One of the few suggestions made in these early books is that of green-manuring. Buck-wheat or 'Brank' is suggested for the purpose. In Tudor times the expedient had a special value; but on village farms it could not be adopted. It smothered the weeds, restored the humus, improved the texture of the soil, and provided manure when dung was scarce. Its use was the greater because the 'seeds' crop, which serves similar purposes more effectively, was still unknown. Buck-wheat is a quick

E

grower and a good weed-smotherer. It is for these reasons also recommended by Child (1651). It was sown in May and ploughed in in July. But Mortimer (1707) considered it a better practice to feed it to dairy cattle when it was coming into blossom. If allowed to seed and ripen, the grain was largely used for pigs and poultry. Milled for human food, it made a very white flour, which in Stuart times was highly esteemed for pancakes.

Child mentions other crops for green manure. Tares were, he says, so employed in Kent. He also recommends lupins, probably from his knowledge of Latin writers. The Romans were fully aware of their value before a corn crop, though the scientific reason for the richness of their fertilizing qualities was a discovery of the last century. In the connexion may be mentioned another form of catch-cropping. William Ellis of Gaddesden, whose writings were famous in the first half of the eighteenth century, attributes the success of Hertfordshire farmers, among other causes, to growing tares on turnip fallows to be grazed in May. Neither mustard nor vetches seem to have been used for catch-crops.

Fitzherbert and Tusser knew no other country than England. Barnabe Googe was both a traveller and a translator. His *Foure Bookes of Husbandrie* (1577) are translated from the Latin work of Conrad Heresbach published at Cologne, and a few pages are added of Googe's own observations on agricultural practices. The farming of the Low Countries with which the book deals, was the most advanced in Europe. But, then as well as subsequently, English farmers looked on foreign innovations with suspicion. They had their full share of the national insularity. In this case they lost an opportunity. Googe gives the first hint of the new resources which, two hundred years later, so marvellously enriched English farmers. He recommended not only the use of rape, but that of what he calls 'Trefoil or Burgundian grass'. 'There can be,' he says, 'no better fodder devised for cattle.' He also suggests, as supplying valuable food for livestock, the field cultivation of turnips. In the Low Countries they were extensively cultivated in the fields. In England, they were only just beginning to struggle into gardens as vegetables for human use to be 'boyled and eaten with flesshe'.

Whether Googe succeeded in converting any English farmers to the value of roots and grasses, is unknown. As he gives a list of men whose farming was an object-lesson to their less advanced neighbours, it is possible that some may have tried the suggestion. If there were any converts, they were few. A dry year may have discouraged the experiment of roots. It may have stiffened the resistance of farmers to their introduction, and confirmed their stereotyped answer that the new crops would not grow in England because their ancestors had never grown them. It was not till more than a hundred and sixty years later that the new resources began, on any general scale, to struggle into use in this country.

In clover and turnips new sources of wealth were thus offered to farmers of land in individual occupation. The want of winter-keep, for instance, accounted for the half-starved condition of English livestock, which only survived the winter as skin and bone. Here was a partial solution of the problem, and a means of carrying a larger and a heavier head of cattle and sheep. The new crops were destined to be the pivots of mixed farming. Throughout the seventeenth century writers kept pegging away at turnips and temporary grasses. Little attention was paid. In the existing system of open-field farming there was no room for either crop. All the partners in the village farms enjoyed grazing rights over the fallows as well as over the other arable fields from corn-harvest to seed-time. Any enterprising man therefore who wished to grow turnips would grow them for the benefit of his neighbours. Up to 1773, it was impossible, without the assent of all the partners, to alter the rotation by which all were bound, or to interpolate either of the new crops. They were, therefore, out of the reach of village farmers. But occupiers of enclosed farms were almost equally backward in their acceptance.

Once again, seventy years after Barnabe Googe, attention was called to the methods of foreigners by an eye-witness. In a clear and concise treatise, Sir Richard Weston described (1645) the field cultivation of artificial grasses and turnips in Brabant and Flanders. At first the book circulated in manuscript, but it was printed in 1649–50 and again in 1651. Arthur Young, with characteristic enthusiasm, calls Weston 'a greater benefactor than Newton', because he offered bread and meat to millions. But the times were unfavourable to progress. Traditionally, Oliver Cromwell interested himself in the introduction of the field cultivation of turnips. He is said to have paid a farmer named Howe a hundred pounds a year for being the first man to grow them successfully in Hertfordshire. Their cause, however, was not helped by the mountebank extravagance of writers like Adolphus Speed (1659), who commends them to farmers as the only food for cattle, sheep, swine, and poultry, sovereign for conditioning 'Hunting dogs', admirable as an ingredient in bread, supplying 'exceeding good Oyl' and 'excellent Syder', and yielding 'two very good crops each year'.

Other writers, on more moderate lines, urged the addition of temporary grasses and turnips to the resources of farmers. Andrew Yarranton, by his personal example and influence, succeeded between the years 1653 and 1677, in establishing clover in Worcestershire and the adjoining counties. He was one of the most interesting men of the time. Starting as a linen-draper's apprentice, he found the 'Shop too narrow and short' for his mind. He took leave of his master, lived a country life for some years, served as a soldier in the Civil Wars, turned consulting engineer in 1652, and studied various means of bettering the condition of the country. Impressed with the exhaustion of the 'rye-lands' by 'long tillage', he suggested clover as the remedy. His *Improvement by Clover* (1663) was 'so fitted to the countryman's capacity that he fell on Pell-mell' and the new crop 'doubled the value of the Land'. Elsewhere, it was long before clover emerged 'from the fields of gentlemen' into common use. Jethro Tull, writing in the reign of George I, says that, if advised to sow clover, 'farmers would certainly reply "Gentlemen might sow it if they pleased, but they (the farmers) must take care to pay their rents"'. He thought, perhaps with reason, that his example and advice carried less weight because he was himself a gentleman farmer. In 1768 clover was still unknown in many counties.

Equally strenuous was the opposition to turnips. It must, however, be remembered that at first they were sown broadcast. The name of the first man, Michael Houghton, who grew them at Hawstead in Suffolk in 1700, is preserved. 'I introduced turnips into the field,' wrote Jethro Tull of Berkshire, 'in King William's reign; but the practice did not travel beyond the hedges of my estate till after the Peace of Utrecht' (1713). In 1716 they were still a source of wonder to the neighbours when they were grown in Scotland by the Earl of Rothes. On the other hand, they made their way more rapidly in Norfolk and Essex where they were established before 1684. Daniel Defoe, who began his tour of Great Britain in 1722, says that Norfolk was the county 'where the Feeding and Fattening of Cattle, both Sheep as well as black Cattle, with Turnips, was first practised'. Hertfordshire may perhaps dispute the claim. Defoe's *Tour* was published in 1738, the year in which died Lord Townshend, whose zealous advocacy of the use of turnips as the pivot of Norfolk farming gained him the nickname of 'Turnip' Townshend.

None of the three Tudor agricultural writers who have been so far mentioned, were men of any scientific pretensions, even in the restricted sense in which the words can be used of our Elizabethan ancestors. Fitzherbert wrote his practical experiences. Tusser recorded facts. Googe reported foreign practices. Sir Hugh Plat was, in the alertness of his mental attitude, more akin to the scientific leaders of the nineteenth century. A man of an ingenious and inventive turn, he farmed near St Albans. Among his suggested improvements was that of drilling, or, as it was then called, 'setting' corn (1600). His attention was drawn to the advantages of the practice by accident. 'A silly wench' dropped wheat seeds into the holes meant for carrots. He claimed that, by dibbing wheat instead of sowing it broadcast, a man could increase his yield per acre from four quarters to fifteen. Few farmers were likely to believe so extravagant a promise. But Plat was on the track of a great discovery, although he and his immediate successors took the dibbing of beans as their model, and intended the seed to be deposited by hand. Others worked in the same direction. Francis Maxey

(1601) described the new manner of setting corn, and invented a machine which punched holes in the ground.

On similar lines Gabriel Plattes championed the new process so eagerly that he gained the nickname of the 'Corn-setter'. He rivalled Sir Hugh in the extravagance of his promises. Those who followed his system and used his drill (patented 1639) were promised a hundredfold increase in their yield. He died shirtless, and starving for want of bread, in the streets of London. But agricultural writers did not lose sight of the suggestion. Worlidge, for example, whose *Systema Agriculturae* (1669) deserved, on the whole, in spite of many defects, its reputation as a standard authority, came nearer the mark. He invented a drill to make the furrow, sow the seed, and deposit the manure. The machine is figured and described in his book. But he appears never to have made or tested his implement. Professor Bradley of Cambridge, who (1727) constructed the machine from Worlidge's drawing, found that the instrument would not perform any of its three functions.

It remained for Jethro Tull to invent and perfect a practical drill. It was used for the first time on his farm at Crowmarsh, near Wallingford in Berkshire, somewhere between the years 1699 and 1709. On the drilling of corn and roots he based much of his system of clean farming. By drilling wheat and keeping the soil clean and stirred between the rows, he grew it for many years in succession without manure. Applied to turnips the process trebled their value. But, as he mournfully says, though he grew better crops, at less cost, and with greater economy of seed than his neighbours, none followed his example. It was not till drilling of corn and roots had been enthusiastically adopted in Scotland and thence had drifted back over the English borders into the northern counties, that it gained any general hold in this country, years after Tull's death.

The most interesting of Sir Hugh Plat's observations are those on manures for arable and pasture land. Once again, it must be noted that, in the use of manure, village farmers were practically restricted to the droppings of their flocks and herds. As a body they were not likely to agree to outlay on the whole of their arable land, and the application to the strips of indidividuals was prevented by the distance which separated the scattered portions of each holding. Sir Hugh's suggestions are contained in the second part of his *Jewell House of Art and Nature* (1594). He is so enamoured of his subject that manure presents itself to his vision as a Goddess with a Cornucopia in her hand. Basing his theories on Bernard Palissy, he argues that perpetual cropping robs the earth of her vegetative salt. Therefore the wise husbandman must continually replace the elements of its fertility. He recommends a valuable list of manurial substances. He urges that existing practices allowed the vegetative salts of dung to evaporate by long exposure to the sun and so waste the richest properties of farmyard manures. He therefore suggests its accumulation in covered pits. He advises the use of marl, with a warning that it should be proportioned to the needs of different sorts of soil. His other manurial substances include lime, street refuse, the subsoil of ponds, and 'watrie bottomes', the brine of Cheshire 'salt pittes', ashes, the hair of beasts, malt-dust, soap-ashes, putrified pilchards, entrails of animals or fish, and blood offal.

Fifty years later than Plat, several agricultural writers were busy on the subject of manures. Among them was a man of ingenious and inquiring mind, Gabriel Plattes, the 'Corn setter'. His *Discovery of Infinite Treasure* was the use of the fertilizing qualities of the substances carried off by water. In the soil of streams, in mud of tidal waves, and in all 'coloured' water, he finds the 'fatness' of the land. He suggests catch-pits to receive the water of the 'land-flouds', especially where they come from fertile fields or paved market-towns. He also advises ditches and sluices to admit tides to run in swiftly and pass out slowly. In both cases, the deposit makes a valuable manure which will fertilize the most barren soil. All 'coloured' water should be similarly utilized on the land instead of being allowed to run to waste.

Contemporary with Plattes, were Walter Blith (1649) and Child (1651). Both give lists of manurial substances which supplement the suggestions of Plat. Putting their recommendations together, we get a fairly complete list of the fertilizers recommended for use by agricultural writers of the seventeenth century. They include marl, lime, and chalk; farmyard manure, which Child says must not be too much exposed to sun and rain; pigeon and poultry dung; swine's dung, which Fitzherbert says was harmful because it bred thistles; ashes, both of wood and 'sea-cole'; soot; malt-dust; 'raggs of all sorts'; 'coarse wooll, nippings, and tarry pitch-markes' (Blith); horn, or shavings of horn; seaweed 'of all sorts, rotted' (Child); salt dross, 'much used on' meadows near Nantwich (Child); marrow-bones (Blith); blood and urine (Child); fish and fish-bones.

Child mentions the New England practice of using on the land a freshwater fish, called the 'Ale-wife, because of its great belly'; very full of bones. It was, he says, caught in weirs, and sold in large quantities to farmers. Both writers suggest mud from rivers, and Child adds 'owse' from marshy ditches and foreshores. Both especially recommend a soil full of small shells, taken out of the beds of certain rivers. Child, who calls it 'snaggreet', says that it was much used in Surrey. Blith, who calls it 'snaylecod', says that one load was worth three of horse or cow dung, that it was found in the Thames Valley and near Uxbridge, and that men gained a 'gallant living' by bringing it to the surface and selling it on the river bank at from one shilling and twopence to two shillings and fourpence a load.

Child also recommends, as has been already noted, the practice of green manuring and the use of lupins for the purpose. Child's *Large Letter* on agricultural improvements is full of useful suggestions. But, in the same breath, he suggests that our livestock and the agricultural wealth of the country should be increased by the introduction of 'Black Foxes, Muske-cats, Sables, Martines', and, above all, the elephant as a useful beast of draught and burden, '15 men usually riding on his backe together'. His advice has not been wholly neglected. In the Cheviots today there already exists a flourishing skunk farm, and elsewhere a farm for silver foxes is projected. The elephant alone, though 'not exceeding chargeable', remains unhonoured on the farm.

Jethro Tull, it may be noted, objected to dung as a weed-carrier. In the writings of William Ellis we find the manures actually in use on a Hertfordshire farm in 1733–50, by an advanced farmer. Chalk was largely employed, pits being sunk to obtain the substance. Among the new ingredients are rabbits' dung and rape-dust. London refuse was freely bought; quantities of 'cony-clippings, horn-shavings, rags, hoofs, hair, ashes, etc.', were bought from 'Mr Atkins of Clerkenwel'. To the manures in use in the country were added, fifty years later, boiled or burned bones, sheep-trotters, and malt-dust.

Before the advent of agricultural chemistry, and the establishment of the principles of plant nutrition, the science of manuring was neither studied nor understood in theory. Probably no farmer in the sixteenth or seventeenth century could have explained the precise action of the different substances which he applied. But observation of results by individuals had built up an imposing list of suggested manures, some of which had taken their place in the traditional routine of the best farmers. It is interesting to note that, though the theory was unknown, practical experiment had provided the essential elements of fertility – nitrogen, phosphoric acid, and potash. All the native resources, except the coprolite deposits, were in fact utilized. It is the method of using these native materials, in their portable form, and in the discovery and use of new or imported ingredients, such as guano, phosphatic rock, the Stassfurt deposits of potash, or basic slag, that the increased command of fertilizing substances mainly consists.

The effect of cattle droppings is so obvious that dung must have been employed as a fertilizer in the infancy of agriculture in every country. Its treatment might be and may be improved. But it was sheer improvidence, or stark necessity which urged farmers to waste their one natural and all-round manure by mixing it with straw, kneading it into lumps, drying it, and burning it as fuel. Standish (1611) notices the practice. It was evidently widespread, for Lawrence (1727) speaks of it as prevailing in Yorkshire and Lincolnshire, and considered it important enough to suggest that all leases should contain a restrictive covenant: 'Cowdung not to be burnt for fuel.' Arthur Young (1770) found the practice in Buckinghamshire and Northamptonshire. 'There cannot,' he says, 'be such an application of manure anywhere but among the Hottentots,' a phrase which he often employs in speaking of village farmers.

To the Romans the value of marl, lime, and chalk were known, not as direct plant food, but as indirect fertilizing agencies. There is some evidence that the original home of their use was Britain. But, with the invasion of the Saxons, many practices were temporarily forgotten. The use of these substances may have lingered on in farming tradition; it may have been revived by ecclesiastical agriculturists from the writings of Pliny, Varro, Columella or Palladius; it may have been discovered afresh from their effect on the land when thrown up in digging ditches or foundations. Marl was certainly used in the thirteenth century in England. But the practice seems to have fallen into disuse. Fitzherbert, who notices its cost – it is, he says, 'exceeding chargeable' – regrets that it was becoming obsolete, and Gervase Markham, writing at the close of the sixteenth century, infers from the age of the timber growing in marl pits that they had been abandoned for two hundred and sixty or three hundred years.

Barnabe Googe recommends the use of chalk in moderation; but he adds the popular saying that 'grounde enriched with chalke makes a rich father and a beggarly sonne'. Its use on the heavy lands of Hertfordshire has been already noticed. 'Mixing earths', such as chalk on heavy clay and 'red clay' on sandy soils, is one of the practices to which Ellis attributes the agricultural success of the county. Large quantities of chalk were also imported into Essex from Kent, whence it was brought up the estuaries and distributed to the farms. The county, it may be added, is said to have owed its high reputation for farming to the early date at which its village farms had been enclosed. Gypsum was another of the substances used, especially in Kent and Sussex. Towards the end of the eighteenth century, its value was more extensively recognized. When Cornish or Devonshire farmers brought sea-sand from the coast on their pack-saddles, they probably did not know the exact nature of its value, or that it mainly lies in the carbonate of lime contained in the broken shells of which it largely consists. But they anticipated the modern market-gardeners of

Penzance in the use of the substance; they had experienced, in some way or other, the utility of its agency.

Other substances more directly contribute to plant food. That the value of soot was soon discovered is natural. Thrown on some waste place, its useful properties would be observed. Whether its effect in raising the temperature of the soil, or lightening its texture, or deterring slugs and snails, or its direct fertilizing qualities, commended its use to the first observer, is uncertain. It was employed, for one or other of these reasons, in the Middle Ages.

More difficult to explain is the discovery of the nitrogenous value of such substances as 'cony-clippings'; hair, shavings of horn, or woollen rags. Their effect is so slow that it might be imagined that it would escape detection. Yet they appear in the seventeenth-century lists of manures, and, as has been noticed, were bought by Hertfordshire farmers from London salesmen in the first half of the eighteenth century. Seaweed was extensively used in counties where it was accessible, and in South Wales the practice is especially noticed. Another nitrogenous manure available in maritime counties was fish-waste, such as the 'putrified pilchards' suggested by Sir Hugh Plat. For more inland counties there were slaughterhouse refuse and dried blood. The valuable properties of malt-dust were, as the lists show, early appeciated and more generally available.

Seventeenth-century writers provided farmers with a considerable choice of nitrogenous manures. They were less rich in their suggestions of substances containing either phosphoric acid or potash. Possibly 'snaggreet', the shelly deposit which is mentioned by Child and Blith, may have been mainly valuable as a phosphatic manure. Some phosphates would also be contained in Cornish sea-sand. Otherwise bones were the only available substance. Traditionally their value was observed by a Yorkshire master of foxhounds on the grass surrounding the kennels. At first they seem to have been roughly broken by hand labour on the farms. But by the middle of the eighteenth century it had become a trade to grind bones for agricultural use, and the value of boiling or steaming them was also recognized. Their use, as has been noted, was recommended by Blith in 1653, and similar advice was given by subsequent writers in the seventeenth century.

For potash, farmers depended entirely on ashes. Their use is recommended in all the early lists of manurial substances. Some evidence exists to show that an industry was established for their production and supply. Thus William Ellis, the Hertfordshire farmer, speaks of a potash kiln in Buckinghamshire. It is also on record that, in the eighteenth century, Kentish hop-growers organized a system of collecting the wood-ashes of neighbouring cottagers. Essential though potash is, it is especially valuable in its effect on some of the crops which were the latest comers in English agriculture, such as mangolds and potatoes, the latter of which were recommended by John Forster (1664), but not adopted outside Lancashire on any extended scale till the last century. Both crops have owed much of their later development to the discovery of the Stassfurt deposits.

The illustrations given from agricultural writers of the sixteenth and seventeenth centuries, show that many of the triumphs of modern farming had been anticipated. The materials had been already collected for the great agricultural advance which took place in the last forty years of the reign of George III. It may be added that, as early as 1645, the necessity of securing to tenants the value of their unexhausted improvements had been pleaded. Where so much had been anticipated, one omission on the part of the 'Rustick Authours' is striking. There is scarcely any suggestion for the improvement of livestock. On this side of their subject, writers are meagre and inadequate. None of them discuss the subject with any completeness, or with much regard for varieties of breed or for the different purposes for which animals are bred. Worlidge's *Systema Agriculturae* (1669), for instance, passed rapidly through five editions. But the subject 'of Beasts' is dismissed in three pages, while one hundred and six pages out of the total number of two hundred and seventeen, are devoted to trees, orchards, gardening, bees, and silkworms.

The neglect of stock-breeding and stock-rearing was not

unnatural, so long as little fresh meat was eaten, and so long
as winter-keep was short, and the stock were herded promis-
cuously on the commons or in the common folds of village
farms. But as the first half of the eighteenth century drew to a
close, these practical obstacles were to some extent removed.
The market for fresh butcher's meat improved. Farms in separate occupation multiplied. Roots and temporary grasses
were creeping into the rotations. When once the improvement
in stock-breeding began, it spread with the utmost rapidity.
Perhaps farmers adopted the principles laid down by Robert
Bakewell (b. 1725; d. 1795) with the greater enthusiasm, because they were the first improvements initiated by one of
themselves. The movement owed nothing to book-farmers.
It met the needs of a growing demand and afforded an outlet
for the natural bent of the genius of English agriculturists;
but it could make no progress on a village farm.

Drainage was the only other essential to farming progress
which still lagged behind. It had been sensibly discussed by
Walter Blith in 1649 and 1652. But the Cromwellian Captain
and Puritan, who brings Scripture to enforce his argument,
commanded none of the modern appliances, and the concerted
use of such methods as were available was difficult, if not impossible, on village farms. Otherwise, the inauguration of the
movement for improved livestock completed the necessary
preparations for a great agricultural advance.

The history of agricultural literature in the times of the
Tudors or the Stuarts is at once an exhortation and a warning
to twentieth-century farmers to keep their eyes open. But it
must continually be borne in mind that the new sources of
wealth, which were revealed by book-farmers and which passed
into general practice, were beyond the reach of the partners in
village farms, unless their organization had been drastically
improved.

2 Agricultural Progress in Open-field Oxfordshire

M. A. HAVINDEN

[This article was first published in the *Agricultural History Review*, Vol. IX (1961).]

It is customary to regard open-field agriculture as backward and static, and consequently it is difficult to believe that any serious farming progress can have been made within the confines of such an unwieldy system. It is true that by modern standards progress was slow. But progress is a relative concept, and although the pace of development within open-field agriculture may seem snail-like to us, when it is seen in its historical context it is less unimpressive. Particularly is this so when it is realized that many of the most important advances in open-field farming were made before the idea of agricultural progress became fashionable in the mid-eighteenth century.

In recent years the crucial importance of the seventeenth century as the germinative period for agricultural improvement has become appreciated.[1] While the most distinctive changes took place in enclosed regions, like East Anglia, improvement was not confined to such regions. There was an advance along the whole agricultural front in the seventeenth century, on open-field as well as on enclosed farms. Indeed, it may well be, as H. L. Gray was the first to suggest, that this early progress on open-field farms was one of the chief reasons why enclosure was delayed for so long in Midland counties like

---

[1] See for instance J. H. Plumb, 'Sir Robert Walpole and Norfolk Husbandry', in *Econ. Hist. Rev.*, 2nd series, v (1952), pp. 86–9; E. Kerridge, 'Turnip Husbandry in High Suffolk', *ibid.*, VIII (1956), pp. 390–2; and A. H. John, 'The Course of Agricultural Change, 1660–1760', in *Studies in the Industrial Revolution*, ed. L. S. Pressnell, pp. 125–55.

Oxfordshire.[1] As late as 1809 Arthur Young was complaining that there were still nearly a hundred unenclosed townships in the county.[2]

In the seventeenth century Oxfordshire was, with the exception of a small area of Chiltern country in the extreme south, an almost entirely open-field county; but this does not mean that it was an isolated backwater of subsistence farming. On the contrary, the fertile lowland area between the Cotswolds and the Chilterns had long been supplying London with wheat and malt, which was shipped down the Thames on barges; while the whole of the upland region in the north of the county swarmed with livestock. Cattle were important as well as sheep, and the cheeses of Banbury were as prized in London as the celebrated Cotswold fleeces.[3] Oxfordshire farmers were thus in the fortunate position of serving an ever-expanding metropolitan market, and therefore had an incentive to improve their methods.

The progress which was made in open-field farming was two-fold. Production was both diversified and increased, the two processes being intimately connected. The growing demand for meat and tallow, as well as for wool, broke down the predominantly arable character of the husbandry and made it more balanced. This, in turn, raised the fertility of the land so that the increase in livestock production was accompanied by an increase in the acreage of wheat and of fodder crops, and a decrease in the area of fallow land. Since the basis of the whole improvement was the diversification of production through the development of livestock husbandry, it is most convenient to consider this aspect first.

Opponents of the open-field system, like Arthur Young, naturally emphasized the rigid features in its use of land. An exaggerated picture was drawn of a system in which land was

[1] See H. L. Gray, *English Field Systems*, pp. 122–37, where farming improvements in the open-field parts of Oxfordshire are discussed from the point of view of field redivision. Gray was a pioneer in the study of improved husbandry practices on the open fields.

[2] A. Young, *General View of the Agriculture of Oxfordshire*, 1809, p. 88.

[3] See Daniel Defoe, *A Tour thro' the whole Island of Great Britain*, ed. G. D. H. Cole (1927), II, p. 430; A. Beasley, *History of Banbury* (1841), p. 586.

permanently divided between arable, meadow, and pasture, and within which no adaptability to changing market demands was possible. This picture has tended to obscure the variety of practice which was followed in different open-field regions, and to over-simplify the whole question of the relationship between improvement and enclosure. Detailed studies of open-field counties, such as that of Leicestershire by Dr Hoskins and that of Lincolnshire by Dr Thirsk, have shown that considerable flexibility and variation had already been introduced into open-field husbandry before the end of Elizabeth's reign.[1] The farmers did not all grow the same crop in the same field, and, more important, a measure of convertible husbandry had been introduced by the practice of sowing leys in the open fields. This useful device had become widespread in Oxfordshire by the early seventeenth century, as can be seen from the terriers of three unenclosed farms in north Oxfordshire, selected at random from the records of New College. At their farm at Hempton in 1624, 25 per cent of the land was described as leys; at Adderbury in 1628 the proportion was 16 per cent; and at Shutford in 1655, 34 per cent.[2]

Because of the problem of common grazing rights on the stubbles and fallow fields, leys were usually sown by all the farmers as part of a general agreement. In this way nobody gave his neighbour unrequited free grazing, and the value of the stubble and fallow grazing was enhanced for all. A good example of such an agreement was that made in the parish of Middleton Stoney in north-east Oxfordshire, near Bicester, in 1638. Nicholas Harmon, the lord of the manor, and Edward Fitzherbert, 'his farmer of the desmesne there', agreed with the parson and the tenants 'to lay down for every yardland of the said farm and demesne, six acres of grass for every second year in North field, and that every one of the said tenants shall lay down for every yardland which they hold five acres for grass yearly in the Cornfield'.[3] The yardlands at Middleton Stoney

[1] W. G. Hoskins, 'The Leicestershire Farmer in the Sixteenth Century', in *Essays in Leicestershire History* (1950); and *The Midland Peasant* (1957); Joan Thirsk, *English Peasant Farming* (1957).

[2] New College, Oxford, book of MS. Terriers (pages unnumbered).

[3] *The Victoria County History of Oxfordshire*, VI (1959), p. 247.

were of about 40 acres each and lay in two open fields, which means that each tenant would have had an average of about 20 acres per yard land in the cornfield each year. By putting 5 acres down to leys each year in the cornfield, the tenants were converting about a quarter of their non-fallow arable land to temporary pasture. The length to which the leys were left down could be varied according to need. When crops were growing near by livestock could be tethered on the leys, or penned in with hurdles.

It used to be argued that the existence of the right of fallow grazing on the open fields prevented the introduction of new and improved crops, particularly the clovers and turnips, since no one could be expected to grow these crops for the benefit of his neighbour's livestock. This argument is however no longer capable of general application, even though it may have been true in certain cases. In fact, a variety of new and improved legumes and grasses were introduced on the open fields in Oxfordshire in the seventeenth century. These included ryegrasses, clover, trefoil, and lucerne; but by far the most important was sainfoin, a deep-rooting legume which is particularly suitable for use on the thin, dry soils which occur in limestone country. It was therefore widely adopted in Oxfordshire, and especially in the northern, Cotswold part of the county. The growing of sainfoin represented an important advance, for it was both more productive and more nutritious than the indigenous grasses. Trow-Smith has said that 'the increase in food value of a stand of lucerne or sainfoin, either pure or in association with some of the improved grasses, over a permanent pasture of indigenous species was one of roughly 100 per cent considered as hay'.[1] Secondly, and perhaps even more important, the nitrogen-fixing mechanism in the root nodules of the legumes increased the fertility of the land on which they were grown.

Sainfoin was introduced into Oxfordshire in the second half of the seventeenth century, and was being grown on the open fields as early as 1673, when it is referred to in a legal document belonging to St John's College, Oxford. This document was

[1] R. Trow-Smith, *A History of British Livestock Husbandry to 1700* (1957), p. 257.

F

drawn up to legalize a private agreement to enclose some common pastures in East Chadlington, but it incidentally reveals
the importance of sainfoin. It seems that the lord of the manor
of East Chadlington, who was a London vintner named Sir
William Rollinson, had sown certain of his strips in the open
fields with sainfoin. His tenants agreed to give him right of way
to move his sheep and cattle from his enclosed pastures to be
tethered on these strips whenever he wished. He, in his turn,
agreed to let the tenants' livestock graze his sainfoin from
1 August until the following 20 March, when it was to be fenced
off with hurdles and allowed to grow for hay.[1]

It is probable that sainfoin was first grown by the more
enterprising lords of manors on their demesne lands, but by
about 1700 tenants were also growing it. This can be seen
from agreements which were drawn up between tenants and
their landlords, somewhat similar to the earlier agreements to
grow leys. These agreements were made because it was more
convenient if everybody agreed to grow sainfoin on all the
strips on certain furlongs rather than on odd strips scattered
about the fields. Thus certain furlongs were withdrawn from
the arable rotation and sown with sainfoin. They were sometimes temporarily fenced off from the rest of the open field and
referred to as enclosures in the agreements, but they lacked the
most important feature of a genuine enclosure, the extinction
of common grazing rights.

Such agreements were made in several townships of the
large parish of Spelsbury, near Woodstock. In one of these
townships, Taston, the twenty-two tenants signed an agreement on 4 January 1700 with the consent of the earl of Litch-
field, who was lord of the manor, to 'enclose' (in the sense
mentioned above) one part of the open fields consisting of five
furlongs, and to sow it with sainfoin. It is made clear in the
articles of agreement, however, that there was to be no enclosing of individual strips within this area, but that each tenant,
or owner, would agree to sow his own land with sainfoin.
Common grazing rights on the sainfoin continued but their
extent and duration were limited. Those with common rights

[1] St John's College, Oxford, Muniments, VI, 56.

were allowed to graze two cows for every yardland they held in Taston. The cows were not allowed in until the first crop of sainfoin hay had been removed. Sheep were not allowed in until 13 October, when six sheep and ten lambs per yardland were permitted. On 2 January the sainfoin was closed to all grazing animals until the following summer. The problem of drinking-water for the stock was solved by a stipulation that all persons having rights of common on the sainfoin must contribute towards digging a pond. Finally, three fieldsmen were appointed to supervise the carrying out of the regulations and to collect fines for non-compliance. Anyone ploughing up his sainfoin could be fined £10 per furrow ploughed.[1]

The details of this agreement indicate that it was intended to leave the sainfoin down for a considerable period, but a similar agreement made by seven yeomen with lands in the common fields of the nearby township of Fulwell in 1715 shows that these agreements were not permanent. In this case an agreement was made to sow sainfoin on a portion of the field which had been temporarily enclosed for that purpose before, but which had later reverted back into the ordinary common-field rotation. The tenants had found that their previous stand of sainfoin had been, in their own words, 'advantageous', and they agreed to sow it again.[2]

Although sainfoin was the most commonly sown of the legumes it was not the only one. For instance, in 1728, when the manor of Chesterton was surveyed for the earl of Abingdon, the surveyor, Robert Whittlesey, noted that there was an acute shortage of meadow. He suggested that this should be relieved not by enclosure but by sowing a third of the arable land with legumes. He recommended clover for the wettest land, sainfoin for the stoniest, and trefoil for the driest.[3]

Turnips, however, do not seem to have been much grown in Oxfordshire at this period. 'I introduced turnips into the field,' says Jethro Tull, 'in King William's reign; but the practice did not travel beyond the hedges of my estate till after

---

[1] Oxfordshire Record Office, Dillon MSS., DIL/II/n/1.
[2] Ibid., DIL/II/t/2.
[3] Bodleian Library, MSS. Top. Oxon. c. 381, 102.

the Peace of Utrecht.'[1] In fact Tull left his Oxfordshire property of Howberry, just across the Thames from Wallingford,
in 1709, when he moved to Prosperous in Berkshire; but he is
probably more or less correct, since the earliest references to
turnips which I have come across in examining thousands of
probate inventories for Oxfordshire is in 1727, when John
Deane, a cordwainer of Brize Norton, had 20 bushels of turnip
seed worth 10s. a bushel.[2] Of course I have not examined every
Oxfordshire inventory, and there were probably some farmers
growing turnips earlier than this, but they were certainly not
common before 1730, nor is there any evidence that they were
grown on the open fields. However, this absence of turnip
husbandry is not necessarily a sign of backwardness, for, as
Trow-Smith has recently pointed out, the turnip has been his-
torically somewhat over-valued. Its nutritive value, weight for
weight, is less than that of barley straw, and it has never been
such an important source of fodder for livestock as clover,
sainfoin, or improved grasses like ryegrass.[3]

The introduction of new crops is only one aspect of agricultural progress, but it is an important one because it sometimes stimulates and makes possible the reorganization of an
old system along more advanced lines. This was certainly the
case with the introduction of sainfoin in Oxfordshire. For
instance, when the farmers of Spelsbury made an agreement to
grow sainfoin in 1708, similar to the ones already cited for
Taston and Fulwell, they took the opportunity to reorganize
their arable rotation by a redivision of the open fields.[4] It was
decided that the land left over after some had been set aside
for sainfoin should be divided into three new fields, two to bear
corn crops and one to lie fallow each year. Spelsbury lies in the
northern upland part of Oxfordshire which was, according to
Gray, traditionally a two-field region; thus the two original
fields were redivided into four new ones, one of which was
always under sainfoin. This redivision of two-field systems into

[1] Quoted by Lord Ernle, *English Farming Past and Present*, Sir A. D. Hall (ed.),
5th edn (1936), p. 135.
[2] Ibid., 170; Bodl. MS. Wills Oxon., 164/3/13.
[3] Trow-Smith, op. cit., p. 256.
[4] Oxford Rec. Off., DIL/II/n/2b.

four or more fields was common all over Oxfordshire in the seventeenth century, and Gray has cited several examples of it.[1] The terrier of the New College farm at Adderbury, previously referred to, shows that there were five fields there as early as 1628.

The primary object of field redivision was to reduce the area of fallow land. Clearly fallow grazing was one of the least efficient ways of feeding livestock, although it served a useful purpose in manuring and consolidating the arable land and also in keeping it free from weeds. It could therefore not be abandoned altogether; but as the fallow land could produce more food for the livestock if it were sown with fodder crops such as peas, beans, or vetches, than it could by growing weeds, the object was to reduce the fallow area to the smallest possible amount. These reductions were possible because the fodder crops which replaced the fallow were legumes, and therefore did not exhaust the land.

The practice of growing fodder crops on the fallow field was called 'hitching'. It was probably first practised in a small way. Perhaps one or two furlongs would be temporarily fenced off from the fallow field and sown with pulses. For instance, in 1612 Robert Loder, who farmed in the two-field parish of Harwell on the edge of the Berkshire Downs, not far from Oxfordshire, had '17 landes hithed with poulse and fatches' (i.e. vetches).[2] The practice spread throughout the seventeenth century, and such small, temporary hitches were gradually replaced by large, permanent fields as the old open fields were divided.

By the early eighteenth century field division had become complex, particularly in the north of the county. An example of this is provided by the parish of Shenington, which was surveyed for Oriel College in 1732. At the end of the survey there is a section headed 'Customs of the Parish' which reads as follows: 'Shenington Field is called Townside Land, Farmside Land, and Cotmanside Land. The Townside is divided

[1] Gray, op. cit., pp. 493-4.
[2] *Robert Loder's Farm Accounts, 1610-20*, G. E. Fussell (ed.), Camden 3rd series, LIII (1936), p. 39.

into four Parts, and three of them are ploughed and sow'd every year, with wheat, Pease and Barley; the fourth part lies fallow; or when it is Sow'd with Pease, it is called Hitch. Part of Townside is every other Years Ground.

'Farmside is ploughed as the Townside.

'The Cotmanside being divided into four parts, one is sow'd with wheat, and one with Barley every year; sometimes the other two parts lie fallow, and sometimes both are hitch, or as the parish agree.'[1]

The open arable land was thus divided into twelve parts in which the tenants' lands lay in intermixed strips. In fact not all these strips were used as arable, since the survey makes it clear that some of them were leys; but excluding the leys, the apportionment of the crops was roughly as follows: a quarter of the land (three of the twelve parts) normally grew wheat, and another normally grew barley, while a sixth (two of the twelve) normally grew peas. The remaining third of the land (four of the twelve parts) was either fallow or hitched with peas, or divided between the two, 'as the parish agree'.

The noteworthy point is the flexibility of this system. The area of pulses could be varied from a sixth to a half of the arable land, and the fallow could be eliminated entirely in seasons when it was felt to be unnecessary. The same degree of flexibility was perhaps not to be found everywhere, but the example of Shenington shows the extent to which the more advanced open-field farmers could vary and improve their system without enclosure.

It is now time to consider what effect the growing diversity of the open-field system had in raising production. We have examined various ways by which the quantity of livestock fodder was increased, and its quality improved; and as we should have expected, these developments were reflected in a growth in the size of flocks and herds during the seventeenth century. This growth can be roughly measured by analysing random samples of farmers' inventories.

Thus, in a sample of 226 inventories relating to the limestone upland region of Oxfordshire, taken between 1580 and

---

[1] Oriel College, Oxford, Muniments, S II.I.19, p. xxxii.

1640, the size of the median average sheep flock was fourteen; whereas in a sample of about the same size for the years 1660–1730 the median average flock was sixty, or more than four times as large. It is true that the proportion of farmers who kept sheep fell slightly between these two periods (from 66 to 56 per cent), but even so it seems clear that the sheep population had considerably increased. Of course, some of the increase must be ascribed to the effects of enclosure, and particularly piecemeal enclosure within open-field parishes; but as nearly two-thirds of this region was still unenclosed in 1730 it seems reasonable to assume that most of the increase occurred in open-field parishes.

In the Thames valley region, between the limestone uplands and the Chilterns, where there is a wide variety of clay and loam soils, and where conditions are less favourable for sheep, the increase was naturally less pronounced. But even here a comparison of the size of the median average flock, taken from two samples containing over 400 inventories each, shows that it more than doubled, over the same period, rising from twenty-four to fifty-one sheep.

The increase in the numbers of cattle was not of a similar magnitude, but they seem to have made a modest advance. Herds were not generally large; the average size was under five, but there was an increase in the proportion of herds containing more than five cattle during the course of the seventeenth century, and this increase was not accompanied by any decline in the proportion of farmers keeping cattle, which remained over 80 per cent during the whole period. In the samples relating to the limestone uplands herds containing over five cattle rose from 33 per cent in the period 1580–1640 to 46 per cent between 1660 and 1730, and the corresponding figures for the lowlands were similar (39–45 per cent). However, herds containing more than twenty cattle did not amount to more than 5 per cent of the herds in either region in 1730, so that the increase in dairy products and beef took the form of a slow but steady advance over a wide area, rather than that of a dramatic increase in specialized production.

From the evidence of the inventories, then, it seems clear

that open-field townships were able to improve their livestock husbandry.

A swing to livestock also reacts upon arable husbandry. It is probable that the acreage of corn crops was reduced, but on the other hand the remaining arable land was given the advantage of better rotations and more manure. This meant that there was an opportunity for the reduction in the arable acreage to be offset by an increase in quality of the corn grown and also possibly in the yield per acre; although detailed evidence for the latter is not available. The evidence of the inventories, however, strongly suggests that the acreage of the inferior bread cereals, like rye, barley, and oats, was reduced while that of wheat was increased. This development was subject to regional variation. The upland areas, which had hitherto been behind the more fertile vales in this respect, showed the greatest rate of advance. The evidence for this comes from a comparison of the crops grown by groups of farmers in the same periods which were used in the comparison of the livestock numbers. For this purpose it is only possible to use inventories which were made in the summer before harvest, and which therefore show the complete acreage of the different crops. Such inventories are not numerous, and the samples used are not as large as I should have liked, but I have used all the surviving Oxfordshire inventories which were available.

On the limestone uplands the crops grown by a group of twenty-three farmers in the period 1660–1730 showed the following changes when compared with those of a group of twenty-six farmers in the period 1590–1640. The proportion of wheat had almost doubled, from about 14 to 27 per cent; the pulses had risen from 15 to 20 per cent, the barley had fallen from 61 to 49 per cent, the oats from 7 to 4 per cent, and the rye, which had only been 4 per cent before 1640, had disappeared altogether. Practically every one of the farmers used in these samples lived in open-field parishes, and although a few of them may have had some enclosed land, there seems no reason to doubt that most of the improvement took place on the open fields. It has to be remembered that this was naturally sheep and barley country, and that the thin 'stonebrash' soil was not well suited to wheat. In the circumstances a doubling of the proportion of land devoted to wheat was an important achievement.

In the more fertile clay vale the advance of wheat was less pronounced (from 25 to 32 per cent) in two similar samples, but it will be noticed that farmers in the vale were already growing twice as much wheat as upland farmers in the early seventeenth century.

Rye, like wheat, was also subject to considerable regional variation. It seems to have lingered longest in the small upland region around Banbury, where a thickly settled peasantry cultivated a useful red soil derived from a localized outcrop of the marlstone, or ironstone, of the middle lias. The farmers' inventories for this region show that before about 1630 the winter-sown cereal was almost invariably rye or maslin (which is a mixture of rye and wheat), and that wheat was seldom sown as a separate crop; but that after about 1630 the position was almost reversed, most of the farmers preferring wheat to rye or maslin. This was true of large as well as small farmers. For instance, William Alcocke, of Epwell, was a substantial farmer who died in 1612 leaving a personal estate of £127 14s. 10d. His crops were worth £44, of which rye and barley accounted for £36, and hay, peas, and oats for £8; but he had no wheat.[1] Neither had Robert Calcot of Burdrop, who died in March 1610 leaving crops worth £50 2s. 8d. Rye was his only winter-sown cereal.[2] This is in marked contrast to the situation twenty years later, when farmers like John Lovell, a yeoman of Bloxham, were more typical. His only winter-sown crop in 1633 was wheat, of which he had 28 acres growing in November.[3]

The way in which the supply of pulse crops was increased by the new rotations has already been indicated from the survey of Shenington, as well as from the comparison of probate inventories. The type of pulse grown depended to some extent on the soil. In the upland regions beans and vetches were rare, and peas almost universal; but in the Thames valley farmers sometimes grew quite a variety of pulses. For instance,

[1] Bodl. MS. Wills Oxon. 1/3/5.   [2] Ibid., 11/3/36.   [3] Ibid., 139/2/7.

Thomas Reading, a husbandman of Shirburn, a parish at the foot of the Chilterns, whose inventory was made on 1 August 1700, had 12 acres of beans and peas, apparently growing together, 9 acres of peas on their own, 2 acres of vetches, and 2 acres of dills, or lentils. In all he had 25 acres of pulses, which was just over a third of his 73 sown acres.[1]

The increase in the production of wheat and pulses took place largely at the expense of barley. This was one of the improvements which agricultural writers like John Worlidge were calling for early in Charles II's reign, when they complained that an excessive acreage was devoted to barley on many open-field farms.[2]

Although there is no reliable evidence that this improvement in the type of cereals being grown on open-field farms was accompanied by an increase in the yield per acre, an interesting development in farm equipment took place at this time, which suggests that harvests may have become heavier; namely, the introduction of the commodious four-wheeled farm wagon in place of the old two-wheeled long-cart. The way in which the use of the wagon was spreading can be seen from the inventories. Dr Robert Plot, writing in 1677, praised the farm wagon, but said that it was little used at this time in Oxfordshire, except by carriers.[3] His estimate is borne out by the farmers' inventories, but they show that he was soon to be out of date; for while there are no examples of wagons in a sample of nearly 800 inventories taken between 1580 and 1640 and only three in a sample of 138 in the 1660s, by the 1690s about 20 per cent of the farmers possessed wagons, and by the 1720s the proportion had risen to 34 per cent. There was hardly a yeoman in George I's reign who did not possess at least one wagon, in contrast to the situation at the Restoration when even the wealthiest yeomen were without them. Although all the reasons for the introduction of wagons at this period are not known, the possibility of higher yields cannot be ruled out.

[1] Bodl. MS. Wills Oxon. 147/2/1.

[2] John Worlidge, *Systema Agriculturae*, 4th edn (1687), p. 36. The first edition was published in 1669.

[3] R. Plot, *The Natural History of Oxfordshire* (1677), p. 257.

It is not possible in a short paper to go any further into the details of the many improvements which occurred in open-field agriculture. I have tried to concentrate upon the main features. These were, of course, abetted by minor changes, such as the exchange and consolidation of strips, which all helped to make the system less inconvenient.

In conclusion, the evidence, when taken altogether, suggests that there was an ascending spiral of progress. It began with an increase in the area of grassland by means of leys. This led to more livestock and more manure. Then the demand for better winter food for the livestock led to the introduction of the legumes like sainfoin and clover. These, in conjunction with the increased supply of manure, helped to raise the fertility of the land, and enabled it to be intensely cultivated by the partial elimination of fallows. As a result of more intensive cultivation, the supply of fodder for the livestock was further augmented (in the form of pulses), while the supply of grain was not only maintained, but actually improved in quality by means of the enlarged wheat acreage. Thus each advance, while small in itself, stimulated further advance in another sector, and the spiral was able to begin again at a higher level.

3 Agriculture and the Brewing and Distilling Industries in the Eighteenth Century

PETER MATHIAS

[This article was first published in *The Economic History Review*, 2nd series, Vol. V, 1952.]

> 'In addition to the stock of the County before described, we must not lose sight of a source of wealth of which the Board, perhaps, has little or no conception: it is in the article of hogs. . . .' (W. James and J. Malcolm, *General View of the Agriculture of Surrey*, London, 1794, p. 33, speaking of the hogs fed at distilleries.)

One of the interesting side-issues that arises from a study of the distilling and brewing [1] industries of the eighteenth century is the close connexion existing between them and the agricultural economy of the country. The most important feature of this connexion is naturally the supply of barley and malt for the raw materials of the industries, but one interesting, if minor, feature of it lies in the use of the waste products as a supply of feeding-stuffs for cattle and pigs, and through that a contribution to the provisioning of London.

Distillers' waste consisted of the spent 'grains' left after the infusion of the barley and malt and the 'wash' from the resulting

---

[1] The grains from brewing had always played a part in the domestic economy of the farm and the country estate. This is mentioned in most of the works on husbandry and agriculture of the time as, for example, Ed. Lisle, *Observations in Husbandry* (2nd edn, 1757), II, p. 330: 'In managing hogs a gentleman has good advantage above a farmer . . . inasmuch as in March (when the corn is almost threshed out) great store of drink may be brewed, with the grains of which many pigs may be maintained till the middle of May when the broad-clover comes in. . . .' This paper, however, is concerned with the commercial utilization of these waste products on a large scale, which developed as brewing and distilling developed as industries during the eighteenth century.

first extraction when the spirits had been distilled from it. The brewery [1] waste consisted mainly of the spent grains alone. As the brewing and distilling seasons were from October to May (the warm months being unsuitable for malting and fermentation) the supply of grains and wash came during the winter when the demand for feeding-stuffs was at its height. In Scotland, where the distilleries were more widespread in the country districts than they were in England, this seasonal cycle was important in itself; in the London area it was combined with a geographical importance, for no small part of London's meat and milk supplies were dependent on the stock fattened and the milch cows fed within the confines of the town area on these waste products of two of the city's greatest industries.

The scale on which the breweries and distilleries were conducted in London – especially as the century advanced – accounts for the great quantities of feeding-stuffs produced and the large numbers of hogs, and later cattle, being kept on them. There were eleven 'capital brewhouses'[2] in the Metropolis at the end of the century, of which the largest – Whitbreads – produced 200,000 barrels of porter in a good year, and the least – Cox, King and Co. – about 45,000 barrels. Similarly, there

[1] This was not including the yeast of the brewery which was the source of a regular trade to the distillers and the bakers, sometimes direct and sometimes through intermediaries – the Yeast Men. All three appear regularly in the Rest Books of Whitbread and Co. which survive at the brewery (I was enabled to see these records through the courtesy of Mr J. E. Martineau). See also *Parl. Papers* (1803–4), IV, Report from Comm. on London Bakers' Petitions, p. 8, and (1808), IV, Evidence before the Comm. on Distilling from Sugar, p. 51. Benwell and Smith say that the great porter brewers supplied corn distillers, and some Scottish distillers.

It does not include either the sludge from the boilers and vats which was used for manure (J. Mills, *New System of Agriculture* (1765), I, p. 94). Combrune complains that there was as yet no use for the spent hops of the brewery which 'might become an object of private emolument to the brewer, as well as of public benefit to the nation' (M. Combrune, *Essay on Brewing* (1758), p. 291), but these are noted as being used with sour grains for manure by 1805 (J. Malcolm, *Agriculture of Surrey* (1805), II, pp. 106–7).

[2] Printed estimates for the production of the first twelve houses exist for 1759–60, 525,674 (Annual Register); 1786–87, 978,200 (Pennant, *History of London* (1790), p. 378 n.); 1794–5, 993,840 (Press Return). These figures are all for the number of 36-gall barrels.

were seven distilleries that produced over 300,000 gallons of spirits in the year 1802–3.[1] The 'length' of a brew of porter – the number of barrels of beer produced from one quarter of malt – was between three and four barrels per quarter,[2] and there are estimates[3] that a quarter of malt produced about 20 gallons of spirits and 110 gallons of 'wash'. Three quarters of grain used produced two quarters of 'grains'.[4] These figures are in no sense exact, but they do indicate unmistakably the great amount of material used in this by-product branch of the industry.

The value of the grains of the distillery was greater than of those from the brewery, largely because of the proportion of unmalted barley used in distilling after 1720. The distillers' grains generally sold at 6s. to 8s. per quarter in 1808,[5] while the brewers' grains fetched only 3s. The ale grains were reckoned richer than the porter grains. But despite this the quantities involved in the brewery were so vast that there was considerable profit in having them as a perquisite, which was the case for persons in charge of the actual brewing at Whitbreads,[6]

[1] *Parl. Papers* (1803), VIII, p. 1039. Papers relating to Distillers. Total numbers in London then were sixteen.

Previous estimates vary greatly. *Corn Distillery stated to the consideration of the Landed Interest* (1783) (Pryme Coll. in the Marshall Library, Cambridge), gives thirty 'Capital Offices' in and about London in 1750 (p. 14), and twelve only after the prohibition of the corn distillery was removed in 1760 (p. 16). When the House of Commons called for a return of the stocks of distillers in and near London in 1782–83 there are only eight firms named (*Commons Journals*, XLIII, pp. 505–6).

[2] Whitbread's Brewing Books, 1800–50, *passim*. F. A. Accum, *Art of Brewing* (1821), p. 125, gives the length of brew of porter from 2½–3 brls per qtr malt. It varied greatly with the quality of the malt.

[3] J. Malcolm, op. cit., I, p.'357. See also *Parl. Papers* (1808), IV, p. 26. Benwell states that 100 gall of wash can be obtained, on average, from 1 qtr grain, and 19 gall of spirits from the 100 gall of wash.

The number of licensed stills and the amount of spirits that paid duty in no sense give total production of spirits, or the total production of these waste products. Fraud was very widespread but impossible to estimate.

[4] *Parl. Papers*, ibid., p. 113.

[5] *Parl. Papers*, ibid., pp. 26, 113, 164–7. *Parl. Papers* (1831), VII. Evidence before Comm. on use of Molasses, p. 69.

A discussion of the ratios of malted to unmalted grain used in distilling is also given in *Commons Journals* (1745), XXIV, p. 833.

[6] Whitbreads: Gratuity Ledger, *passim*, 1800–50. When calculating how much David Jennings, the brewer, has benefited from perquisites there is the entry

and appears to have been the general practice. These were all
sold off the premises to the cow-keepers and to cattle dealers,
as was the case with the waste from the breweries and distilleries near Edinburgh; so that with this scale of selling the generally assumed picture of the milk-cows of London being driven
into the town daily or feeding on the grass of the open districts
within London is misleading.

In England the organization of the distilling industry was
primarily metropolitan, and, with it, the utilization of the
waste products of distilling. This had been encouraged by a
deliberate fiscal policy which discriminated against the small
producer of both beer and spirits and, in addition, the high
rate of duty levied, which was payable before returns from
sales were received, told against the small unit of production,[1]
throwing the trade into the hands of those people with capital.
This applied above all to the brewers and the primary distillers,
the rectifiers (redistilling the raw spirit made by the primary
distillers) being more numerous and more widespread.[2] The
primary distillers kept hogs themselves about their distilleries
rather than sell their 'offals' off the premises as did the brewers.

By 1736 the scale of this feeding of hogs at the distilleries,
and the low price at which they could afford to sell them was

(1801) '. . . for Money received of Cowkeepers and which he has not brought to
account – £779, which sums are set against his 2 years Gratuity. Besides which he
had perquisites in Hops and Grains suppose between £300 and £400.'

[1] This is illustrated by counsel in *Rex* v. *Brown, Parry and Co* (1808, Goldsmith's
Library) Golden Lane Brewery, 1808, in Ct. of Exchequer, Sgt. Vaughan (re.
12 Ch. II, Ch. 23, s. 22 and later acts giving allowances to Common Brewers):
'. . . the legislature thought it was better for the Crown to have these breweries
conducted on a more extensive scale, and that it was considered a great object to
prevent as much as possible brewing privately and in small quantities – the Legislature felt perhaps that from the magnitude of the concern in the one case it
would be easy to collect the duty and difficult to evade the payment of it: –
whereas in the other the collection of the duty would be troublesome and expensive and the revenue daily liable to be defrauded. . . .' And also Mr Nolan, 'It
is important [for the Crown] that the breweries should be confined as to their
numbers but extensive with regard to their concerns. . . .'

[2] *Parl. Papers* (1803), VIII, p. 1039. There were then 133 rectifying distillers of
which sixty-one were in the London area. There were only twenty-two licensed
primary distillers in the whole country (England) of which sixteen were in London, and the others in Bristol (two), Colchester, Maidstone (Bishop's 'Geneva'
distillery), Stanstead, and Worcester.

raising opposition[1] among the home-county and Shropshire hog-farmers. Farmers were having to send unfattened 'stores' to the distilleries in London rather than fattening them themselves and were opposed to giving the distillers the estimated profit of 20s. that the fattening put on the price of each pig. It is difficult to discover the actual numbers involved, because, before the end of the century brought the reports to the Board of Agriculture and the more sober evidence of Parliamentary Papers, the main sources of printed evidence is in pamphlet literature and petitions to Parliament – both highly tendentious. But, at all events, they must have been considerable, and the distilleries were already large units of production.[2] One estimate was of 50,000 fattened annually, and the writer[3] was interested in playing down the claims of the farmers who were exaggerating the menace to their profits. The point at issue was that, since the distillers had begun to use unmalted grain[4] a short time before, they were enabled to feed the hogs completely on their grains and wash without any reliance on beans or pease that were necessary with the grains left over from only malt. Thus they by-passed the farmers completely and were enabled to undercut them in the markets and for the valuable victualling contracts for the Navy. These matters were brought before the House of Commons in January 1740, when petitions from the home-county farmers were presented, a Committee was detailed to investigate the complaints, and a report given to the House in 1745.[5]

[1] *Impartial Enquiry into the Present State of the British Distillery* . . . (1736) (Pryme Coll.), pp. 37–8, and *Distilled Spirituous Liquors the Bane of the Nation,* which is on the farmers' side against the distillers.

[2] *General Description of all Trades* (1747), p. 79: '. . . Malt Distilling, which vies with the Brewery for Return of Money and Profit, for most of them are very large concerns indeed, adding to the Distilling Malt Spirits chiefly for the use of Rectifiers, that of fatting Hogs, an Advantageous Article, which together are not to be undertaken without some thousand Pounds in Cash. . . .'

[3] *Impartial Enquiry,* p. 38.

[4] Ibid. This was a measure that profited them fiscally by escaping the malt duty, as well as enabling them to feed their hogs more effectively. James and Malcolm in 1794 suggest that they began to keep hogs in order to recoup some of the excise payments. (*State of the Agric. of Surrey* (1794), pp. 33–4.)

[5] *The Case of the Malsters, Farmers and Graziers in General* (Goldsmiths' Library, c. 1750). *Commons Journals,* XXIII, pp. 584, 630; XXIV, pp. 833–6. This latter section

It was generally admitted[1] at the time that the 'country-fed' pork was superior to the distillery pork, and this was part of the reason for the difference in price between them – but not entirely, as the petitioners knew. The competition had forced down the prices to a point where it had become uneconomic for the farmers to fatten, and dropping rents in the Fen Lands (largely leased out for hogs it was said), slackening of demand and falling prices for beef and mutton are together blamed on the distillers' hogs. This difference in price was variously estimated to be between 2*s*. 6*d*. per stone (for country-fed) and 1*s*. 6*d*. per stone (distillery-fed), 2*s*. and 1*s*. 4*d*., 5*d*. and 3½*d*.[2] per lb. One dealer, after a long tirade about the bad quality of distillers' hogs, admitted that he made but 2*d*. per stone discrimination against them in his buying price and none in his selling price. Since the distillers had entered the market for the victualling contracts it was stated that the Commissioners had 'not dealt with the farmers for many years' and that the West Country hog farmers no longer drove to Portsmouth as they did. Conceivably this driving long distances put the farmers at a disadvantage with the distillers who were enabled to 'fat' near the yards at Deptford, and it was probably

---

includes the evidence of witnesses summoned before the Committee and the following passage is largely based on this.

The original petition ran '. . . and that with the Grains of Unmalted corn (i.e. whose use they wished to prohibit altogether) now used in brewing and preparing spirituous liquors, Distillers and others do feed and fat a great number of Hogs; which would otherwise be better fed and fatted in the Country by Farmers or would necessarily consume a great Quantity of Pease and Beans, and coarse corn mixed with Grains, if the said Distillers and others were obliged to use malted corn only' (XXIII, p. 584).

[1] The inferiority of the distillers' meat was the common charge in all pamphlets against the distillery. See *Spirituous Liquors the Bane* (1736); J. Tucker, *An impartial Inquiry into the Benefits and Damages . . . of low-priced Spirituous Liquors* (1751); *Impartial Enquiry*, op. cit., p. 39; *Commons Journals*, loc. cit. This evidence includes that of an ex-distiller, Harvest. Jennings, a contractor buying for the naval Victualling Commissioners, says that the distillery-fed hogs could give good keeping pork if they were managed properly and the favourable report of J. Middleton in 1813 (*General View of the Agriculture of Middlesex*, p. 486) suggests that this proper management came with experience and experiment – although he is still combating consciously a common opinion.

[2] *Impartial Enquiry*, op. cit., p. 39. He suggests that the distillers sold at this 1½*d*. per lb less because 'they can afford it so cheap'.

G

advantageous for the naval authorities to deal directly with persons who could guarantee large-scale deliveries at a low price, rather than with graziers and others who would collect the hogs round the farms in the hinterland and drive them to the ports.[1] This had its disadvantages, however, for the distillers were few enough in number to combine together in order to protect their market – much as the 'ring of timber contractors did at a later period'.[2] And in so far as the low price did reflect any difference in the keeping quality of the pork (through the distillery pork being gross and not 'taking' salt in curing as effectively as the country-fed pork), 'saving the public money' partly explains the perennial complaints about rotten provisions in the fleets. John Jennings, one of the contractors buying hogs for the Navy,[3] described how:

> The Distillers have entered into a combination and advanced a large Sum of Money, in order to prevent other Persons from contracting at the Victually Office and that because the Witness [i.e. himself] contracted for hogs with some farmers, the Distillers afterwards refused to sell him any.

Writers in the latter part of the eighteenth century thought that the British distillery reached its peak about 1750. The stoppage of the Corn Distillery from 1756 until 1760 and rising rates of duty from 1751[4] had further concentrated the industry

---

[1] *Commons Journals*, p. xxiv, 835. There are few precise references to the contractors with whom the Navy dealt in the printed Calendar of Treasury Books and papers. Reference is made to a grazier who petitioned against a contract that had proved unprofitable through a sudden rise in prices of country-fed hogs (C.T.B. August 1697–8, p. 210). And there appear to be regular purchases made in Ireland in 1743. (C.T.B. 1743, pp. 260–1, 264, 274.)

[2] R. G. Albion, *Forests and Sea Power* (Cambridge, Mass., 1926), pp. 55–60, 320–4.

[3] *Commons Journals*, xxiv, p. 836.

[4] 'Immediately upon passing the Act (1751) the Distillery was lessened a full Third.' *True State of the . . . Distillery* (1760), Pryme Coll. 24 Geo II, Ch. 40. 2 Geo III, Ch. 5. This new duty of 7 guineas per tun meant that when the Corn Distillery was allowed to start again in 1760 the total nominal duty was £24 10s. per tun, increased by £4 18s. per tun in 1762. The 1756 stoppage had been partly in response to pressure from the West Indies interest to encourage the sale of molasses and 'low Sugars'. This running fight continued into the nineteenth century, intensifying when the West Indies ran into bad times.

Corn Distillery stated to the Consideration of the Landed Interest (1783). (Pryme

and limited the numbers of hogs kept by the distillers while providing an incentive for the exploitation of waste products. The round figure of 100,000 is given [1] for the numbers annually fattened in 1750, with 20,000 to 25,000 in addition sold in a winter to the Victualling Office 'for the use of the Navy, at a low price, deducting the Discount on the Navy Bills'. This account is coloured by the conditions of 1783 being those of a depression year.[2] The writer does emphasize the effect that the distillers' pork has upon the market prices, favouring the abundance of distillers' hogs in order to get the prices down. The farmers had complained of just this in 1740–5 and Burke, pointing out the way a bad grain harvest in 1794–5 increased the prices of country-fed hogs and threw an increased demand upon all other flesh, argued against the stoppage of the corn distillery which increased it – '. . . . another cause, and that not of inconsiderable operation. . . . It is an odd way of making flesh cheap to stop or check the distillery.'[3] Dixon claimed[4] that the high price of Norfolk hogs in 1810 was partly due to the stoppage of the distillery in 1808.

As the distilleries became fewer and larger, so the organization of pig-keeping became scientific, and evidence more reliable than the round numbers of the pamphleteers becomes available. John Middleton, a more independent observer,

---

Coll.), p. 16, states that apart from the twelve distilleries that reopened on corn distilling in 1760, '. . . all the rest [were] shut up or demolished without receiving any recompence or reward from Government under whose sanction they were erected at the expence of many thousands of pounds.'

[1] *Corn Distillery stated to the Consideration of the Landed Interest*, pp. 43–4.

[2] There is the double complaint that fat hogs were too dear for the Victualling Office to buy and that there were too few in the hands of the distillers to be sold. The bad harvest meant less corn for the 'lean stores' on the farms and affected the parent industries of brewing and distilling also in the high grain prices and in the decline of purchasing power through unemployment. The writer emphasizes that the need is for employment, not charity (p. 49). Production of malt that paid duty fell from 28 million bushels in 1782 to 17·23 million in 1783. (*Parl. Papers* (1835), XXXI, 15th Report of Commissioners of Excise Enquiry, p. 4.)

[3] *Thoughts and Details on Scarcity* (1795), Works, 1834, II, p. 243.

[4] W. Dixon, *Inquiry into the Impolicy . . . of the prohibition of Distillation from Grain* (Liverpool, 1810), p. 41 (Pryme Coll.). *Corn Distillery stated . . .* (1783), p. 44, claims that the decline of the distillery was responsible for the increase in the price of hog-fat for the soap boilers from £24 to £34 per ton.

reported to the Board of Agriculture in 1813, for Middlesex,[1] that the distillers fattened 50,000 hogs for bacon annually, and in doing so increased their value £4 each, making £200,000 each year. And, moreover, he now praises the quality of the pork. Dixon had put the numbers at 'over 41,000' in 1810, and James and Malcolm say that, for Surrey:

> . . . the numbers which . . . are annually fattened, shews to what an extent it is carried on, and, as a branch of commerce, [it] is of considerable value: it is, besides, of material benefit to those counties from whence they draw their supplies; and inasmuch as it makes a part of agricultural economy, deserves every encouragement that can be given to it. There are also great numbers fed in the starch yards, which we shall distinguish from those of the distilleries. . . .[2]

They continue to give the numbers as 3,000 fattened annually at Messrs Johnson's Distillery at Vauxhall; 3,000–4,000 at Benwell's, Battersea; 2,000 at Bush's, Wandsworth. Stenard's starch manufactory fattened 2,700 yearly, on an average, and Randall and Suter's 600–700. The starch yards, however, were under the disadvantage of having to use a proportion of beans and pease in addition to their offals. All these figures are in excess of the numbers of cattle that the distillers had begun to keep, as described below, and they total for Surrey 11,700 hogs annually, value £46,215.

As with the cattle this was now 'capitalistic' meat production in a systematic way. Finchley Common[3] was the great market, both for the butchers who bought 'fat' and for the distillery feeders who bought the 'lean stores'. Finchley was the selling point for those coming from the Midland counties – Yorkshire Lincolnshire, Leicestershire, Berks, and Shropshire – while the counties to the North-East of London – Norfolk, Suffolk, and Essex – sent their breeds to[4] Romford market after the harvest. At market they were sorted into sizes by the salesmen

---

[1] J. Middleton, *General View of the Agriculture of Middlesex* (1813), p. 579.
[2] W. James and J. Malcolm, *State of the Agriculture of Surrey* (1794), p. 33.
[3] Ibid., pp. 36–7. J. Malcolm, op. cit., p. 486.
[4] D. Defoe, *Tour thro' the whole Island* . . . (1722), Everyman edn, I, p. 37.

(the distillers wanted them at about 15 months and they needed too many each to be able to buy all of the same breed) and sent to the various feeders. In 1813 the average buying price was about 55s. and they sold fat, according to weight and quality, in about 18 to 26 weeks time. James and Malcolm print[1] a table of weights and prices showing the great profit obtainable from this business, and comment on the way in which they are kept 'with all imaginable care and cleanliness in one progressive state of increase. . . . It must be observed that no pains are spared to keep them clean and sweet, which the superior construction of their very extensive premises enables them to do.'

With both meat prices and the rate of duty rising at this time there was every incentive for the distillers to become as efficient as possible in their feeding arrangements. One estimate[2] reckoned upon being able to pay all the running expenses of the concern on the receipts from keeping stock, others[3] supposed the gain to be about 2s. per week for each pig and 10–15s. a week per head of cattle. This advantage may have been the incentive for the distillers to begin keeping cattle themselves once it had been proved feasible – beef was more in demand and the price was higher. Middleton describes how it began and how a mixed diet which included the distillery offals now had made this side of meat production highly efficient.[4] A certain Mr Man of Bromley first fed meat cattle on the wash and grains in 1789.

[1] Op. cit., p. 35. 'Table of hogs at Messrs Johnson's Distillery:

Breed	Age bt.	Value	Weeks kept	Weight and value when sold	
Salop. Herefd. Glos. Berks.	15 mths.	55s.	18–26	32–5 st.	£4–£5
From Essex	15 mths.	60s.	,,	34–6	£4 15s.–£5 10s.
Norfolk. Suffk.	Younger	42s.	,,	21–4	£2 15s.–£3 3s.
Yorks	15 mths.	46s.	,,	21–8	£3–£3 10s.

[2] *Parl. Papers* (1816), IX, Report on Illicit Distilling in Ireland, p. 143. The reference is to a large distillery.

[3] James and Malcolm, op. cit., p. 35. Stephenson, *Agriculture of Surrey* (1815), p. 522.

[4] Middleton, op. cit., pp. 579–90.

During the first three or four years of this practice Mr Man obtained the wash for nothing, the secret then began to extend, and the wash is now fetched from the distilleries to all the environs of the town, and even to the distance of 10 or 15 miles, although it is now sold for 2s. 6d. per butt. The whole quantity of wash used to be drained off into the river as of no value; it is now sold and so desirous are the cow-keepers and cattle feeders of obtaining it that carts to the numbers of ten or twenty at a time may be seen waiting to be filled up in turn, when the wash is turned on.

On the strength of this Man had, by 1813, enough accommodation to feed 1,000 bullocks at a time; and between 4,000 and 5,000 passed through his hands each year. Cattle on the King's farms at Windsor were also fed on distillery grains; the bailiff considering[1] them a 'very valuable food indeed'. While selling off the premises was still general where there was a market in the neighbourhood for their waste products, it appears that it was becoming general, for the larger distillers to keep cattle themselves on the 'wash' after 1800. Thomas Smith, a distiller of Brentford, thought[2] that about 4,800 to 5,000 were kept by them in 1808, but that the greatest proportion fed by the distillers was still for milk. They themselves, at Brentford, did more fattening than others because they had no cow-keepers near them, and as late as 1808 they found difficulty in selling their grains outside. 570 cattle were kept there in stall.

By 1813, in Surrey, Stephenson writes,[3] that

> Most of the cattle . . . fattened for the butcher in this country are in the hands of the great distillers at Battersea,

---

[1] *Parl. Papers* (1808), IV, Evidence before the Comm. on Distillation from Sugar, p. 120, N. Kent, the King's Bailiff.

[2] Ibid., p. 29. One of the main issues raised by this Committee and argued by the witnesses is the potential dislocation of the cattle-feeding branch of the distillery if distilling from corn should be prohibited. The wash from distillation from molasses could be utilized if need be, but it would not be feasible to keep stock without the grains that were produced only from corn distillation. Beans and pease would have to be purchased from other sources if the corn distillery were closed, pp. 33, 135. Also *Parl. Papers* (1806–7), II, Report from Comm. on distilling from Corn and Sugar, Report, p. 6, and Evidence, pp. 24–6.

[3] W. Stephenson, *Agriculture of Surrey* (1813), p. 522.

Vauxhall, etc. . . . The practice of carrying cattle is adopted by many of the feeders, particularly at the distillery in Vauxhall, and is found to answer remarkably well.

James and Malcolm note this as being the case at Hodson's as early as 1794, when special accommodation had lately been built and the management made thoroughly efficient. By 1805 they had begun to fatten 600 each season – from October to May – while at Brentford the distillers' cattle were evidently one of the agricultural sights of the county. At Smith and Harrington's premises there were nearly 500 tied up '. . . and kept in the highest possible stile; so fine a sight is no where in England to be met with, and these gentlemen take much pleasure in shewing them to persons properly introduced'.[1]

There were, as then, none at Cook's new distillery but Calvert, Clarke, Dunkin, and Scott were preparing to keep large numbers and had already 100. William Adam, a farmer at Streatham, had arranged his farm to keep cattle specially on the offals from the distilleries, having the same system of management as Hodgson's but sending the 4 miles daily to Vauxhall and Battersea for the grains and wash.[2]

This system is itself revealing – and is as efficiently planned and operated as any 'high farming' in Norfolk. At Hodgson's

> . . . almost circumscribing their premises a range of houses have been built, of almost 600 ft in length, by 32 ft in width for the oxen. There houses are divided longitudinally into separate stalls for each beast. . . . The oxen are placed in two rows standing with their heads opposite each other, and in the middle between the two rows is a passage 6 ft wide the whole length, and one at each end of the same width, where the cattle go in and out. Latterly they have introduced an open wooden trellis,[3] or grating, made strong . . . to keep

[1] J. Malcolm, *Agriculture of Surrey* (1805), I, pp. 355–9.
[2] James and Malcolm, op. cit., p. 32. Malcolm, ibid.
[3] This was discontinued in 1805 because of the trouble it caused to the feet of the cattle. The stalls had then been entirely paved with brick. Malcolm thought that some of the cattle kept by the other distillers were cleaner than Hodgson's, being well strawed. Malcolm, loc. cit.

the animals from the pavement, that they may not only be
kept dry but also that they may with greater facility be kept
clean; which, as often as they want to do, the soil is drawn
out from under the grating by means of a broad hoe. . . .
For every 100 oxen two men are kept . . . the allowance is
one bushel of grains put into a triangular trough filled with
wash, to each, and one truss of hay per diem to every 15, to
which is added sometimes, some of the meal dust that flies
from the malt in grinding.[1]

William Adam also had these special houses 'conveniently
constructed and sufficiently capacious' to feed 600 bullocks on
the same mass-produced, stall-feeding pattern. They bought in
September at Kingston and the other West Country cattle
fairs, preferring the Welch to the Herefords, for about £5 each,
and sold, according to the market, after 14 to 16 weeks to the
carcass butchers for about £16 per head. Despite this efficiency
there was a certain waste that the reports to the Board of Agriculture regret. The profits were directly from the meat sold to
the London market, and the manure resulting was largely
wasted in those establishments within the town – 'not for
want of a market for it, but because the collecting it in any of
the large distilleries would be attended with some trouble, and
their premises are too confined and valuable to allow of their
affording sufficient room for such an article . . . '.[2] Here lies
one of the big differences in emphasis between England and
Scotland – for the keeping of livestock at, or on the produce
of, the distilleries was common to both. In Scotland the point
always stressed is that the livestock kept through the distilleries
provided manure essential for maintaining, and extending, the
general fertility of the farms. The connexion between the agricultural economy of the country and the distilleries was there
more intimate and widespread – for the distilleries were not
confined to the towns.[3]

This increasing exploitation of the waste products of
breweries and distilleries is concomitant with the development

[1] James and Malcolm, p. 31.   [2] J. Malcolm, op. cit., II, p. 26.
[3] This is brought out in a large number of pamphlets, books and Parliamentary
Papers, and is more conveniently dealt with separately.

of the parent industries during the same years. They were becoming organized on a large scale, and consequently facing problems of industrial organization more general in the next century – with capitalization, buying policy for stock, pricing and so forth. Because they were functioning on such a large scale it became profitable to use systematically the quantities of valuable by-products remaining from the primary manufacture. And this incentive which arose merely from the scale on which they were working was increased by the opportunity it afforded of off-setting in some degree the rising rate of taxation and spreading a loss in a bad year when raw material prices were high. The long-term influence of the duty was very sharply increased by a bad harvest. It was not customary for retail prices of drink to move in response to one bad harvest, and when the distillers had to bid for barley at a scarcity price, the knowledge that they could command a profit from the sale of their stock which would also be that of scarcity must have been a big compensating factor. Also the move into keeping cattle comes at a time when the greatest fluctuations and difficulties were affecting the breweries and distilleries. It is probably not coincidental that this new phase of livestock keeping comes at the same time as the tied house system was rapidly spreading among the brewers. Both are a likely response to bad times. The practice raises interesting points about the stage at which profit can be calculated for a firm spreading its commitments and being vertically integrated in this way.

Apart, however, from these more particular questions, the general fact is important. This livestock kept by industries emerging in their own way through an industrial revolution, made a significant, if unnoticed, contribution to feeding the city population which they supplied with drink.

4 Enclosure and Labour Supply in the Industrial Revolution[1]

J. D. CHAMBERS

[This article was first published in *The Economic History Review*, 2nd series, Vol. V (1953).]

Until the advance, a generation ago, in the study of the demographic aspect of the Industrial Revolution, the function of enclosure in regard to labour supply was regarded as crucial. Its special importance in recruiting the industrial labour force was developed in a series of important studies as the result of which it came to be generally regarded as a basic postulate of the new large-scale economy.[2] More recent examination of the growth and movement of population has done something to modify this view, but the conventional picture of catastrophic change effected by enclosure continues to find adherents. Any alternative to it, says Mr Maurice Dobb, implies the assumption that 'the appearance of a reserve army of labour was a simple product of growing population which created more hands than could be fed from the then cultivated soil. If this were the true story, one might have reason to speak of a proletariat as a natural rather than an institutional creation and to treat accumulation of capital and the growth of a proletariat as autonomous and independent processes. But this idyllic picture

[1] Based on a paper read to the Annual Conference of the Economic History Society, Easter 1951.

[2] For the most explicit statement of this view see Marx, *Capital* (Everyman ed. G. D. H. Cole), ii, p. 793, and M. Dobb, *Studies in the Development of Capitalism* (1947), p. 223. 'The capitalist system pre-supposes the complete separation of the labourers from all property in the means by which they can realize their labour. . . . The expropriation of the agricultural producer, of the peasant, from the soil is the basis of the whole process.' See also H. Levy, *Large and Small Holdings* (1911), p. 38: 'The expropriated small farmer, degraded to the position of labourer . . . swelled the rural exodus being driven into the towns.'

fails to accord with the facts.'[1] This formulation of the problem invites discussion on several counts, but from the angle of
the regional historian (from which it is viewed here) it general-
izes a process which he sees in terms of its separate parts, i.e.
as actual movements of population in particular places; and he
is impelled by the force of his methodology to test the abstract
formula of 'institutional creation' by fitting it to the local
facts as he knows them. Such is the purpose of this article; but
some clarification of the formula is necessary at the outset.

The question which is raised here is not the institutional
origin of the proletariat, but whether enclosure is the relevant
institution; not whether the growth of the proletariat can be
treated in isolation from capital accumulation, but what form
the relationship took. It centres on the emergence of what Professor Tawney has called 'a residual population' of property-
less free labour,[2] and the factors, in addition to enclosure and
eviction, which accounted for its growth; and a brief résumé of
the early stages of the problem is necessary to indicate the
context of its later stages with which we are here concerned.
It is relevant, for instance, to recall that as early as the thirteenth century, among the limiting conditions for the growth
of a free labour force, were the localized customs of partible
and impartible inheritance and the influence they exerted on
the age of marriage. In the area of open-field or 'Champion'
England, where, we are told, holdings usually descended un-
divided to one son, the rise of a free labour force from younger
sons and daughters would have taken place more rapidly but
for customary restraints upon their marriage.[3] These, it has

[1] Dobb, op. cit., p. 223. But see pp. 257, 272-3, where the increase of population is attributed to the fall of the death-rate owing to improvements in public
health, and 'natural increase' is stated to 'have powerfully reinforced' the pro-
letarianizing process. There remains, however, the question of the 'institutional'
creation of the proletariat, by which is meant the forcible dislodging of the
peasantry from the soil.

[2] R. H. Tawney, *The Agrarian Problem in the Sixteenth Century* (1912). 'A residual
population, which cannot fit itself into the moving mechanism of industry without ceaseless friction and maladjustment', p. 104, and especially pp. 104-6, n. 3,
and pp. 21-3, n. 2.

[3] G. C. Homans, *English Villagers of the Thirteenth Century* (1940), p. 137. A
'husbond' held a substantial tenement and could therefore afford to be a husband
and parent. For the rest 'no land, no marriage'. Mr Homans notes elsewhere

been suggested,[1] would be relaxed when alternative means, e.g. the domestic woollen industry, were offered for rearing a family. Here was a potential source of labour power that could be expected to respond to the stimulus of investment all the more freely for the absence of the counter-attraction of partible inheritance.

These sources of growth operated silently and perhaps we may say organically, i.e. they were not the direct or indirect product of compulsion; and for that reason there is a danger that they may be overlooked. For opposite reasons enclosure and eviction may be given too much importance: they operated, in Mr Dobb's phrase 'institutionally', i.e. compulsorily, as the result of the exercise of power, and stirred the social conscience to protest and the victims to riot and rebellion. But their effectiveness as a recruiting agent for the labour army remains a doubtful quantity, especially in the light of the knowledge we now have of the scale on which they worked. Sixty villages 'wiped out', fifty of them by enclosure between 1450 and 1600 in Leicestershire alone; the desertion of ninety-three sites in Warwickshire and 'other hundreds to be discovered':[2]

---

that Norfolk and Suffolk were areas of partible inheritance and here 'there were large numbers of small and perhaps impoverished landholders and the two shires where the revolt of 1381 held most imperious sway'. Homans, 'Partible Inheritance of Villagers' Holdings', *Econ. Hist. Rev.*, VIII (1937), p. 48. In Kent 'a parcel of 1½ acres would pass to co-heirs'. H. L. Gray, *English Field Systems* (1915), p. 292. See also J. C. Russell, *British Medieval Population* (Albuquerque, 1948), pp. 31, 65–6.

[1] See J. Granat, *The Disappearance of the Peasantry in England* (Moscow, 1908), where special importance is given to the part played by the heavy English soils which, the author thinks, necessitated the use of numerous cattle for the plough-team and thus provided a barrier to the subdivision of the holding. This in turn would produce a class of landless labourers long before the capitalist era from younger sons and daughters (cf. Homans on the heavy soils of 'Champion' England). Granat also thinks this accounts for the slow rate or population growth until the rise of the wool industry which attracted labour from the soil (see especially Chapters II and V kindly translated for me by Mr J. Twardowski, B.A.). See also summary by E. A. Kosminsky in *Econ. Hist. Rev.*, I (1928), p. 222.

[2] W. G. Hoskins, *Essays in Leicestershire History* (1950), p. 101; W. G. Hoskins, 'Leicestershire Farmer in the Seventeenth Century', *Agricultural History*, January 1951, p. 16; M. W. Beresford, 'Lost Villages', *Geographical Journal*, June 1951. Mr Beresford's statement that 'each represents a landowner pursuing his advantages to the point of destroying a farming community' (loc. cit., p. 129) is

changes of this order must have made a sizeable contribution
to the army of the landless; but it seems to have provided only
a temporary alleviation of the labour shortage and did little
to stimulate population growth.[1] 'The problem of population,'
says Professor Tawney, 'was the problem of under-popula-
tion'; and contemporary writers were beginning to explore
the possibilities of rewards for parents of large families and
penalties for bachelors.[2]

The period immediately preceding the era of parliamentary
enclosure with which we are primarily concerned here, seems
to have followed a not dissimilar pattern; it was marked by
the buying out of freeholds and leases for lives as a prelude to
enclosure on such a scale as to give rise to the erroneous view
that the yeomanry had already disappeared by 1750.[3] But rapid
and ruthless as this process may have been, it failed to meet the
labour needs of the time or to accelerate substantially the
processes of proletarian reproduction. 'The fear of scarcity
of labour,' we are told, 'seems constantly in the minds of
eighteenth-century employers';[4] and 'for a century following
the Restoration', says Mr Dobb, 'the growth of capitalist
industry must have been considerably handicapped by the
comparative weakness of the labour army';[5] but, from the
middle of the eighteenth century, 'the pace of dispossession

---

somewhat modified later when he suggests other 'non-institutional' factors which
might have operated; and it would not be difficult to add to them, but the aggregate of the evicted must have been large.

[1] Mr Dobb notes that the surplus of labour thus produced was turned into
a deficit in the next century owing partly, he thinks, to the slackening of enclosures. But the evidence for this in the seventeenth century is lacking. Dr
Hoskins finds that in Leicestershire it was greatly accelerated ('Leicestershire
Farmer . . .', loc. cit., p. 17) though I think his figures are necessarily swollen by
his inclusion of all enclosure by agreement in the pre-1730 period. There was
certainly no slackening in Nottinghamshire; see my *Nottinghamshire in the
Eighteenth Century* (1932), pp. 147, 187. The explanation for the shortage of labour
seems to be that the 'residual population' failed to reproduce itself until rural
demographic conditions became more favourable in the next century.

[2] Tawney, op. cit., p. 109 n., quoting Starkey.

[3] Marx, op. cit., ii, p. 800, quoting a letter of 1795, but see p. 100 n. 2,
below.

[4] J. Lord, *Capitalism and Steam Power* (1923), p. 204.

[5] Dobb, op. cit., p. 227.

quickens';[1] and enclosure at last takes place on a scale sufficient
to perform its allotted task of reducing the peasantry to a
landless proletariat and removing the last prudential checks
upon their increase.

At this point, the existence of census returns, enclosure
awards, and land tax duplicates makes possible the application
of more exact tests to the claims which are made for enclosure
in recruiting the labour force, and to this aspect of the discussion we may now turn.

The first effect of bringing the method of quantitative inquiry to bear on the problem seems to be to diminish the role
assigned to enclosure. Professor Gonner, in his exhaustive
study of census returns, could find no general connexion between enclosure and movement of population.[2] Professor
Redford finds that the impact of agricultural change at least
during the war years was more often to stimulate the growth of
rural population than the reverse, and that side by side with the
growth of urban communities, there was also a growth of

[1] Mr Dobb's citation in this connexion of Lord Leicester's remark: 'I am like
the ogre in the fairy tale and have eaten up all my neighbours' calls for comment.
Marx says it was made when he contemplated 'the solitude' which he had created
as a result of building his famous house at Holkham (loc. cit., Vol. II, p. 767. See
also A. M. W. Stirling, *Coke of Norfolk and his Friends* (1912), p. 38). To cite this
as an example of enclosure producing a 'solitude' is a particularly unfortunate
choice. The builder of Holkham found his estate 'open and barren' when he
succeeded to it in 1707. He reclaimed 400 acres from the sea and began planting
trees as a wind-break; he grew turnips as early as 1723 and wheat, clover, and
lucerne by 1731 and probably before. See Naomi Riches, *Agrarian Revolution in
Norfolk* (Chapel Hill, 1937), p. 95, and J. E. T. Rogers, *History of Agriculture and
Prices* (1902), VII, pp. 636–704. As early as 1752 it was said that where these
practices were followed 'there is three times as much work for labourers in
plowing, hedging, threshing, which supports twice as many families'; quoted
Riches, op. cit., p. 77. See also C. W. James, *Chief Justice Coke and his family at
Holkham* (1929), p. 265. His great-nephew continued these improvements. He is
said to have increased the number of farms on his estate by twelve, and to have
spent half a million on palatial farms and – for those days – model cottages, and
even earned a rare encomium from Cobbett. See E. Rigby, *Holkham and its
Agriculture* (1817), p. 52; Stirling, op. cit.; Cobbett, *Rural Rides* (ed. G. D. H.
Cole), I, p. 47. The population of Holkham, which was said to be 200 in 1770,
was returned as 550, 585, 810, 792, 683 between 1801–41. The decline from 1821
is a reflection of the post-war slump, especially disastrous in North Norfolk with
its inferior soils. To apply the words 'ogre' and 'solitude' in this context would
be a case of post-Coke propter-Coke thinking!

[2] E. C. K. Gonner, *Common Land and Inclosure* (1912), pp. 441 *et seq.*

entirely new agricultural communities as well as the reinforce-
ment of those already existing.[1] Among the examples he gives
we might refer especially to Lincolnshire, where the distressing
lack of originality in rural nomenclature emphasizes the
novelty of the new creations: East Ville, Midville, West Ville,
Langrick Ville, to mention only four entirely new rural communities emerging as a result of an enclosure act of 1812.
There was a parallel movement in Cheshire where the enclosure of Delamere Forest was the midwife of a new community.
And the enclosures of Sherwood Forest, Charnwood, Enfield
Chase, Bere Forest, Beeley Heath, Hampton Common, of
wastes in Cumberland, Dorset, Derbyshire, Lancashire, Yorkshire, Northumberland, continued to stimulate the growth of
population in rural areas almost up to the middle of the century.

But it may be objected that the peopling of the waste places is
merely a variant in a rural setting of the movement of expropriated peasants from the old established rural centres under
the expulsive force of enclosure. It is also possible that such
a movement was masked by the growth of rural industries,
and that the extruded peasantry were being transformed into
a rural industrial proletariat as the first step to their recruitment
in the army of urban labour.

An attempt has been made to examine this objection within
a limited area of 119 villages in Nottinghamshire with results
seen on Chart 1. It shows that the population of the predominantly agricultural villages rose only less fast than that
of the villages in which manufacturing or mining industry
prevailed; and that of the agricultural villages, those that had
been enclosed by act of parliament before 1800, rose faster than
any.

[1] A. Redford, *Labour Migration in England* (1926), p. 63: 'It appears,' Professor
Redford writes, 'that the agrarian changes of the early nineteenth century were
part of an evolutionary process by which the rural population of each district
was specializing in the kind of agriculture to which the district was physically
and climatically suited. . . . During Cobbett's life-time no single county . . .
reported a decreased population at *any* of the successive census returns. Cobbett
countered this argument by flatly refusing to believe the census returns; but in
this he was narrowly anticipating Dame Partington's opposition to the Atlantic
Ocean' (p. 69). See also G. E. Fussell, 'English Countryside and Population',
Econ. Geography (1936), p. 296.

Such evidence, however, leaves the larger question un-answered. The increase in population which is seen to be take-ing place in all types of villages, whether enclosed or not, may well be compatible with the reduction of the small-scale pro-ducer to the level of labourer and a stripping of the cottagers of their last remaining vestiges of independence. In regard to the section loosely called the yeomanry, that is (to adopt the work-ing definition of Sir John Clapham) the farmer-owner with a holding sufficient to occupy his whole time, it would appear that he held his own or even made something of a recovery, at least during the war-time boom, and that the post-war de-cline was not catastrophic, as the Agricultural Reports of 1833 and 1836 show.[1]

In regard to the earlier period when it is suggested the yeo-manry actually made something of a recovery, we need make no more than a passing reference to the many examples quoted by the Agricultural Reporters[2] to show that economic condi-tions were not always unfavourable to the independent owner-occupier and that there was a widespread tendency to buy on the rising market. Where the soil was favourable to the small freeholder, enclosure might permit him to develop a form of mixed husbandry, as in South Wiltshire, where 'there are so many parts of the land, that, when enclosed, may be applied to the purposes of a small farm, without the necessity of keep-ing a flock of sheep to manure it; viz. by keeping that part which will be necessary to remain in arable, on a turnip system . . . by laying the wet parts to grass . . . and by apply-ing the sand lands on a garden system'.[3] An interesting con-firmation of this opinion is provided by Rutlandshire where great varieties of soil occurred at short distances so that nearly

[1] See J. H. Clapham, *Economic History of Modern Britain* (1926), 1, pp. 103–5.
[2] See A. H. Johnson, *Disappearance of the Small Landowner* (1909), Chapter VIII; Ernle, *English Farming Past and Present*, pp. 292 *et seq.*; Clapham, *Economic History of Modern Britain*, 1, pp. 99–104; W. Hasbach, *History of the English Agricultural Labourer* (1920), pp. 70–7; and H. C. Taylor, *Decline of Landowning Farming in England* (Wisconsin, 1904) for valuable summaries of this evidence. For an interesting contemporary summary see Thomas Robertson, *General Report upon Size of Farms submitted to Board of Agriculture* (1796), county by county, including Scotland.
[3] T. Davis, *General View of Wiltshire* (1794), p. 139.

all the farms had suitable land for all kinds of husbandry 'thus producing everything useful in themselves', which helps to account for the continued survival of the small farm, e.g. of 20–50 acres after enclosure.[1] An example of a different kind of

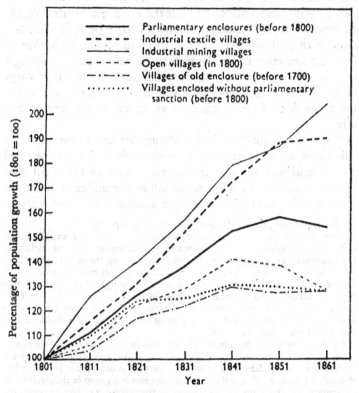

CHART I. Growth of population in Nottinghamshire: changes 1801–1861.

advantage enjoyed by the small farmer at this time comes from Knaresborough Forest where, after enclosure, the small proprietors, we are told, 'took the lead and brought their small shares into the completest state of cultivation', while the larger proprietors were handicapped through shortage of labour and extravagantly high wages demanded, so that many of the

[1] R. Parkinson, *General View of Rutlandshire* (1807), pp. 17 and 30.

H

larger allotments had not even been fenced fifteen years later.[1]

Most of these examples refer to the small owner. The small tenant was in a far worse case and contemporary opinion leaves us in no doubt that this class generally suffered in numbers heavily from enclosure;[2] but the economic context of enclosure cannot be assumed always to have been fatal to the small man at this time; it varied in its incidence according to local circumstances. Enclosure marked only a phase – though an important one – in the ascendancy of the large farm with its lower comparative costs; it was not the signal for the extinction of the small farm as an economic unit everywhere.

If we turn to the statistical evidence, we find confirmation of this supposition. A number of localized inquiries may be cited which tend to show that the survival-value of the small man under the impact of enclosure should not be underestimated. In Professor Lavrovsky's exhaustive analysis[3] of eleven villages

[1] G. Rennie, etc., *General View of Yorkshire* (1794), p. 76.

[2] See, for example 'Chalk Wiltshire', where the small farmer was eliminated through the destruction of the common sheep-fold system. In some enclosures the commissioners saved the small farmer by retaining the commons without which he was doomed, an example of institutional factors coming to his rescue. On the other hand 'Cheese Wiltshire' remained the stronghold of the small family farm. See Davis, op. cit., p. 85, and forthcoming chapter of the *Wiltshire V.C.H.* on 'Agriculture and Estate Management 1609–1793' by E. Kerridge who has kindly permitted me to read this important study based on hitherto unused material of the manorial surveys.

[3] V. M. Lavrovsky, 'Parliamentary Enclosures in the County of Suffolk (1797–1814)', *Econ. Hist. Rev.*, VII (1937), pp. 193, 207–8. He points out that the penetration of capitalist elements into the English village did not always take place through the medium of capitalist farming. Sometimes a group of rich, well-to-do peasants arose from among the peasantry themselves, i.e. before enclosure. See also *Econ. Hist. Rev.*, XII (1942), p. 92, for review of his important book on *Parliamentary Enclosure of Common Fields in England* by Christopher Hill, where he confirms the view of students of the land tax returns that the late seventeenth and early eighteenth centuries, rather than the age of the French Revolutionary wars, was the most critical period for the peasantry and concludes that by the time enclosure took place there had been a growth of the largest peasant holdings (those over 50 acres) and the smallest (less than 25 acres), but the middle category had become relatively insignificant. 'And this had occurred in unenclosed parishes.' In old enclosed parishes the process had gone much further. E. Davies found that 'the occupying owners had almost ceased to exist in the old enclosed parishes' before 1780, *Econ. Hist. Rev.*, I (1927), p. 103.

in Suffolk enclosed between 1797 and 1814 he finds that
the peasantry, in the form of small owners and leaseholders,
were very numerous before enclosure, and that the former
were somewhat more numerous afterwards. Moreover, owners
and tenants were so intertwined that it was difficult to distin-
guish between them, as they frequently held land from each
other besides occupying their own, and a surprisingly large
number were absentee landowners. After enclosure, the copy-
holders as well as the freeholders received allotments in compensation for loss of common rights; common-right owners
without land were compensated and so came into the category
of landowners for the first time, thus increasing the numbers of
the smallest owners, i.e. the cottagers with an average of rather
less than an acre each and the small farmers with an average
just under 10 acres each. But in size of properties the average
amount held by the smallest owners remained unchanged while
that of the handful of larger owners was substantially increased,
the effect of enclosure thus being to accentuate the economic
differentiation between large and small owners while adding to
the numerical advantage of the latter. In a further study[1] of
twenty enclosure awards in different parts of the country he
finds there were few large farms but (except in four of the
twenty) a numerous peasantry. Moreover, the awards indicate,
he says, 'an extraordinary development of peasant ownership'
as a result of the sale and division of some of the large farms;
and he refers especially to the village of Newbold in Leicestershire, where at the auction of land held by the Commissioners
to defray expenses, nineteen small owners, who he thinks were
new to the parish as their names were not found among those
receiving allotments at the enclosure, acquired an average of
three acres each. Whether the small tenants came off equally
well is another matter. As Professor Lavrovsky says, they were
more immediately affected 'as parliamentary enclosure signified
the temporary suspension and annulment of leases, though it is
true on a basis of some "compensation" to lessees'. There may
have been consolidation and a reduction in numbers; 'doubtless,

[1] V. M. Lavrovsky, 'Tithe Commutation as a Factor in the Gradual Decrease
of Landownership by the English Peasantry', *Econ. Hist. Rev.*, IV (1933), p. 273.

large farms might have been formed under favourable circumstances', to quote this scrupulously careful author again, but the
fact that so many of the tenants were also small owners would
serve as a brake upon any catastrophic fall into the category
of landless labourers.

Nothing, however, is said of the lowest group of all, the
cottage labourers with customary usage of the common; and
nothing statistically can be said. Since they had no proprietary
rights to defend they do not appear in the enclosure award
or land-tax returns though they occasionally occur in estate
accounts, as is the case of the Duke of Kingston's accounts of
Gedling, Carlton and Stoke Bardolph where sixteen cottagers
paid rent before enclosure but none afterwards;[1] these landless
or semi-landless workers, together with the small tenants who
disappeared through consolidation, represent the real victims
of enclosure, and unless they are constantly kept in mind, they
may also become the victims of the statistical method. It is
of such – tenant cottagers and small tenant farmers – that Dr
Hasbach can truthfully say: 'Enclosure was the last act in the
drama of proletarianization'; but it does not seem that this
was necessarily true even of the smallest owner or copyholder
who could substantiate a legal claim to the satisfaction of the
enclosure commissioners; and in the light of recent research
it would seem that the commissioners were not too difficult to
satisfy. Indeed, they stand in striking and pleasing contrast to
the squires and rich yeomen of the fifteenth and sixteenth
centuries who 'wiped out' the villages of the Midlands by the
hundred, turning the dispossessed away 'tearfully' and 'into
idleness'. Whatever may be said of the method of enclosure

---

[1] G. Mingay, *Duke of Kingston and his Estates*, p. 91 (Dissertation for B.A.,
University of Nottingham). In Cotgrave the twenty-one cottages continued on
the rent roll after enclosure as before, but with no provision for loss of the usage
of the common. Enclosure Awards sometimes give examples of houses and tofts
in occupation of tenants who would lose the use of the common by enclosure,
e.g. forty-nine at East Keal, but there is no means of giving an over-all statistical
picture of this 'stripping of the cottagers'. Arthur Young cites thirty-seven
enclosures in twenty-five of which the poor lost their cows: 'a mischief that
might easily have been avoided'. See *Inquiry into the Propriety of Applying Wastes
etc.* (1801), p. 19.

by act of parliament, it represents a milestone in the recognition of the *legal* rights of humble men.[1]

So much for the immediate effects of enclosure in these thirty-six examples examined by Professor Lavrovsky. What of the delayed effects – the fencing of allotments and paying the expenses of enclosure? Unfortunately, no answer can be given to this question for the villages under review, and in order to throw light on it the results of inquiries elsewhere must be explored. There is for instance the interesting study – the most extensive yet made – by Mr Swales of seventy Parliamentary enclosures in Lindsey in which he finds that the number of owners receiving allotments reached a total of 1,374 of whom 82 per cent were owners of less than 50 acres.[2] The burden of

[1] See W. H. Hosford, 'Some Lincolnshire Enclosure Documents', *Econ. Hist. Rev.*, 2nd series, II (1949), p. 73, where it is shown that the Commissioners accepted verbal claims, although the official notice stated that claims must be made in writing. 'They appear to have been honest men – careful, conscientious and even considerate' (p. 78). See also T. H. Swales, 'Parliamentary Enclosures of Lindsey', *Lincolnshire Arch. Soc. Rep. and Papers* (1936), where examples are given of allotments of small men being more conveniently placed than those of large. Arthur Young in 1770 speaks of their 'ignorance, knaving and self interest . . . combined with despotic power' (*Northern Tour* (1770), I, p. 256), but in 1799 gives an example of a Commissioner of twenty-eight years standing who made it his invariable custom 'to begin to line out and allot for the smallest proprietors first . . .'. *General View of Lincolnshire* (1799), p. 85. See also Davis, *General View of Wiltshire*, p. 85, for attempts by enclosure Commissioners to protect the small owners. For 'Policy and humanity forbid that they should be injured even with their consent'. Gonner thinks the Commissioners were men of experience and integrity, op. cit., pp. 94–5. For generally favourable verdict based on exhaustive study of Commissioners' Minute Books, etc., see M. W. Beresford, 'Commissioners of Enclosure', *Econ. Hist. Rev.*, XVI (1946), p. 130, and W. E. Tate: 'Oxfordshire Enclosure Commissioners 1737–1856', *J. Mod. Hist.*, XXIII (1951), p. 138. But of the poor *without* legal rights it remains true that 'by nineteen enclosure bills out of twenty they are injured, in some grossly injured' (Young, op. cit., p. 42).

[2] Swales, op. cit. A point which has not been investigated is the proportion of absentee owners. It was usually high, and some of them would no doubt be among those who sold. The range in the size of holdings was as follows:

Over 100 acres	Between 50–100 acres	Between 20–50 acres	Between 10–20 acres	Between 5–10 acres	Between 2–5 acres	Between 1–2 acres	Under 1 acre
150	103	169	201	214	255	124	158
10·9%	7·5%	12·3%	14·6%	15·6%	18·6%	9%	11·5%

The total acreage was 81,502.

expenses was heavy on the small owners and he cites between
seventy and eighty examples of sales in nine villages either
before or after enclosure. There may have been more of which
he has no knowledge, and there is evidence, in the case of the
earliest examples, of substantial decline after enclosure; but
the author has no doubt from the evidence of the land-tax returns that this loss was more than made up afterwards by the
influx of fresh purchasers during the period of high prices,
especially in the Fen parishes.

Elsewhere, in Lincolnshire, the small owner, wherever economic conditions favoured him, was very strong, whether subject
to enclosure or not; Arthur Young,[1] writing in 1799, notices
146 proprietors at Kirton enclosed six years before: 120 at
Barton, enclosed at the same time; Laceby, apparently a village
of old enclosure, 'where every man lives of his own'; in the
Fens where half the area was in the hands of small freeholders.
The Lincolnshire historian Canon Massingberd was certainly
correct when he said, as early as 1910,[2] that small owners were
numerous where the land lent itself to small-scale production,
as in the overwhelmingly peasant villages of the Isle of Axholme, but were at a disadvantage where the essential condition
of success was large capital expenditure as in the warp lands
alongside the Trent.

It will be noticed, however, that all these examples are drawn
from the predominantly arable areas where corn growing
continued to flourish after enclosure under the scarcity conditions of the Napoleonic wars, or where cash crops could be
grown under specially favourable conditions as in the Fen
parishes of Lincolnshire and in the Isle of Axholme. What of
the pasture areas where corn growing gave way to grass and
the age-old economy of the open village passed under the
yoke of the grazier and fatstock dealer?

Even William Marshall, who can usually see no ill in enclosure, was prepared to admit that in the Vale of Evesham
corn growing and population had been severely reduced as a

---

[1] Young, op. cit., pp. 19–20.
[2] *Lincolnshire Notes and Queries*, xi, p. 31. Warp lands owed their fertility to the
deposit of silt by regulated flood water – an expensive process.

result of enclosure owing to the conversion of rich deep-soiled arable grounds to permanent pastures; there were other areas where these results were felt: the Vale of Berkeley, the country round Horncastle and – for special reasons – Downland Wiltshire. But it would be unwise to assume that the enclosure of rich arable always had the results commonly attributed to it even in the classic pasture county of Leicestershire, as the following inquiry into the twelve villages in the north-east of the county clearly proves. The area was chosen, in the first place, because it is singled out by Dr Slater[1] as an example of the evil effects of enclosure of rich arable for conversion to pasture, a process which was calculated, according to a well-known pamphlet quoted by Dr Slater, to reduce the population by fifteen families per 1,000 acres. Of the twelve parishes cited, enclosure awards exist for five and the land-tax returns for all, so that a statistical picture can be drawn of what was happening.

The main impression from this localized inquiry is one of remarkable stability. Here was no spectacular growth of cottage property, as in so many of the Lincolnshire villages;[2] but neither was there any marked advance by the large owners. The pattern of property distribution of 1780 remained basically unaltered in 1830. The large owner – the Duke of Rutland – in 1780 paid in land tax £290 out of £647 (45 per cent); in 1830 he paid £366 out of £665 (55 per cent). The remainder was divided among 250 small owners in 1780; in 1830 there were 305, of whom 128 were resident in 1780 and 157 in 1830. The small owners were getting smaller but there were more of them. The tenants showed a decline from 211 in 1780 to 198 in 1830 which indicates some degree of consolidation, perhaps a higher degree than the figures themselves suggest, since they would include a number of tenant tradesmen as well as tenant farmers. Of the villages which have enclosure awards only one shows any marked change in property distribution; this is Harby where forty-four owners received allotments at the enclosure in 1790 and fifty-eight paid land tax in 1830.

A question which calls for examination at this point is the nature of the evidence on which these figures are based. The land tax was a tax on land as measured by its annual value, taking into account the value of the buildings on it as well as the land. It was therefore levied on tradesmen, shopkeepers, innkeepers, canal proprietors as well as landowners in the strict sense of the word. But since the villages under review were essentially rural and boasted of their immunity from the incubus of poverty-stricken industrial workers, especially stockingers, the number of property units at any given time may be taken as a true reflection of the rural community, though not exclusively of property in land. Moreover, since many land-tax payers bought themselves out under the redemption act of 1798, the returns are actually an understatement of the number of property owners after that date.[1] The figures quoted for these villages show that the ownership of property, most of which was landed property, was almost as widely distributed in 1830 as in 1780 though the tenancies were more consolidated; but they hardly bear out Dr Slater's assumption that enclosure, even of the richest arable, necessarily resulted in wholesale consolidation of farms and depopulation.[2] He might

[1] Freeholders were known to be reluctant to get themselves put on the land-tax lists. There were said to be 700 in Holland and 300 in Lindsey who had escaped notice in 1825, see Stapylton, '*A list of Freeholders of Lincoln 1825*'. This would be a deficiency of between 8 and 9 per cent. (Kindly brought to my notice by Dr J. W. F. Hill.)

[2] The explanation seems to be that Dr Slater included these enclosures among the enclosures for pasture of the first half of the eighteenth century which may very well have had the effects he described. He notes (p. 97) that the enclosures took place between 1766 and 1792 and it would appear that he is transposing the effect from the earlier to the later period. The dividing line should probably be 1770–80 or even earlier. See Fussell, quoted below, p. 113, n. 2. A more intriguing example of confusion in the matter of periods is provided by his citing of Wistow and Foston (Slater, op. cit., p. 100). They are said, on the authority of Rev. John Howlett, quoting a correspondent, to have been enclosed and almost entirely depopulated. But both of them are classed as deserted villages of the period 1450–1600. See Hoskins, *Essays in Leicestershire History*, map opposite p. 72. L. A. Parker, 'Depopulation Returns for Leicestershire in 1607', *Trans. Leics. Arch. Soc.*, XXIII, pt. II (1947). The Hearth Tax Returns of 1670 (kindly made available to me by Dr Thirsk) give eight householders in Foston and seven in Wistow. Perhaps these villages were in process of being repopulated, only to be redepopulated within the century, or perhaps Howlett's correspondent was drawing on a folk-memory of 200 years earlier!

---

have been more cautious if he had paid greater attention to the account given by the Reporter to the Board of Agriculture in 1809.

> The Duke [he writes] is a kind landlord, never oppresses and seldom removes a tenant. The advanced rent has been in part produced by the enclosure, but in part certainly by a change of time and circumstances; the land has been much improved by laying the richest part to grass, and by drainage, etc.; the occupations are mostly small, few individuals rent above £100 in an estate of £21,000 per annum. A numerous and able bodied peasantry is now supported; no stockingers or other manufacturers, and care taken that there shall be none; poor rates low, rents well paid. . . . The enclosure of this Vale has not at all, I believe, hitherto lessened the number of its inhabitants, as the farms are small and few changes of tenantry have taken place.

The writer anticipates that as old farm-houses fall into decay and new ones are erected in their place, farms will be consolidated on principles of economy and let to the the more active and diligent farmers, and the rejected occupier and his family will have to emigrate into towns or elsewhere for employment.[1] This melancholy result, however, seems to have been delayed for another forty years for the area in question shows a steady rise of population until the middle of the century when the rate of increase begins to slow down.[2]

If we go over the border into the neighbouring county of Rutlandshire we find again that enclosure was by no means incompatible with the survival of the small farm. The Agricultural Reporter[3] himself refers to the great number of very small farms, and these were found equally – or even more

---

[1] W. Pitt, *General View of Leicestershire* (1807), p. 15.

[2] The relative increase for the first five census periods was 100, 111, 131, 147, 167 and 172, counting 1801 as 100.

[3] R. Parkinson, *General View of Rutland*, pp. 2 and 29. The decline of the small farmer in Rutlandshire seems to have taken place later in the century. In 1886 there were still 743 farms under 50 acres out of a total of 1,163. In 1914 there were 496 out of 907; in 1944 there were 254 out of 631. (Information kindly supplied by Mr Green, School of Agriculture, Sutton Bonington.)

frequently – in the villages where pasture predominated as in the mainly arable villages. Thus out of twenty-nine villages where pasture and meadow together were three times as extensive as arable, 27 per cent of the villages had farms of 20 acres or less compared to 18 per cent in the twenty-seven predominantly arable villages. It is also worth noting that out of twenty-eight villages enclosed between 1774 and 1801, eleven still had copyhold tenure when the Report was written in 1809. Many small farmers had withstood the shock of enclosure in Rutlandshire because the basic condition of agrarian success, wide variety of soil in close proximity, enabled them to survive until the agricultural crisis of the 1880s.

A far more typical example of enclosure in the pasture area than any yet mentioned is that of Queniborough, enclosed in 1794. Here a large part of the arable had been converted to pasture, and the Reporter, a strong critic of enclosures, tells us[1] that productivity was no greater in any department, no more corn nor cattle, nor increased produce of butter or cheese or beef. The output of grain remained about the same on a smaller acreage owing to an increase in yield by about 50–100 per cent; the sheep were fewer in number but were fed on green fodder crops and sold fat instead of lean; and there were far fewer losses from disease to which they were liable on the open fields. Indeed, he quotes a local farmer to the effect that the losses had been so heavy that there was some doubt whether the occupiers could have gone on in the open fields; and when we hear, as we do again and again,[2] of flocks being halved or entirely swept away by sheep-rot on the undrained and disease-ridden commons, of the scourge of abortion among cattle on the

---

[1] Pitt, op. cit., p. 71.

[2] Among many examples see Young, *Oxfordshire* (1809) (quoting a local farmer), 'I have known years when not a single sheep totally kept in open fields has escaped the rot. Some years within my memory rot has killed more sheep than the butchers have. Since enclosure has not lost one sheep from rot in nineteen years.' C. Vancouver, *Cambridgeshire* (1794), pp. 87 and 208 – 'owing to abortion among cows due to foulness of pasture twenty-three cows have lost ninety calves in five years'; and (p. 107) 'half the sheep in Dry Drayton and 1,000 out of 1,400 in Croxton carried off last season from rot due to bad drainage'. See also T. Rudge, *Gloucestershire* (1807), p. 250; G. Rennie, etc., *Yorkshire* (1794), p. 32; W. T. Pomeroy, *Worcestershire* (Appendix 2) (1794).

commons, of the frequent outbreaks of cattle plague to which the Quarter Sessions Minute Books refer, we can well believe it. Our concern, however, is not with the mortality of sheep and cattle on the commons, but with that of peasants in the enclosed villages. In Queniborough there was no benevolent Duke of Rutland to temper the harsh winds to the shorn lamb; on the contrary there were two large owners who pressed their tenants hard by raising their rents from 12*s.* to 23*s.*, greatly reduced the arable area, and diminished the head of stock. Here we have all the circumstances that might be expected to result in a sharp decline of the small cultivator and to a reduction of population. But an examination of the enclosure award and the land-tax returns does not confirm this expectation. For ten years before and after enclosure there is no sign of change either in numbers of tenants or of owners or in amounts of tax paid; the names of the allottees at the enclosure recur in the land-tax returns and remain substantially the same until about 1810 when new owners and tenants come in, possibly as a result of an invasion of the villages by stockingers to which the Agricultural Reporter had referred in 1809; and it may be that we must look to this source for the steady increase of population – 25 per cent between 1801 and 1851 – which the census figures reveal. The number of farm tenancies seems to have declined somewhat, from twenty-four in 1790 (three years before enclosure) to twenty-one in 1810 and twenty in 1830 though there was an increase of very small tenancies which again may be due to stockinger influx.

But the case of Queniborough does not dispose of the problem of enclosure and depopulation in Leicestershire. The census returns show many cases of declining population during one or more of the census periods, an average in fact of between forty and fifty in each period. The responsibility of parliamentary enclosure for this result is, however, hard to establish, since most of the villages in question belong to the area of old enclosure, i.e. before 1700. Of the twenty-one villages enclosed by act of parliament after 1790, the census returns show some evidence of decline in ten, but all of them seem to belong to the area of stiff clay which was too heavy for mixed agriculture based on turnips. Like the Vale of Evesham, they seem to fall into the category of deep rich grazing grounds which lent themselves to permanent pasture. In villages such as these, e.g. East and West Langton, Slawston, Bringhurst, Drayton, Great Easton, enclosure was rounding off two centuries of adaptation to the special circumstances of the soil; but even here, where, as Dr Hoskins has shown,[1] the authentic voice of depopulation is unmistakably heard, the fall is far from catastrophic, the highest figure being 24 per cent decline in Slawston between 1801 and 1811, the others oscillating between 4 and 17 per cent, though they show a slight over-all increase in the period 1801–51.

Perhaps we may inquire at this stage what were the factors that tended to keep the rural population on the soil and indeed to increase it even where the opposite results might have been expected.

One important factor contributing to the stability of the agrarian population during this period was the high level of employment which was maintained both in enclosed and open parishes where the improved agriculture was adopted. The explanation seems to be that new agricultural practices had developed in advance of the technical devices for dealing with them.[2] Thus the yield of corn per acre went up (e.g. at Queniborough from 50 to 100 per cent) after enclosure but the methods of ploughing, sowing, reaping, and threshing were not substantially speeded up until the 1830s and 1840s. At the same time the spread of turnip cultivation and green fodder crops both in open and enclosed villages called for labour throughout the year in field, barn, and stackyard; the main-

[1] 'Leicestershire Crop Returns' in W. G. Hoskins's *Studies in Leicestershire Agrarian History* (Ed.).

[2] It is not always realized that the widespread use of drilling machinery was a feature of the nineteenth century, not the eighteenth. It was vehemently opposed by Arthur Young in 1770, and by Sir John Sinclair as late as 1817. Corn was dibbled when not sown broadcast. Wheat was dibbled in Norfolk as late as 1831, see Riches, op. cit., p. 116. As Naomi Riches feelingly writes: 'When one considers that all the work of ploughing, sowing, harvesting was done with little agricultural machinery, the complexity of labour organization on these [Norfolk] farms becomes intriguing. Imagine harvesting 800 acres of barley by hand, i.e. by scythe and sickle and hand-made straw bands.'

tenance of a milking herd or fatstock involved continuous field-
work throughout the year in pasture districts as well as in
arable, except where the land was too stiff for mixed farming
as in south-east Leicestershire; and the hedging and ditching
of the new enclosures found winter work for casual labour to
a greater extent than the open villages. As for enclosure of
forest, moor, and fen, labour was attracted from far and wide.
As a result of the enclosure of the Forest of Knaresborough
we are told,

> the poor cottager and his family exchanged their indolence
> for active industry, and obtained extravagant wages; and
> hundreds were induced to offer their labour from distant
> quarters; labourers of every denomination, carpenters,
> joiners, smiths, and masons, poured in, and met with con-
> stant employment. And though before the allotments were
> set out, several riots had happened; the scene was now quite
> changed; for with all the foreign assistance, labour kept
> extravagantly high. . . . In consequence the product is in-
> creased beyond conception, the rents more than trebled and
> population advanced in a very high degree.[1]

In regard to parishes mainly given over to pasture like
Queniborough and other Leicestershire parishes, we should
remember that much of it was in convertible leys, i.e. an arable
form of grass farming. William Marshall speaks[2] of the grass

[1] G. Rennie, etc., *General View of Yorkshire* (1794), p. 76. For other examples
of energetic attack on moorland waste, see A. Young, *Northern Tour*, II, pp. 263–
75; *Eastern Tour*, I, pp. 213–20. See also 'Inclosure of Open Fields', a poem
celebrating enclosure, translated from the Latin by Dorothy Halton, *Northamptonshire Past and Present* (1951), p. 35, and Lord Tennyson, *Northern Farmer*
(Old Style), verse x.

[2] Marshall, *Rural Economy of Midland Counties*, I, pp. 115, 187, 213, and Hoskins,
Agric. Hist. (1951), loc. cit., for seventeenth-century ley farming in Leicestershire. See also G. E. Fussell, 'Animal Husbandry in Eighteenth Century',
Agricultural History (April 1937), p. 99: 'The topographers whose evidence is
too scattered to cite in full [lead to the conclusion] that the effect of eighteenth-
century progress was not to lay the Midland counties to grass, but on the contrary to restrict the acreage devoted to grazing and make them primarily corn-
growing counties by the middle of the nineteenth century', and *Economic Geography* (July and October 1936) p. 296: 'It is doubtful whether any such drastic
change from cornfield to grass was the consequence of enclosure in the second
half of the eighteenth century.'

farms of the old enclosures being subjected 'to an alternacy of grass and arable the land having lain six or seven years in a state of sward, it is broken up for oats', then wheat and barley and then a further six years under grass; and mentions the practice of growing wheat on a clover ley even in the open fields. Moreover, in ley farming on heavy land, grass may take the place of turnips, so that although in many parishes in Leicestershire turnips were not grown, this need not imply that the new farming was unknown there. Indeed, I am told there are still parishes in Leicestershire where convertible leys are preferred to turnips owing to the high cost of producing them on heavy soil.

In regard to the numerical increase of cottage owners revealed by the land-tax returns at a time when the most cautious authorities – e.g. Sir John Clapham and Professor Gonner – are of opinion that they were stripped of their small properties, it should be remembered that in addition to the reasons already given – the recognition of the claims of the smallest owners, who may have thus come into the land-tax returns for the first time; the sale of land in small lots to pay expenses; the influx of purchasers from outside – there was also the stimulation of rural trades and industries as a result of the greater productivity of farming, the rise of population, and the increasing traffic on the roads. The Agricultural Reporter for Leicestershire, in accounting for the maintenance of rural population in the Vale of Belvoir in spite of enclosure, speaks of the mechanics, blacksmiths, wheelwrights, tailors, weavers, who with the labourers and their families together may equal ten or twelve to every 100 acres. Moreover, the £5,000,000 or £6,000,000 spent in poor relief would represent a redistribution of rural incomes most of which, as the Hammonds do well to remind us, would find its way into the pockets of rural tradesmen who had an interest in supplying the pauperized labourers with the goods which they could have partly supplied, before enclosure, for themselves.

For all these reasons, there seems no doubt that the cottage-owning population continued to grow in the newly enclosed villages, though in character and personnel it may have been very different from the cottagers of the pre-enclosure village.[1] The figures given below, in which the inquiry is taken down to the Tithe Awards of 1840,[2] provide merely one of many warnings against the assumption that the cottage-owning population suffered eclipse at this time. On the contrary, it seems certain that there was a net increase, and that in the areas where waste was plentiful, their numbers continued to grow even during the post-war depression.

It will be seen, therefore, that the enclosure acts had the effect of further reducing, but not of destroying, the remaining English peasantry. They came at the end of a long period of attrition by consolidation and purchase and direct eviction which practically eliminated the peasantry from the parishes of old enclosure; but in the open villages, although there had been differentiation among the peasantry themselves, especially

[1] This differentiation between the cottage-owning class and the proletarian labourer helps to throw some light on the problem which puzzled the foreign traveller, Louis Simond, who wrote: 'I do not know where the common labourers live. . . . There is no appearance of poverty anywhere . . . it is impossible to look round without the conviction that this country is upon the whole one of the happiest, if not the happiest, in the world. Every cottage with roses and honeysuckle and vines' (*sic*). Then he is told that the labourers live in some small town or village in the neighbourhood and walk several miles to work. 'There are, it seems, obscure corners where the poor are swept out of the way.' Simond, *Journal of a Tour, 1810–11*, quoted W. Smart, *Economic Annals of the Nineteenth Century*, I, p. 312. Besides the closed and open villages there were also the villages where model landlords were trying to attach the labourers to the soil by cottage and cow-pasture schemes (see below, p. 118).

[2] P. Perry, *Trends in Population and Landholding in Nottinghamshire* (Dissertation for B.A. of Nottingham University), p. 43.

Distribution of Owner Occupiers in 21 Nottinghamshire parishes, 1792–1840

Year	1792	1816	1825	1832	1840 (Tithe awards)
Mixed farming district (six parishes)					
Average number per parish	16·0	15·3	16·6	16·6	13·6
Pastoral district (three parishes)					
Average number per parish	1·3	0·6	0·6	0·6	0·3
Natural Waste district (twelve parishes)					
Average number per parish	12·9	13·5	14·0	16·3	17·9

The over-all total had risen from 255 to 296. The villages were entirely rural in character.

at the expense of the middle peasant, as well as attempts at consolidation by the landlord, the small owners and tenants were still remarkably strong. With the upward turn of rents in the fifties (of which accelerating enclosure was a symptom) there was further loss of tenants by consolidation and of owners by purchase; but when prices took their war-time leap and the attack on the waste got under way, there were gains of both as well as losses. What the net loss in farming units was it is not possible to calculate, but it was catastrophic only in particular localities;[1] and where large areas of waste were involved or where conditions were especially favourable to small-scale cultivation, there was considerable increase in numbers. Professor Clapham has reminded us that the ratio of labouring families to farming families rose slowly, and that while it was 1·74 to 1 in Gregory King's time, it was still only 2½ to 1 in 1831. He concludes that 'the Census Figures are entirely destructive of the view, that as a result of agrarian change and class legislation, an army of labourers toiled for a relatively small farming class; we have not a proletarian army under officers'; . . . 'numerically the average agricultural unit must be compared, not with the factory, but with handicraft workshops – master, journeyman or two, prentice or two'.[2]

---

[1] The effect on the small tenant seems to have been disastrous whenever the soil was unsuitable for mixed farming. See p. 102, n. 2. No attempt can yet be made to represent this statistically, but its social effect has received classic expression in Dr and Mrs Hammond's *Village Labourer*, especially Chapter VIII, 'The Isolation of the Poor'. The purpose of this article is not to question the existence of this problem: on the contrary; but to suggest that its contribution to the industrial labour supply calls for further investigation.

[2] J. H. Clapham, 'Growth of an Agrarian Proletariat 1688–1832', *Camb. Hist. J.*, I, p. 92, and *Economic History of Modern Britain*, I, p. 113. See also *Concise Economic History*, p. 115, where he says: 'To [Davenant] a typical cottager was obviously landless and possibly a claimant on the rates.' Dr Hoskins reminds me that the Hearth Tax Returns of 1670 provide a statistical basis for a consideration of the relative proportions of the social classes. The figures for Leicestershire give a total of 13,833 assessed to the Hearth Tax, of whom 4,249 were excused payment on grounds of poverty, i.e. 30·7 per cent of the whole. This implies that a great many labouring families in Leicestershire must have paid hearth tax or Gregory King's proportion of 1·7 to 1 does not apply to that county. Cf. also Professor Tawney's figure for Gloucestershire in 1608 of two independent producers to one labourer. See 'An Occupational Census of the Seventeenth Century', *Econ. Hist. Rev.*, v (1934), p. 53. Rapid as the growth of the agricultural

Moreover, in view of the great amount of enclosure for pasture in the first half of the eighteenth century a large proportion of the fall in the number of farming units had occurred before the great era of parliamentary enclosures opened; 'Sweet Auburn, loveliest village of the plain', the deserted village of Goldsmith's poetic imagination, was written in 1770, and had few if any authentic successors.[1] Since the rural population in general was unmistakably on the increase during this time, the contribution which the dispossessed made to the industrial labour force came, in the majority of cases, from the unabsorbed surplus, not from the main body.

But to say this – and much else that might be said in clarification of the statistical picture – is not to minimize the social consequences of the loss of the commons. The appropriation to their own exclusive use of practically the whole of the common waste by the legal owners meant that the curtain which separated the growing army of labourers from utter proletarianization was torn down. It was, no doubt, a thin and squalid curtain, for it will be remembered that Gregory King classed them all as actual or potential paupers who 'decreased the wealth of the country'; but it was real, and to deprive them of it without providing a substitute implied the exclusion of the labourers from the benefits which their intensified labour alone made possible.[2] The conscience of an age which had felt the impact of Wesley as well as of Rousseau could not remain unmoved by a form of injustice that aroused fear of consequences in the next world as well as this, and the ethical protest which it evoked had its champion if not its

semi-proletariat may have been in the seventeenth century, it is difficult to believe that the proportion of labouring families to independent producers went up from 0·5 to 1·7 to 1 between 1608 and 1688. There is need for closer scrutiny of Gregory King's figures on a regional basis before final conclusions can be drawn.

[1] It may be noted that the twenty-nine villages in the Vale of the Wiltshire Avon which Cobbett found so shrunken had suffered a collapse of the carding and spinning industries. 'It is now wholly gone,' says Cobbett, and the women and girls had to find work outside. *Rural Rides* (ed. Cole), II, p. 376.

[2] See Riches, op. cit., p. 133, for speeding up on big Norfolk farms.

I

martyr.[1] Side by side with this emotional response, a character-istically empirical approach to the problem was being made by practical men – experts like Kent, Stone, Davies, Arbuthnot; landlords like the Earl of Winchelsea, Lord Carrington, Lord Egremont, and Lord Sheffield had schemes for endowing the labourers with cow-pastures and other forms of self-help. They converted such influential figures as Eden, Arthur Young, Sinclair, Wilberforce, and even Pitt himself;[2] and some of the more enlightened landlords were already doing it.

In Rutlandshire, almost entirely an enclosed county, cot-tagers frequently had sufficient land to enable them to keep one or two cows. 'This practice,' we are told, 'does not prevail in all parishes' but was sufficiently general to account for the comparatively low poor rates. After citing numerous cases in Lincolnshire, Arthur Young refers especially to Sir John Sheffield's estate covering twenty miles of country where the cottagers paid a rent of 40*s.* a year for house, garden, a rood or a half acre of land, and feeding for two cows and two or three pigs. Moreover, the landlords wisely kept the cottages in their own hands, knowing well that the farmers would use them to give a further twist to the screw which already pressed so hard upon the labourers. But in his enthusiasm for the growing 'cow-ocracy' of Lincolnshire, Arthur Young unwittingly let a portentous cat out of his rather hastily packed bag when he wrote that as a result, the 'population increases so that pigs and children fill every quarter; in the last twenty years the baptisms at Burton have exceeded the burials by 136. The women,

[1] Samuel Whitbread, who introduced the Minimum Wage Bill in 1795 and again in 1800, a 'large and comprehensive Poor Law Bill in 1807', and opposed the Peninsular War 'for his compassion for the miseries of the English poor. . . . He spent his life in hopeless battles and he died by his own hand of public despair'. Hammond, *The Village Labourer*, 1, p. 136 (Guild Books, 1948). See also Smart, *Economic Annals of Nineteenth Century*, 1, pp. 37, 444.

[2] At any rate, he included in his Poor Law Bill of 1797 a clause permitting loans to be made by the parish for the purchase of a cow or other animal if it seemed likely that such a course would enable the recipient to maintain himself. But he bowed to the storm from ratepayers and magistrates and to 'the objection of those whose opinions he was bound to respect', of whom the most noteworthy was Bentham (Hammond, op. cit., 1, p. 147). For an excellent summary of the ideas of Lord Winchelsea and others see Hasbach, op. cit., pp. 164–8 and Hammond, 11, pp. 154 *et seq.*

however, are very lazy; they do nothing but bring children and eat cake'.[1] He was soon to be made to realize that he had confounded himself out of his own mouth. In a subsequent edition of the famous *Essay*, Malthus invoked against him, partly with the aid of his own evidence, the inexorable logic of the *Principle of Population*, and endeavoured to prove that the labourers' most ardent champions were in the long run their worst enemies.

Whether the influence of Malthus was decisive there is no means of knowing. He was swimming with the tide of interests – tradesmen, farmers, and most landlords – but against the main current of sentiment if not of ideas. The volume and virulence of the opposition showed the strength of the 'philanthropic Jacobinism' which he challenged, and we are left wondering what might have happened if his basic humanitarianism had taken a Tory instead of a Utilitarian form. In the upshot, he helped to cement an alliance between vested interests and economic theory which was sufficient to kill the scheme for cow-pastures for labourers, and the opportunity to reverse the verdict of the enclosures was lost: the labourer was now separated in theory as well as in fact from all proprietary interest in the product of the soil which he tilled.

That this was a social calamity brought into relief all the more by contrast with the contemporary land settlement in Denmark[2] – may be conceded without admitting the measure

[1] A. Young, *Lincolnshire* (1799), p. 462. He was obviously impressed by the Malthusian argument when he wrote: 'It might be prudent to consider the misery to which the progressive population might be subject when there was not a sufficient demand for them in towns and manufactures, as an evil which it was absolutely and physically impossible to prevent' (quoted Malthus, *Essay on Population* (edn 1890), Appendix, p. 557). The dilemma with which Arthur Young and other agrarian reformers like Sir Thomas Bernard were faced should be considered before final judgement is passed on the statesmen and policies of the time.

[2] B. O. Binns, *The Consolidation of Fragmented Agricultural Holdings*; F.A.O.; Washington (1950), p. 41. The scheme was carried through under the inspiration of the Counts of Bernstorff and strengthened the proprietary rights of the peasants while giving them the benefit of consolidation, but it destroyed the village as a community. 'It was an attack from above,' as Mr Dobb says, but it was undertaken in the interests of the peasants themselves who later put a memorial up to the man who had made it, see Binns, op. cit., p. 42. In England the influence

of responsibility it is usually given for the recruitment of the reserve army of labour. As we have seen, the cottage-owning population seems actually to have increased after enclosure. Even the proletarianized labourers continued to remain on the soil in increasing numbers in most areas until the 1830s and in some parts to the 1840s, when improved farming techniques and railway transport caught up with the new farming practices. It was then that the real flight from the countryside began.

If agrarian change, as symbolized by enclosure, cannot be regarded as the chief recruiting agent of the industrial proletarian army, where did the new drafts come from which not only manned the expanding industries but the expanding agriculture also; and manned them in such strength that in some departments, the very plethora of labour was itself a brake upon technological innovation?

Economic historians are generally agreed that the fever of technical improvement in the early phases of the Industrial Revolution was partly occasioned by labour shortage even though enclosure was reported to be emptying the villages and bringing desolation to the countryside. What happened to transform the situation so that in the last quarter of the eighteenth century labour became available for an unprecedented expansion of industry and agriculture, for fighting a twenty years' war and for summoning up the grim spectre of the Malthusian population formula to the terror of statesmen who might otherwise have been prompted to remedial action? The only answer can be that at some unspecified time in the eighteenth century the movement of population had taken an upward turn in village and town alike and provided an entirely new supply of human material beside which the dislocations

---

of Malthus was a powerful – perhaps decisive – barrier to landlords' reconstruction within the village community which the enclosure acts transformed but did not destroy. See especially Hammond, op. cit., Chapter VIII, and pp. 124–6. Humanitarianism in England was thus left to oscillate between the cheap-jack benevolence of Speenhamland and the pursuit of the net social product by Chadwick.

caused by enclosures were of secondary importance. The Isle of Axholme, an example unique in England, of a peasant community of the continental type, is a case in point.[1] There was no question here of the institutional pressure of enclosure and the large farm. The inhabitants, small cultivators growing successive crops of corn, potatoes, hemp, flax, on their little farms of from 4 to 50 acres, with a few large ones of 200 or more, worked like Negroes, says Arthur Young, and the smallest of them lived worse than the occupants of the poor house, but 'all is made amends for by *possessing* land'. An examination of the land-tax returns shows that between 1783 and 1800 the numbers of freeholders rose from 829 to 1,326, an increase of 60 per cent; and between 1800 and 1829 to 1,444, a further increase of 9 per cent.[2] But while the property owners were increasing by 9 per cent, in the same period the population went up by 33 per cent (from 7,214 to 9,626). Thus in this classically peasant region, the population rose faster than the units of property; a proletariat was coming into being by the natural increase of the peasant population. Moreover, it will be seen, by comparing the growth of these villages with the non-peasant villages around, that they grew in numbers side by side with the landlord villages until the 1840s and then they diverged, the landlord villages showing a steady decline, the peasant villages going on for another two generations until they, too, began to falter in the teeth of the blizzard which blew up for farmers of all kinds in the last quarter of the century. The difference of institutional structure seems to have made no difference to the contribution made to the reserve

---

[1] W. B. Stonehouse, *History of the Isle of Axholme* (1839), writes: '. . . these small freeholders are generally very badly off (far worse off than the generality of labourers – p. 33). Further inheritances have become so incumbered with mortgages that the interest is a very high rent, an inconvenience necessarily attending the descent of land not entailed in the same family from the provision which has to be made, at different times, for the younger children. . . . The worst landlord must give way to the circumstances of his tenant; but a mortgagee is a perfect land shark, his heart is as hard as that of a political economist' (Preface, p. x). 'Had the Isle of Axholme continued in the sole property of one Lord Paramount, such as the present Duke of Northumberland, the Earl of Yarborough . . . what a different state would it now be in' (p. xiii).

[2] W. O. Massingberd, *Lincs. Notes and Queries*, xi, loc. cit.

army of labour: it may, for all we know, have been proportionally the same: no more and no less, until the second half of the century when the non-peasant villages entered on their numerical decline.

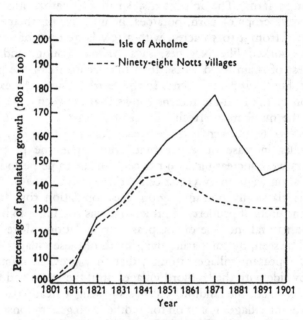

CHART 2. The population of the Isle of Axholme and of 98 Nottinghamshire villages.

If it be conceded, as I think it must, that the period 1780–1840 saw only a sporadic exodus (apart from the migration of the surplus) from the rural areas which have formed the subject of this paper, and side by side with it, an actual filling up of empty spaces and a steady rise in the great majority of established centres of rural population, we are tempted to ask, from what hidden springs did this surge of rural population come, a surge that not only flowed over into what had formerly been empty and almost desert places – the black lings of Tideswell and Castleton, the heights of Mam Tor, and a score of sparsely occupied forests and marshes and yet had a surplus to spill over into the growing centres of industry in towns and industrialized villages? This phenomenon of rural fecundity is all the more remarkable since it follows a period marked by enclosure and the consolidation of farms on such a scale as to persuade many observers that the rural population was actually on the decline, being driven from their homes by the improving farmer and the rent-hungry landlord.

The remarkable paradox of visible population growth side by side with lamentations of rural desolation engaged the attention, among others, of John Howlett and Arthur Young. Both agreed that in so far as enclosure was associated with capital investment in improved agriculture, it was followed not by a decline but by a growth of population. Arthur Young elaborates on this theme again and again and expounds, with a wealth of illustrations, the theory that an expanding economy will call into being its own labour supply by providing incentives to early marriage. In his *Northern Tour*, written in 1770, he says 'the only complaint he met with was the high price of agricultural labour, the causes of which he attributes to turnpikes, navigations, drainages, and enclosures: all these conspired to make hands scarce and to depress the farmer'. But he goes on:

> It is employment that creates population: marriages are early and numerous in proportion to the amount of employment. In a great Kingdom there must always be hands that are idle, backward in the age of work, unmarried for fear of having families, or industrious only to a certain degree. Now an increase of employment raises wages and high wages changes the case of all these hands; the idle are converted to industry; the young come early to work; the unmarried are no longer fearful of families and the formerly industrious become so in a much greater degree. It is an absolute impossibility that in such circumstances the people should not increase. . . . Provide new employment and new hands will inevitably follow.

In more measured language, Adam Smith was writing in much the same strain and at the same time pointing out that 'the real recompense of labour' had risen which 'enabled them to provide for their children and consequently to bring up a greater number of them'. Twenty years later, Eden and Malthus related population growth to the greatly increased demand for labour 'combined with a greatly increased power of production, both in agriculture and manufactures'.[1]

Later historians have been inclined to look for the reason in the institutional factors of enclosures and poor law, which, they tell us, reduced the dispossessed peasantry to hopelessness and despair and removed the last remaining restraints upon 'unbridled impulse'.[2] The regional historian has no competence to discuss these views in their wider implications, but he may be able to set them within the context of the local economy in so far as the special tools of his trade enable him to re-create it. In addition to those already used in this article there are others, such as marriage registers, estate accounts, testamentary inventories, and the history of cottage architecture, together with the London prices – in the absence of local ones – of wheat and capital. By these means it may be possible to attempt a comparative study of regional demographic and secular trends during this crucial period of rural population growth, and in Charts 3 and 4 an experiment of this kind is presented rather for the potentialities of its approach than for the finality of its results.

A study of the marriage registers of 117 Nottinghamshire villages, shown in Chart 3, suggests that about the middle of the century the marriage rate took a decisive turn upwards, not only in the partially industrialized villages where the stocking industry and mining were entering on a phase of rapid expansion, but also in the agricultural villages whether sub-

---

[1] Young, *Northern Tour*, iv, pp. 411 *et seq.*; Adam Smith, *Wealth of Nations*, Book I, Chapter VIII; F. M. Eden, *State of the Poor* (1797), i, p. 407; Malthus, op. cit., p. 243.

[2] See especially Hasbach, op. cit., pp. 170, 361, 390, where impressive evidence is cited showing the part played in the increase of population by the large farm with its out-cottages and the spread of rural slums in the 'open' parishes. But he omits the very numerous examples of increase of population in response to the widening market for labour resulting from drainage of heavy soils and fens, etc. See also important discussion by T. Griffith, *Population Problems in the Age of Malthus* (1925), especially Chapter VI.

ject to enclosure or not.[1] The rate of increase slowed down in
the latter but accelerated in the former to the end of the century,
but there seems to be no doubt that among the sources of the
demographic revolution of the eighteenth century was the
slow-moving but immensely powerful tide of agricultural

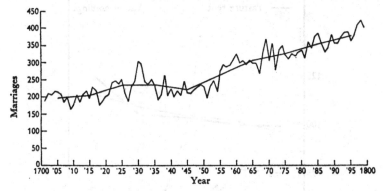

CHART 3. Annual totals of marriages in 117 Nottinghamshire parishes
1700–1800. The yearly average.

change. Some light on the nature of this under-swell is thrown
by Chart 4 in which is shown the movement of prices, rents,
arrears, and farm vacancies on the Nottinghamshire estates of
the Duke of Kingston.[2] A comparison of this with the marriage trend suggests that about 1750 there was a simultaneous upward movement of the agricultural series and the marriage
series after a period during which agriculture appears to have
been depressed and marriages showed only a slight tendency
to rise. Evidence of another kind – the widespread rebuilding

[1] P. W. Phillimore, T. M. Blagg, and others, *Marriage Registers of Notts* (1898–
1937), Vols. I–XXI; *Marriage Registers of Lincolnshire* (1905–21), Vols. I–XI.
  The relative change in the average number of marriages per village (ten-yearly
average) is as follows:

	1745	1755	1765	1775	1785	1795
Notts. (26 industrialized villages)	100	137·3	154·6	167·5	205·1	224·1
(91 non-industrialized villages)	100	115·7	138·6	147·1	144·4	151·0
Lincs. (65 non-industrialized villages)	100	108·5	124·5	119·8	116·9	130·7

Further details will have to await the completion of a study of marriage rates on
a regional basis which is now proceeding.
[2] G. Mingay, op. cit. For similar rent trends in Wiltshire see Kerridge, loc. cit.
In both counties there were cases of land tax being transferred to tenants.

of Midland farm-houses in a solid brick and tile which survives today and the rising value and variety of testamentary inventories left by yeomen and husbandmen[1] would suggest that

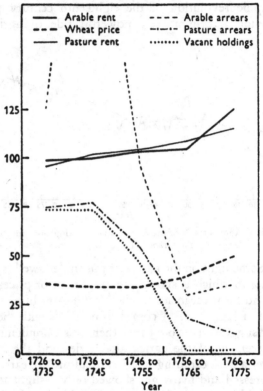

CHART 4. The Kingston estates accounts. Ten-yearly average figures 1720 to 1780.

agricultural investment and living standards were moving upwards in the region from the late seventeenth century in spite of the evidence of depression shown in the account books of the Duke of Kingston. The low level of food prices in the

[1] M. W. Barley, *Cottages and Farm houses in Lincolnshire and Nottinghamshire* (M.A. thesis, 1952). The author speaks of 'a revolution in housing standards' which began in the sixteenth century and entered on its second phase after 1660 when bricks began to take the place of traditional materials. The cottages of the labourers remained generally of stud and mud until the nineteenth century except where squires rebuilt their villages in brick. Part II, pp. 7 and 256.

1730s might be expected to bring about a fall in the infant death rate which may be reflected in the rise in the marriage trend twenty years later, a rise that the general expansion from the 1750s would sustain. With the slight upward turn from 1750 of rents and prices, the fall in rent arrears and farm vacancies, the expansion of industry in the rural and urban centres, together with the maintenance of low interest rates,[1] the context for a parallel movement in the secular curve of prosperity and population was complete, and the conditions for an adequate labour supply were at last fulfilled.

Whether this inference will bear the test of wider inquiry remains to be seen, but the evidence is such as to cast doubt on the *a priori* assumption that the reserve army of labour for large scale industry was an 'institutional creation' in the sense of being a response to the exercise of power by a ruling class; it may also be seen as the outcome of the complex of forces represented by an expanding economy which offered inducements as well as compulsions, e.g. to inventors to supplement the labour force and to parents to augment it, while making possible for their offspring a more favourable chance of survival than had ever before been known. A demographic change was thus set in motion which itself became a fact of history, and has to be taken into account if a balanced picture is to be drawn of the social stresses of the time;[2] and in a recognition of this lies the best hope of reconciling the apparent inconsistencies of the sociological and the economic approach with which this article began.

[1] For the effect of a rising rate of interest on the farmers of Norfolk during the American War compared to what it was fifteen or twenty years earlier see W. Marshall, *Rural Economy of Norfolk* (1787), II, pp. 104–7. 'Through the present high rate of interest to be made on government security, the monies which were dispersed . . . among farmers and tradesmen are now called in. . . .'

[2] See also E. F. Heckscher, 'Swedish Population Trends before the Industrial Revolution', *Econ. Hist. Rev.*, 2nd series, II (1950), p. 270: 'The progress in production was taken out first and foremost in the form of an increase of population, not in raising the standard of living . . . the lives of pre-revolutionary people were insecure and irregular; they felt helpless victims of the inexplicable and unpredictable freaks of nature.' Also W. Sombart, *Der Moderne Kapitalismus* (Leipzig, 1928), III (i), p. 361: 'Der Kapitalismus ist es also letzten Endes selbst, der sich sein Proletariat herbeischafft, wenn auch nicht in der Weise, wie Marx es wollte.' And pp. 363, 373–7 for a valuable discussion of the evidence prior to the appearance of T. Griffith, op. cit.

5 The Cost of Parliamentary Enclosure in Warwickshire

J. M. MARTIN

[This article was first published in the *University of Birmingham Historical Journal*, Vol. IX (1964).]

In estimating the social effects of the parliamentary enclosure movement of the eighteenth and early nineteenth centuries, the cost of the process is a major consideration. So far only one modern writer has attempted to investigate the evidence in any detail.[1] His main conclusion was that the cost of enclosure was not in general excessive even for the smallest owners, and ends up with the remark that 'in this, as in several other matters, it appears that parliamentary enclosure has been saddled with a responsibility which does not properly belong to it'[2] (i.e. driving the small man out of business).

This opinion was, however, contrary to that of many contemporaries, of whom perhaps Arthur Young was the most vocal in denouncing 'the absurd extravagance' of the method of enclosure.[3] It was opposed also to the views of many later writers from Cunningham to Ernle.[4] Even Gonner,[5] who generally views the parliamentary enclosure movement favourably, remarked that 'the general expenses were heavy' and goes on to make the further point, that 'in some instances little or no increase in value could be perceived for many years'.

[1] W. E. Tate, 'The Cost of Parliamentary Enclosure in England (with reference to the County of Oxon)' in *The Economic History Review*, 2nd series, v (1952), pp. 258–65.　　　　[2] Ibid., p. 265.

[3] A. Young, *The Northern Tour* (1770), I, pp. 254–60; *General Report on Enclosures*, pp. 12 ff.

[4] A. Cunningham, *English Industry and Commerce* (1892), p. 487; Hasbach, *English Agricultural Labourer* (1908), pp. 63–6; H. Levy, *Large and Small Holdings* (1911), pp. 24–5; J. L. B. Hammond, *The English Village Labourer* (1912), p. 74: E. C. K. Gonner, *Common Land and Enclosure* (1912), p. 78; Ld. Ernle, *English Farming Past and Present* (1917 edn), p. 251.

[5] Gonner, op. cit., p. 78.

In Warwickshire, whatever the reasons, there is evidence that, very commonly, the social consequences of enclosure in the eighteenth century were both considerable and painful. It seems reasonable, therefore, to conclude that a further study is necessary of the financial burden which this transformation of the landscape imposed on rural society.

We have emphasized that little detailed investigation has been made of the actual evidence of enclosure costs. In particular, almost nothing is known about the outlay of capital required for the actual making of the enclosures, as opposed to those expenses usually included in the schedule drawn up by the enclosure commissions.

In fact a considerable amount of evidence about enclosure costs can be gleaned from the Warwickshire awards themselves. From these we can discover the total general expenses of each enclosure, and thus work out the average cost per acre. In some awards where the cost of making the enclosure, that is 'ring-fencing' or 'outfencing', and 'infencing', or subdividing, of the tithe owner, or the Poor's allotment is undertaken by the proprietors, we can estimate the average cost of this item also. Then we can take this further and note the relative expense of enclosing large and small estates. Finally, in a fair number of enclosure awards, schedules are included which reveal the distribution of the various expenses under their separate heads, and this can be useful for calculating the proportional expense of officials' fees, legal and parliamentary expenses, and so on.

The Warwickshire awards are unusually informative about the cost of parliamentary enclosure. W. E. Tate has mentioned on two occasions the paucity of detailed information about enclosure expenditure in the enclosure awards which he has examined. In one article he declared that 'accounts of expenses involved in enclosure are very rarely entered in abstract in the awards, though these rather more commonly include a schedule showing the expenses charged upon each separate proprietor'.[1] In a later study dealing with the cost of

[1] W. E. Tate, 'Some Unexplored Records of the Enclosure Movement' in *English Historical Review*, no. 57 (1942), p. 256.

the process he again mentioned his dearth of evidence, and was unable to find any detailed accounts for Oxfordshire, and only one example for Nottinghamshire.[1]

For Warwickshire, on the other hand, enclosure commissioners' expense totals have come to light in no less than eighty-nine awards.[2] Furthermore the detailed distribution of enclosure expenses has been located in some thirty-four awards.

The commissioners' schedule did not take account of anything but the public expenses of the act and award which were to be borne by the landowners as a body. These included the fees of the various officials, parliamentary and legal fees, the travelling and subsistence allowances of all those concerned with carrying out the enclosure, and the cost of any ancillary improvements such as new bridges, roads, or drainage schemes which might be launched at the time of the enclosure.

Those costs included in the commissioners' schedule were only a part of the total financial burden which the landowners would be required to shoulder. It is clear from an examination of the awards that the commissioners' accounts make no mention of the costs of actually enclosing the land. This is not surprising, since it is clear from the remarks of the commissioners, that the allotments remained unfenced or ditched, at the time they made their award. They went no farther than to demand that these enclosures should be made within a stipulated period of time. The time allowed was often very short. In the parish of Willey,[3] for example, the commissioners required that 'all enclosures shall be within two calendar months after the execution of this award, inclosed, hedged, fenced, and ditched by the several proprietors'. It would bear most heavily on the small owners, since the entire holdings would be included under this injunction, whereas the subdividing of holdings which could be carried out in more leisurely fashion, would affect the larger proprietors, in the main. The 'infencing' or division of large enclosed estates into farms would take a

---

[1] W. E. Tate, 'The Cost of Parliamentary Enclosure in England', p. 261.

[2] See Appendix A.

[3] Enclosure Award of parish of Willey, 1769, in Warwickshire County Record Office (henceforth referred to as W.C.R.O.).

considerable time. In a recent study of the parliamentary enclosure movement in Yorkshire the author remarked that 'only the skeleton framework of the modern field-pattern came into being within twelve months or so of the making of the award.'[1]

The total cost of the public transaction which enclosure involved could vary considerably between one award and another. Tate calculated that the total sum included in the commissioners' schedule could amount to £1,800–£2,000.[2] In one-fifth of the eighty-nine expense schedules for Warwickshire, the total sum was well over £2,000. Most of these came towards the end of the enclosure era; the movement got off to an early start in this county, and the cost in the early phases was very much lower. Thus we find that it is after 1779 that the majority of the heavy enclosure costs appeared: in sixteen out of twenty-five schedules made after this date, the total cost was over £2,000; in some cases very considerably more. The reasons for this greatly increased cost of enclosure will be discussed later.

In forty-five of the eighty-nine accounts, the total public costs amounted to more than £1,000, but these noticeably appeared, with two exceptions, in the period after 1760.

The average cost per acre of meeting the public expenses of enclosure increased in a most striking manner during the course of the eighteenth century. Between the period 1730–59 and the end of the century the cost more than trebled, as we see from Appendix A.

The expense of enclosure doubled again after 1800 so that, in all, we see a sixfold increase over rather more than a century.

In Table I we summarize the evidence for the growth in enclosure expenses.

The extent of this increase has been underestimated by some modern writers.[3] But it was not confined to Warwickshire.

---

[1] Alan Harris, *The Rural Landscape of the East Riding of Yorkshire, 1700–1850* (1961), University of Hull Publication, p. 68.

[2] W. E. Tate, 'The Cost of Parliamentary Enclosure in England', p. 259.

[3] For example, R. A. C. Parker speaks merely of 'costs tending to rise towards the end of the eighteenth century'. 'Enclosures in the Eighteenth Century' in *Helps for Students of History*, publication of The Historical Association, no. 7, 1960.

TABLE I

No. of awards	Dates	Average cost per acre (in shillings)
17	1735–59	11·0
20	1760–69	13·7
29	1770–79	19·6
6	1780–89	19·7
9	1792–97	34·08
8	1801–65	61·9

The average cost of thirty-eight Oxfordshire awards was higher, and saw a similar pattern of change.[1]

From Thirty-eight Oxford Enclosure Award Schedules

Parishes	Dates	Average cost of enclosure per acre (in shillings)
12	1757–73	15
12	1789–96	39

In Leicestershire H. G. Hunt found the average costs per acre were lower, though the rise was almost 100 per cent over the later eighteenth century.[2]

Eighty-eight Leicestershire Enclosure Award Schedules

Parishes	Period	Average cost of enclosure per acre (in shillings)
10	1755–59	12
38	1760–69	12
24	1770–79	16
11	1780–89	11
5	1790–99	23

The average cost of enclosure in Warwickshire over the whole period was 22*s.*, higher than that of Leicestershire, and of Lindsey (18*s.*),[3] but not so high as that of Oxford (25*s.*). The relatively low average cost in Warwickshire was due to the large amount of early enclosure which took place, prior to the inflationary years of the 1790s.

One important point revealed both in the Leicestershire and Warwickshire awards is that costs changed little before the

[1] W. E. Tate, 'The Cost of Parliamentary Enclosure in England', p. 264.

[2] H. G. Hunt, 'The Chronology of Leicestershire Enclosures' in *Economic History Review*, 2nd series, x, no. 2 (1957), p. 269.

[3] L. Swailes, 'The Parliamentary Enclosure of Lindsey' in *Reports of Papers of the Architectural and Archaeological Societies of Lincolnshire and Northamptonshire*, XLII (1957), pp. 233–74: also ibid., N.W. Lincs., II (1938), pp. 85–120.

later 1780s. This fact, once the economic advantages of the
first private act had made themselves apparent, must have been
a strong incentive to landowners to seek an enclosure. The
pattern of cost increase also gives a clue to the factors involved:
clearly the rise in prices did not fully account for it. Largely it
must have been due to the conditions prevailing during the
French wars, which offered a favourable setting for many
ambitious economic schemes on the land: not only the enclosure of parishes, where the cost, prior to 1790, had been pro-
hibitive, but also experiments with drainage, new farming
methods, and new machinery. It was in the war years that
many Midland landowners and farmers began to overcome
their caution in experimentation.[1] It is clear that parishes
where the cost of enclosure would be small were, not surprisingly, enclosed first. The parishes which were left over to
the period after 1780, and in particular the war-boom years,
were those where the quality of the land was poor, and enclosure would have brought, perhaps, little return unless it
had been associated with expensive improvement schemes.
Examples of this type of parish were 'Hungry' Harbury (where
the soil was cold clay and notoriously unproductive) and
Sutton Coldfield. Many other parishes where enclosure necessitated vast new road schemes are detailed in Appendix B. Or
else they were of the large 'open' type, where re-allotment of
the land would be very expensive and involved, and not in any
case desired by the large number of smaller proprietors. Such
parishes were Napton, Harbury, Ilmington, and Lower
Eatington. Lastly, in the nineteenth century, came the enclosure, less urgent, of the North Warwickshire fields.

As a consequence of all these differences, enclosure, from the
1790s onwards, seems to have been a long drawn-out and complicated business. This is reflected in increased fees paid to the
various officials, who received their money at a fixed daily
rate. In particular, though the number of commissioners declined to three, two, or one, the average sums they received in

---

[1] For an account of these activities in the Midlands see J. M. Martin, 'Social
and Economic Changes in the Rural West Midlands', unpublished M.Com. thesis,
University of Birmingham (1960), Chapter III.

K

fees more than doubled. This was due, partly to the larger amount of work involved, partly to the doubling between the 1760s and the 1790s of their daily rate of remuneration.

The rate of payment of commissioners' fees seems to have increased over the years as illustrated in Table II below.

TABLE II

Award	Date	Daily fee received by commissioners
Wixford	1767	£1 1 0
Stretton on Fosse	1771	
Quinton	1773	
Lr Shuckburgh	1778	
Warmington	1778	
Fenny Compton	1779	£1 11 6
Napton	1779	
Shottery	1787	
Stockton	1792	
Little Compton	1795	
Lower Pillerton	1795	£2 2 0
Erdington	1802	

A big increase in the actual sums received by commissioners was noted by Henry Homer, as early as 1765.[1] He said that formerly they had been paid a lump sum of £200–£250, but that 'now (1765) it is at least £400'. At Brailes (1787) and Eatington (1795) the commissioners' fees alone amounted to £652 and £629 respectively, leaving aside the reimbursement of their expenses.

The increase in the sums received by the commissioners in the form of fees is quite clearly revealed by the distribution of enclosure costs (Appendix B). The average sum received in fees alone by commissioners in nine awards dated 1744–67 was £99 12s. However, the average sum received by commissioners in twelve awards between 1779 and 1801 had risen to £338 4s. 2d. Furthermore we find that in the first twelve awards recorded in Appendix B, the commissioners received in fees a total of £1,332 6s., but in twelve awards between 1779 and 1801 this was increased to £4,058 10s. In addition they received a further substantial sum in payment for journeys and

[1] H. Homer, *Nature and Methods of Ascertaining Specific Shares of Proprietors upon Enclosure of Common Fields*, 1765 (Oxford, 1766).

subsistence. The payments made to other officials, in particular to the enclosure surveyors, were increased in like manner over the course of the eighteenth century. Homer confirms that all fees 'had been enhanced, and some extravagantly' in 1765.[1]

Fee increases were clearly one factor which contributed towards the rise in enclosure costs during the later eighteenth century. It is possible that those paid in other parts of the country were even higher than in Warwickshire. R. A. C. Parker, in a recent essay, said that commissioners normally received £3 3s. for each meeting (plus travel and subsistence allowance),[2] while the Committee of 1808 considered that four guineas was extortionate,[3] implying that this was occasionally demanded by commissioners.

This rise in fees must have been connected, in part, with the growth of professionalism among the commissioners and surveyors as the eighteenth century advanced. In the early days when the commissioners' panel was composed of gentlemen amateurs, there is evidence that in Warwickshire they occasionally worked for a nominal fee.[4] For example, at Wolfhamcote (1745) five commissioners received only ten guineas each (the surveyors on the other hand received £130).

The increasing complexity of the commissioners' and surveyors' task is reflected not only in the rise of the highly skilled professional, and the rising level of fees, but also in the amount of time which the enclosure process consumed. This unquestionably increased during the later eighteenth century. In the early days the application for the act was usually followed in the next year by the commissioners' award. But in the late eighteenth century, and more particularly in the early years of the nineteenth, four or five years' interval was common.

As an illustration of this tendency we might look at the enclosure of Bickenhill and Little Packington which was spread

---

[1] H. Homer, op. cit., p. 105.
[2] Parker, 'Enclosure in the Eighteenth Century', p. 8.   [3] Reprint, p. 85.
[4] First enclosure award of Wolfhamcote, a wholly small-Freeholder village (1745) in W.C.R.O. Presumably the commissioners were influenced by the general poverty of this rural community which is stressed in a document dated 1730. See W.C.R.O., Z Collection (Photostat copy of original).

over the five years 1819–24. Under the award 1,663 acres were re-allotted at a cost of £3,733, that is 45*s.* per acre on average.

It is clear from Appendix A that even from the early eighteenth century the cost of enclosing the open fields of North Warwickshire, where ownership was often widely divided among a number of small proprietors, was very much higher than in the Feldon South. Thus in the first phase of parliamentary enclosure, the average cost in seventeen Feldon awards, 1735–39, was only 11*s.*, but that of Barston (1735) and Wilnecote (1738), both North Warwickshire parishes, was 17*s.* and 20*s.* respectively.

It is not therefore surprising that most of the enclosure left over till the nineteenth century was of open fields, as at Bickenhill and Little Packington, lying in North Warwickshire. The open fields in this part of the county were in any case of secondary importance: they were small and surrounded by enclosed land.

The Enclosure Minute Book[1] and the Commissioners' Personal Account Book[2] relating to Bickenhill and Little Packington record that the first meeting to launch the enclosure took place on 1 May 1818. Between this date and October 1824 there were no less than thirty-one series of meetings. At least four of these meetings lasted six days, nine lasted five days, and five meetings three days. At each meeting, in addition to the daily fees, expenses were incurred by each official at the daily rate of 12*s.* for lodgings, and 17*s.* 6*d.* for servants, a total of £1 5*s.* 6*d.* per day.

It is not surprising that the total cost of these meetings, spread over six and a half years, was enormous. On the other hand, the fairly straightforward enclosure of a Feldon parish usually occurred at an early date, and commonly took only a fraction of the time. Typical of such an enclosure was that of Wixford and Exhall in 1767, when a total of thirty-three days' attendance by the commissioners is recorded in the award.

Another item which helped to swell the costs at Bickenhill and Little Packington was payment for culverts needed to form

---

[1] Bickenhill Enclosure Minute Book, 1818–24, in W.C.R.O. Ref.: H.R.5.
[2] Commissioners' Personal Account Book in W.C.R.O. Ref. as above.

a watercourse, and for building new roads. This brings us to another major factor responsible for the greatly accelerated cost of enclosures from the 1790s onwards both in the Feldon, where this decade saw the last big wave of private acts, and in North Warwickshire.

Enclosure in the French wars frequently included very considerable expenditure on new roads, drainage operations, and so on,[1] in this respect it marked a considerable point of departure from the earlier enclosure movement. In twelve awards in which such expenditure was noted, the first dated 1792, the total outlay on such ancillary operations was £5,615 out of £25,308, that is 22 per cent of the expenditure included in the commissioners' schedule. At Oxhill in 1798, the capital outlay on new roads was £1,010 out of £2,898. At Wolverton in 1831 a special rate[2] was drawn up by the commissioners to cover the cost of new roads which amounted to £612 and was one of the most important items in their schedule of expenses. It is, therefore, no surprise to discover that the cost of enclosure both at Oxhill and Wolverton was very high, working out at 51.7s. and 122.7s. per acre respectively (exclusive of the cost of forming the enclosures).

In addition to the work already mentioned, Henry Homer, the Warwickshire cleric and commissioner, wrote a second essay in which he emphasized the opportunity which enclosure offered for building new roads.[3] In this latter tract, though it was meant to have relevance to the country as a whole, it is worthy of note that it was addressed and dedicated to the leading landowners of the county, who formed the Trust of the two important Turnpike Roads from Dunchurch to Stonebridge, and from Ryton to Banbury. The initial objective was probably to influence the leading gentry of his own county.

We can conclude that where opportunity allowed, enclosure could have a considerable effect on the movement to secure improved communications in Warwickshire, and presumably

[1] See, for example, the awards of Stockton 1792; Wolvey 1794; Shotteswell 1794; Little Compton 1795; Lr Pillerton 1795; Oxhill 1798; Wolverton 1831.

[2] See W.C.R.O. H.R.6 for this document.

[3] H. Homer, *An Enquiry into the means of preserving and improving the public roads of this Kingdom* (Oxford, 1767).

also in other counties. Clearly Homer had a significant influence in forming the opinion of the local landowners in favour of transformed communications as an absolute necessity if full advantage of enclosure were to be realized. The favourable boom conditions of the French wars provided an opportunity for canalizing surplus capital into such a necessary investment.

These seem to be the major factors responsible for the inflation of enclosure costs from the later eighteenth century. However, there were others in some cases; for example, it is clear that opposition was a factor in the later enclosures (probably one of the reasons why enclosure had been delayed). Where the advocates of change had to overcome such opposition, this could very considerably enhance the expense of the process. For example, at the enclosure at Wolverton in 1831 the 'appeal' fund amounted to £631, probably the most important single item in the expense schedule.

It is to be observed that the rising cost of enclosure is related to social change. Not unnaturally where the public expenses of the enclosure alone amounted to between £1 14s. and £3 per acre (from 1790) compared with 11s. (in the 1750s), the social consequences would tend to be more quickly apparent.

Thus from the 1780s the selling up of small estates in large numbers was common, in the years prior to, during, and immediately after the enclosure. Evidence of this is forthcoming both from the commissioners' awards, and the Land Tax assessments. The smaller proprietors did, in any case, pay more, acre for acre, than the great landowners, as is shown by the following analysis of twenty-seven awards, in the apportionment of the commissioners' general expenses.

In nine awards owners of under 40 acres paids over 5s. per acre more than those of over 180 acres.

In six awards owners of under 40 acres paid 2s. to 5s. per acre more than those of over 180 acres.

In five awards owners of under 40 acres paid up to 2s. per acre more than those of over 180 acres.

In seven awards owners of under 40 acres paid the same or less per acre than those of over 180 acres.

TABLE III *Size of Holdings*

		Over 180 acres			40–80 acres			0–40 acres		
Parish	Encl. date	No.	Acre-age	Av. cost per acre in s.	No.	Acre-age	Av. cost per acre in s.	No.	Acre-age	Av. cost per acre in s.
Bidford	1766	1	561	10·6	1	60	15·2	14	67	15·7
Wixford	1767	2	885	12·2	5	344	11·8	18	141	18·2
Ilmington	1781	3	569	18·1	5	308	20·0	4	124	23·3
Brailes	1787	1	2,496	16·6	4	256	23·9	12	185	24·2
Little Compton	1795	1	1,094	37·6	2	122	47·9	1	1½	75·2

Thirty-three Warwickshire awards include detailed expense schedules from which we can estimate the relative importance of the different items in the public costs (see Appendix B). In the table below we summarize the evidence of the schedules.

TABLE IV

[*Note.* As will be seen from the Appendix, not all thirty-three schedules specify every item. Hence the percentages below relate to different totals.]

Item	Total awards	Total sum	Cost of item	Proportion of total cost
Cost of enclosing tithe owner's allotment	21	£38,317	£6,131	16%
Commissioners' and Surveyors' fees and expenses	21	£28,471	£9,619	34%
Legal and Parliamentary fees	30	£41,614	£15,419	37%

Thus, while the cost of obtaining the act and the various legal payments was the largest expense item, the commissioners' and surveyors' fees and subsistence expenses were almost as great, and moreover were increasing, as a proportion of the total, in the course of the eighteenth century.

We shall see later that, in addition, the cost of making the enclosures for the smaller holdings was very much greater per acre than for the large estates. Vast sums of money were paid out by the landowners in parishes undergoing enclosure to meet the cost of enclosing the tithe-owners' allotments. In twenty-two awards £6,431 was paid out for this purpose, an average of £292 per award.

It is difficult to say whether the statements of contemporaries like Arthur Young about the cost of enclosure were exaggerated or not, since we do not usually know precisely to what expenses they refer. Young suggested that the average cost of parliamentary enclosure over the whole period was £2 5s. per acre. The Hammonds cite as an example of the costliness of the process[1] an Oxfordshire parish where 4,000 acres were enclosed at a cost of £20,000–£30,000, an average cost of £5 to £7 10s. per acre. They claimed that general expenses were usually about £3 per acre in a lowland parish and £2 10s. in an upland one.

If they referred only to the general expenses covered by the commissioners' account, then their estimate if applied to the Midlands, was clearly too high. If, however, the cost of making the enclosures is added to this, then this was by no means so. The evidence shows that the capital outlay required to fence, hedge, and ditch holdings was very heavy indeed. This leaves aside the additional burden of 'infencing' holdings, which was as much again.

An idea of the sums involved in physically making the enclosures is forthcoming both from the awards and the accounts of individual landowners. Where the cost of making the rector's enclosures was borne by the remaining proprietors the bill for this operation was sometimes included in the commissioners' schedule. This furnishes an illustration of the cost of such a task, which would apply equally to the holdings of other landowners.

In thirteen awards the average cost of making the incumbent's fences was 24s. per acre. The cost varied considerably over the eighteenth century, from 16s. to 37s. It also, and this is very significant, varied inversely with the size of the allotment. Thus at Shottery, enclosed in 1787, that land received by the smaller tithe owners cost a good deal more to enclose than that received by the lord of the manor, Lord Beauchamp.

Cost of ring-fencing			*Av. cost in* s.
Lord Beauchamp's tithe allowment of 298 acres	£226 16	4	15·2
Mr Sidebottom, 8 acres 1 rood 27 perches	£30 15	0	76·7
Mr Daniel, 2 acres 1 rood 16 perches	£20 15	0	207·6

[1] See W. E. Tate, 'The Cost of Parliamentary Enclosure in England.'

Where we have evidence of the cost of making the inward mounds and fences it suggests that this was even more considerable. For example, at Warmington in 1777 the expense of making the 'out fences' of the rector's glebe and tithes was £99. That of forming the 'infences' and mounds was £450.

From documents in the Leigh collection we can see in great detail how the various costs in making the enclosures in the parish of Adlestrop in Gloucestershire were incurred. The enclosure took place in 1776 and involved 960 acres in all.[1] From the account book of James Leigh we find that the total expense of enclosing the whole was £2,820, that is £3 per acre. The cost of the timber used between Michaelmas 1775 and the Autumn of 1776 alone amounted to £409, that is an average of 8·5s. per acre.

The other major item was the labour cost estimated at one shilling per day over several years. The total expenditure under this head was £794 4s. 2d. Thus the cost of labour would work out at 16s. per acre. The final cost of the enclosure to the landlord was £4,020, because two new farm-houses were built at an outlay of £400, and two others were fitted up at £200 each. Such new buildings were a common item in enclosure expenditure.[2] It would, therefore, be quite misleading to consider that the total cost of enclosure, or even 50 per cent of the immediate capital outlay, was represented by the sums recorded in the commissioners' accounts.

If, however, we take the average cost per acre of those general expenses included in the commissioners' schedules (that is twenty-two shillings for Warwickshire) and to this add the average cost of making the ring-fences (estimated from thirteen Warwickshire awards at twenty-four shillings), we get a total of £2 6s. per acre in this county, taking enclosures over the whole period. There is contemporary confirmation of this figure: it is near to that quoted by Arthur Young (£2 8s.): it receives the support of Homer, the celebrated

[1] Leigh MS. in The Birthplace Library, Stratford. Adlestrop Papers, Box I, Bundle III. 'Account Book for the Enclosure of Adlestrop.'

[2] For the vast scale of rebuilding of Midland farm-houses and the construction of mansions from the 1760s onwards, see J. M. Martin, 'Social and Economic Changes in the Rural West Midlands', in particular the Appendices.

Warwickshire commissioner who stated, as early as 1766, that the cost lay between £2 and £3 per acre.[1] This was estimated, of course, before the sharp rise in costs of the Napoleonic war years. Lastly, it was calculated that the prospective enclosure of Adlestrop would cost Mr Leigh, the proprietor, at least £3 per acre, and this was in the middle 1760s.[2]

The figure we have arrived at to cover the cost of enclosure per acre of land in Warwickshire is considerably in advance of those quoted by Tate or the Government Report of 1808 which give the average cost as one pound.[3] It also establishes that the estimate of average enclosure costs advanced by the Hammonds and quoted earlier was subtantially correct. This is without taking account of the cost of subdividing or 'infencing' of holdings. From the 1790s the cost of enclosure would be between £2 10s. and £5 per acre in Warwickshire. There seems to be no evidence to support the further statement of the Hammonds that the costs were different in low-lying and hilly parishes. More significant, it seems, was the date of enclosure, and the structure of landownership, as a determinant of costs.

The consequences of these conclusions are more considerable yet. If we take £3 per acre as the cost of enclosing the smaller allotments (bearing in mind that the expense has been found to be much greater for them than for the great landowners), then the total cost of enclosing even a small estate of 5 acres would be fifteen pounds, almost equal to a labourer's wages for one year. The financial burden would certainly be heavy from the 1780s onwards, and must go some way in explaining the evidence of the selling up of small estates in many parishes coming under enclosure in these years. It is really no answer to say that the small owner could afford enclosure because of the high prices prevailing in these years, and the favourable markets for

[1] H. Homer, 'An Essay on the Condition . . .' (1766) p. 12.

[2] Leigh MS. in The Birthplace Library, Stratford. Adlestrop Papers, Box I, Bundle III. Entitled 'Memoranda 1765'.

[3] General Report on Enclosures 1808, Appendix XVII, p. 97. In the example given, although the average cost was only one pound, the expense of the fences was included, rising to £550 out of £1,650; that is to say, one-third of the total expenses. W. E. Tate regards the pound quoted in this General Report as 'a convenient average figure'. See 'The Cost of Parliamentary Enclosure in England', p. 261.

agricultural produce. High prices were more likely to affect him as a purchaser than as a marketer of surplus produce. We are reminded by Gonner that an increase in value did not always accrue immediately from an enclosure; [1] and this was particularly so in the case of small, uneconomical holdings in the hands of men who lacked the capital to exploit the opportunity for further improvement of the land which enclosure offered. The recouping of enclosure costs was also delayed where land was rented out (as the land-tax assessments show that many small estates in Warwickshire were at the end of the 1780s). Owners of rented land could only receive the benefits of increased value when leases fell in.

In view of this evidence it is at least questionable whether W. E. Tate's conclusions can be upheld, namely that contemporaries and later historians had greatly exaggerated the cost of enclosure, and that the monetary outlay was not 'enough in itself to have any serious effect in driving the (small) man out of business'. [2]

Though evidence is not forthcoming from Warwickshire, it has been found in other parts of the country, for example the Yorkshire Wolds, where landownership and farming were perhaps less highly developed at this time, and the small man more significant in forming local policy, that 'alternatives to a full enclosure were sought in many Wold villages'. One such scheme, aimed at introducing seeds and roots into the rotation, without the 'immense expense' of an enclosure, was described by Isaac Leatham in a report to the local Board of Agriculture written in 1794. [3]

In conclusion we can assert that in Warwickshire, at least, the cost of enclosure increased perhaps sixfold during the eighteenth century under the influence of a number of factors which have been detailed; not the least of these was the growth in the work and professional status of the commissioners and other officials connected with enclosure, leading to a rise in fees and expenses. From the later eighteenth century, that is

[1] E. C. K. Gonner, op. cit., p. 78.
[2] W. E. Tate, op. cit., p. 265.
[3] Alan Harris, op. cit., pp. 64–5.

from the enclosure of the large 'open' parishes, the expense of the process became formidable, and it is difficult to escape the conclusion that from this time, if not before, the cost to the smaller landowner would be a serious burden, which would be all the heavier for the small man, owing to the relatively high cost of enclosing tiny, uneconomical allotments. He had, further, to pay his share of the cost of enclosing and fencing the tithe-owner's allotments, a very considerable expense rising to at least 16 per cent of the commissioners' general schedule of costs. Almost all Warwickshire enclosures entailed this method of surmounting the tithe problem.

The expense of actually making the enclosures, normally, doubled at least the total cost. Such expenses were not in any instance, in Warwickshire, included in the commissioners' account of general expenses, a point which has not always been made clear by students of enclosure costs. The completion of this operation was normally required by the commissioners within a month or two of the award, on penalty of forfeiture of the allotment.

There has been a tendency for some time, reacting to the general condemnation of an earlier generation of historians, to minimize the social injustice which enclosure brought. We must, however, be aware of the heavy financial burden which the change necessarily imposed on the lower classes of rural society. In one large Warwickshire parish, at least, the memory of the eighteenth-century enclosure left a bitterness which remained for generations. We will end with the comment of one of the villagers of Tysoe in Warwickshire that 'enclosures would have done good if there had been justice in 'em. They give folks allotments instid o' ther rights – on a slope so steep, a two-legged animal can't stand; let alone dig!'[1]

---

[1] M. K. Ashby, *Joseph Ashby of Tysoe* (Cambridge, 1963), p. 38. Miss Ashby recalls many interesting conversations and observations from the days of her father's childhood in Warwickshire.

APPENDIX A. ENCLOSURE COST TOTALS, 1730–1860

Date	Award	Total expenses	Average (gross)	Av. cost per acre in s.	
1735	Hunningham	£216	645	6·7	
1735	Barston	£331	400	16·5	
1742	Stivichall	£305	594	10·2	
1740	Brinklow	£480	1,198	8·0	
1744	Wolfhamcote	£825	1,692	9·7	
1754	Hillmorton	£759	1,822	8·4	
1755	Gt Harborough	£564	945	11·9	
1756	Churchover	£640	1,120	11·4	
1757	Newton in Clifton	£680	700	19·4	
1757	Wolfhamcote	£798	1,800	8·8	
1757	Radway	£454	1,335	6·8	
1758	Morton Morrell	£546	962	11·2	
1758	Wilncote	£1,016	978	20·6	
1758	Priors Marston	£1,471	3,800	7·6	
1758	Priors Hardwick	£430	770	11.2	11·0
1758	Loxley	£524	962	10·8	17 awards
1759	Honington	£396	897	8·76	1735–59
1760	Preston on Stour	£572	1,073	10·6	
1760	Barford	£673	1,409	9·5	
1760	Willoughby	£889	1,500	11·7	
1761	Southam	£1,100	2,165	10·2	
1761	Ryton	£1,205	1,324	18·1	
1761	Princethorpe	£751	1,000	15·0	
1761	Exhall	£521	669	15·5	
1762	Pailton	£733	1,272	11·5	
1766	Snitterfield	£1,319	1,610	16·3	
1766	Bidford	£395	720	10·8	
1766	Grandborough	£680	1,756	7·7	
1765	Atherstone	£850	616	27·5	
1765	Chilvers Coton	£786	1,003	15·6	
1767	Exhall and Bidford	£1,099	1,918	11·6	
1767	Ryton in Bulkington	£756	900	21·6	
1767	Draycott	£861	1,209	14·25	
1768	Cubbington	£984	1,893	10·5	
1768	Leamington	£571	990	11·5	13·7
1767	Haselor	£863	1,380	10·9	20 awards
1769	Willey	£550	745	14·7	1760–69

Date	Award	Total expenses	Average (gross)	Av. cost per acre in s.	
1770	Bulkington	£1,337	1,600	16·7	
1771	Stretton on Fosse	£940	1,122	16·7	
1771	Bedworth	£1,004	505	39·7	
1771	Butlers Marston	£500	615	16·3	
1771	Alcester Heath	£931	616	30·2	
1772	Alveston	£1,210	1,953	12·3	
1772	Waverton	£1,142	1,143	19·8	
1772	Monks Kirkby	£500	738	13·1	
1772	Knightscot and Northend	£964	1,792	10·7	
1773	Warwick St Nicholas	£1,456	1,547	18·8	
1773	Shilton	£638	717	17·7	
1773	Quinton	£1,025	866	20·0	
1774	Newbold on Avon	£859	1,203	14·2	
1774	Rugby	£1,390	1,671	16·3	
1774	Halford	£1,083	893	24·2	
1776	Long Itchington and Bascote	£1,857	2,000	18·5	
1776	Lea Marston	£680	770	17·6	
1776	Wootton Wawen	£2,150	1,900	22.6	
1776	Dorsington	£536	869	12·3	
1777	Little Kington	£623	642	19·4	
1778	Shuckburgh Field	£978	898	21·7	
1779	Clifford Chambers	£689	337	40·9	
1779	Stratford and Bishampton	£1,407	1,600	17·6	
1779	Binton and Drayton	£749	1,900	8·8	
1779	Foleshill	£1,062	995	26·7	
1777	Barton and Martcleeve	£1,243	1,194	20·75	
1777	Warmington	£1,714	1,060	32·3	19·6
1779	Fenny Compton	£1,368	2,047	13·3	29 awards
1779	Napton on the Hill	£2,861	3,672	15·5	1770–79
1780	Harbury	£2,609	3,180	16·3	
1780	Coleshill	£2,466	2,046	24·3	
1781	Ilmington	£1,504	1,712	18·2	
1783	Burton Hastings	£1,100	831	26·4	19·7
1787	Shottery	£1,436	1,600	17·8	6 awards
1787	Brailes	£2,751	3,562	16·0	1780–87
1792	Stockton	£2,066	1,323	31·2	
1792	Gt Kineton	£1,295	800	30·8	
1794	Shotterwell	£1,614	1,200	26·5	
1794	Wolvey	£5,330	2,524	40·0	
1795	Eatington	£3,728	2,520	29·6	
1795	Ratley	£1,705	900	37·9	

Date	Award	Total expenses	Average (gross)	Av. cost per acre in s.	
1795	Little Compton	£2,412	1,588	30·5	
1795	Lr Pillerton	£2,226	2,352	28·6	34·08
1797	Oxhill	£1,010} £1,888}	1,120	51·7	9 awards 1792–97
1801	Welford	£2,384	645	73·9	
1812	Hampton in Arden	£1,304	600	43·4	
1805	Sutton under Brailes	£2,646	895	59·1	
1824	Bickenhill	£3,753	1,663	45·1	
1831	Wolverton	£3,259	531	122·7	
1850	Whitnash	£2,324	1,090	42·6	61·9
1850	Blackwell	£1,420	767	37·0	8 awards
1865	Armscote	£3,598	1,003	71·7	1801–65

APPENDIX B. DISTRIBUTION OF ENCLOSURE COSTS

Parish and date of award	Cost of enclosing tithe-owner's allotment	Fees to commissioners	Expenses of officials (entertainment and journeys)	Fees to surveyors	Fees to clerk or solicitor	Obtaining act and legal expenses	Sundries, i.e. stakes, seeds, and other equipment	Quantities, parish clerk and labour expenses	Ancillary expenses – road, bridges, drains	Total sum
1744 Wolfhamcote		52 10 0		130 19 4		} 641 0 0				825 0 0
1754 Hillmorton	70 2 8	108 3 0	66 19 4	121 15 7	72 11 7	60 3 7 / 248 8 6		11 15 2		759½ 0 0
1756 Churchover		73 10 0	109 16 0	26 13 0	112 13 2	187 17 6		20 9 6		640 0 0
1757 Gaydon		57 15 0	40 3 6	115 13 0	26 1 10	234 7 10		12 12 0 / 15 7 8		502 0 0
1758 Priors Marston		152 5 0	64 5 4 / 138 10 3	31 10 0 / 214 4 0		28 16 9 / 80 19 6	125 7 0	43 5 5		1,471 1 3
1758 Priors Hardwick		63 0 0	35 12 6	55 13 0	27 19 10	185 6 6 } 591 0 0		30 0 0		430 11 3
1760 Willoughby		124 0 0	127 0 0	162 0 0	457 0 0			19 0 0		889 19 9
1762 Pailton	226 1 10	92 8 0	44 10 9	81 14 3	46 3 6	233 12 2		6 9 0		733 0 0
1767 Wixford, etc.	(9 19 8 part only)	173 5 0	164 4 5	195 5 0	189 1 7	205 13 2		5 3 6	37 . 15 . 3 (2 roads and 1 bridge)	1,120 11 1
1771 Alcester Heath	282 3 1	74 13 0	7 7 0 / 26 18 10 / 66 0 1	67 17 0	242 7 10			0 11 0		931 18 4
1777 Warmington	549 15 6	164 0 0	127 0 0		1,002 0 0		231 7 3 (ploughing, seeds and sowing)			1,714 3 7
1777 Barton and Montcleeve	(30 3 4½)	96 17 0		160 8 6	499 10 0				57 . 9 . 5 (causeway and a bridge)	1,243 13 1½
1779 Fenny Compton		250 0 0			1,368 13 10					1,618 0 0

1779 Binton	(15 0 0 part only)	36 0 0	70 0 0	227 10 0 ⎫	4 4 0		337 18 8
1779 Drayton	(40 0 0 part only)	92 8 6	61 1 2	227 0 0 ⎬	6 6 0	8 8 0 (bridge)	410 18 8
1755 Gt Harborough		80 17 0	65 19 2	79 4 0	97 18 8 / 185 3 0	14 7 4		564 0 0
1757 Newton in Clifton		75 15 0	25 0 0 / 78 16 6	51 3 0	102 13 0 / 342 12 9	8 17 6		680 17 9
1761 Exhall	26 0 0	70 7 0	53 9 9	61 10 10	61 10 8 / 196 10 10	12 4 11 / 12 4 11		521 15 2
1761 Southam	100 0 0 (part cost of subdivision)						50 0 0 (repairs of roads and bridges)	1,100 3 2
1771 Stretton on Fosse	50 0 0 (Poors' All.) / 249 9 6							940 19 7
1773 St Nicholas Warwick	396 12 0 / 40 8 0 (Furze plot for Poor)	153 0 0	29 17 0 / 84 10 2	154 3 0	297 9 1 / 28 12 4¼ / 191 8 2¼	10 10 0 / 19 15 0 (valuers) / 39 19 10 (labour)	67 7 10 (private roads and bridges)	1,456 0 0
1774 Halford	329 12 0	357 0 0						1,083 0 0
1779 Napton								2,861 0 0
1781 Ilmington	(438 acres) 600 0 9	241 15 10 (journeys to London) / 10 4 6 / 25 3 6	299 0 0	216 0 0	11 10 0 / 179 6 0	233 4 0 / 9 7 7 / 14 18 0	0 16 0 / 24 18 0	2,104 0 0
1787 Brailes	(493 acres) 630 0 0	652 1 0	57 1 9 / 39 14 0 (journeys)	501 13 1	497 9 7¼ / 266 2 4¼	27 2 4 / 1 1 0	60 14 6	2,751 18 2

Parish and date of award	Cost of enclosing tithe-owner's allotment	Fees to commissioners	Expenses of officials (entertainment and journeys)	Fees to surveyors	Fees to clerk or solicitor	Obtaining act and legal expenses	Sundries, i.e. stakes, seeds, and other equipment	Quantities, parish clerk and labour expenses	Ancillary expenses – road, bridges, drains	Total sum
1794 Shotteswell	132 2 3½	293 0 0	72 19 6 / 57 7 0 (journeys)	199 18 10	217 15 1½ / 180 12 6	193 0 9		127 0 0	288 13 5½ (repair of roads)	1,614 15 11½
1792 Gt Kineton		140 14 0	27 3 10 / 33 1 0	150 19 1	271 7 7	199 9 3	8 3 6 / 137 8 6	5 2 0	230 10 0 (making roads)	1,235 16 6
1792 Stockton	282 0 0	281 18 6		184 1 0	172 8 8	136 6 6 / 201 8 8		145 0 0 / 85 0 0	195 5 8 (roads)	2,066 13 0
1795 Little Compton	224 6 9½	355 0 0	39 6 2 / 27 6 0 (journeys)	201 5 5	229 11 11	492 19 8	182 9 7	17 4 0 (labour) / 14 11 6	454 6 4	2,412 0 0
1795 Lr Pillerton	69 6 0 (poor, etc.) / 248 12 0	252 10 8	4 5 10 / 4 16 0	259 18 1	285 4 6	285 3 9	1 1 0 / 183 7 0		358 16 0	2,225 0 0
1787 Shottery	501 0 0	192 19 0	6 11 0	196 19 0	332 18 11	129 4 4		21 19 0	96 14 3 (Surveyor's fee for highways)	1,436 2 9
1801 Welford on Avon	288 5 1	375 18 0	133 0 0	181 1 9	312 11 10	319 2 5 / 225 0 0 (Act Parl. Fees)	41 16 0	14 14 4 (fees) / 20 11 0	633 12 2 (Public roads)	2,384 12 8
1795 Eatington, hamlets of Upper & Lower	276 0 0	629 0 0	133 0 0	409 0 0	444 0 0	647 0 0		14 9 5	1,020 7 8	3,728 0 0
1803 Whatcote	300 0 0									
1795 Ratley	363 0 0	252 0 0	14 0 0	224 0 0	582 0 0		24 0 0	21 0 0	225 0 0	1,705 0 0
1779 Clifford Chambers	106 0 0	74 0 0		54 0 0	430 0 0			9 3 0		689 0 0
1818–24 Bickenhill					488 0 0	1,103 0 0			1,164 0 0	3,753 0 0
1826–31 Wolverton (471 acres)	239 0 0	250 0 0		750 0 0	(inc. 2,440 0 0 'Appeal Rate')				612 0 0 (inc. 632 0 0 'Appeal Rate')	3,295 0 0

APPENDIX C. THE COST OF FENCING, HEDGING, AND DITCHING WARWICKSHIRE ENCLOSURES

Parish	Date of award	Tithe and glebe allotment in acres	Comment	Cost of making fences	Cost per acre in shillings
Wellesbourne Hastings and Newbold Pacey	1735	23	'Outfencing' of small tithes only	£22 0 0	19·1
Hillmorton	1754	81	Sir J. Astley recd. 81 acres glebe, and the vicar was to receive £34 14s. od. rent charge on it	£70 0 0	17·4
Pailton	1762	193	For fencing of tithe allotments of Brasenose College and Incumbent	£226 0 0	23·4
Stretton on Fosse	1771	227	Great tithe and Glebe to Rector	£249 0 0	21·9
		14	Poors' Allotment	£50 0 0	71·4
Alcester Heath	1771	94	Rector's six allotments for Great and Small Tithes	£282 0 0	60·0
Halford	1774	180	Rector's Glebe and Great Tithes	£329 0 0	36·6
Barton and Montcleeve	1777	33	Two allotments for Glebe	£30 0 0	18·2
Warmington	1777	184	Rector's Glebe and Tithe 'Outfences'	£99 0 0	} 59·7
			'Inward mounds' and Glebe	£450 0 0	
Ilmington	1781	352	Glebe and Great Tithes	£354 0 0	20·1
Brailes	1787	362	Great Tithes	£633 0 0	34·9
Shottery	1787	356	'Ring-Fencing' Ld. Beauchamp's Tithe – 298 acres	£226 16 4	15·2
			'Ring-Fencing' Corp. of Stratford – 45 acres	£223 15 0	92·5 } 28·1
			'Ring-Fencing' Mr Sidebottom – 8-1-27 acres	£30 15 0	76·7
			'Ring-Fencing' Mr Daniels – 2-1-16 acres	£20 15 0	207·6
Stockton	1792	225	Tithe and Glebe	£262 0 0	23·3
Shotteswell	1794	92	Vicar's allotment	£132 0 0	28·7
Little Compton	1795	274	Rectorial Tithe	£224 0 0	16·4
Lower Pillerton	1795	223	Duke of Rutland's Gt and Small Tithes	£248 0 0	22·3

In the following parishes, a contribution only was made towards the cost of enclosure by the proprietors

Parish	Date of award	Tithe and glebe allotment in acres	Comment	Cost of making fences	Cost of acre in shillings
Southam	1761	339	Rector's two allotments 'towards the cost'	£100 0 0	5·9
Great Harborough	1755	183	Rector's allotment	£40 0 0	4·3
Exhall	1761	25	Vicarial tithe. 'In part' made at the general expense	£26 0 0	20·8

6 Agriculture and Economic Growth in England, 1660–1750: Agricultural Change

E. L. JONES

[This article was first published in *The Journal of Economic History*, Vol. XXV (1965).]

Between the middle of the seventeenth century and the middle of the eighteenth century, English agriculture underwent a transformation in its techniques out of all proportion to the rather limited widening of its market. Innovations in cropping took place on a wide, though not a universal, front and independently of any great expansion of demand, which was to stimulate the extension of improved methods during the classic agricultural revolution of the late eighteenth century. Except in the sphere of stock breeding, the remainder of the century really had little to offer in the way of techniques which were new in principle. Yet the initial introduction of the most important advanced techniques had come during the late seventeenth and early eighteenth centuries, when the slow and ultimately uncertain growth of population and the modest rise in *per capita* national income combined to produce only a gradual growth of demand.

The problems posed are of two kinds: one relating to the economic conditions which induced the developments within agriculture, the other relating to the economic consequences of agricultural change. First, how, in a restricted market, did substantial technical innovation, a rise in output, and an expansion of agriculture's capacity to meet the subsequent burdens of an expanding economy come about? Second, how serious was the fall in agricultural investment and incomes which is thought to have taken place during the second quarter of the eighteenth century, and what were the effects on the course of economic growth? What I shall attempt, therefore, is a thumbnail sketch of the timing and distribution of technical changes before 1750 and of their effect on output. I shall then offer two complementary explanations of these achievements and mention briefly the implications for the aggregate levels of investment and income in agriculture, matters which are germane to any incomes-effect explanation of industrial growth. A fuller discussion by Arthur John of the impact of the agricultural changes on the growth of the whole economy is the subject of the following article.

It will be plain that my aim is threefold: first, to give a brief overview of present knowledge on the topic,[1] although it must be insisted that limitations of space prevent any but the most cursory discussion of the evidence, and this must therefore be pursued through the footnote references; second, to relate the fragments of evidence so far available in a provisional and speculative explanatory scheme; and third, by the necessary tenuousness of any model constructed at this state of research, to indicate the programme needed to fill the most critical gaps in our information.[2]

I

What were the early husbandry changes and how were they inserted into the agriculture of preindustrial England? During the sixteenth and seventeenth centuries, the range of plants at

[1] Especially as revealed in the following key sources: H. J. Habakkuk, 'English Landownership, 1680–1740', *The Economic History Review*, x (February 1940), pp. 2–17; A. H. John, 'The Course of Agricultural Change, 1660–1760', in L. S. Pressnell (ed.), *Studies in the Industrial Revolution* (London: Athlone Press, 1960), pp. 122–55; G. E. Mingay, 'The Agricultural Depression, 1730–1750', *The Economic History Review*, 2nd series, VIII, No. 3 (April 1955), pp. 323–38. The present article is a slightly revised version of a paper given to the joint conference of the Economic History Society and British Agricultural History Society, at the University of Reading, 10 April 1964. Comments by Gordon Mingay and Donald Whitehead, and by B. H. Slicher van Bath and his staff at a seminar in the Department of Rural History, University of Wageningen, Netherlands, have been most helpful.

[2] In order to extend our knowledge of agricultural output, an analysis of eighteenth-century farm accounts has now been started at Nuffield College, Oxford, under the direction of R. M. Hartwell and the writer.

the farmer's disposal had been extended beyond any pre-
cedent. The discovery of the Americas, for example, had
greatly increased the vegetable species available to England,
although most of the introductions to this country were made
from or through the more intensive agricultures of the Low
Countries, and most of them not until the seventeenth century.[1]
By that time, as recent work has shown, farm organization even
in the common fields was sufficiently flexible to utilize the
new crops. The most influential newcomers were all fodder
crops – two legumes (sainfoin and clover) and a root (the
turnip).

The most rapid survey of published sources alone shows that
the introduction of these plants as field crops came earlier and
over a much wider area of England than was once thought.
Sainfoin, for instance, was established at Daylesford, Worcestershire, in 1650, and about the same year at North Wraxhall, in north-west Wiltshire, by one Nicholas Hall of Dundry
in Somerset.[2] The turnip, after being introduced as a vegetable
by Dutch immigrants to Norwich soon after 1565, later spread
until by the reign of Anne, according to Defoe, it was to be
found 'over most of the east and south parts of England'.[3]
Even in western counties, turnips were being grown during
the seventeenth and early eighteenth centuries, and by the
middle of the eighteenth century they were grown in Cornwall,
the westernmost English county (by 1771, farm accounts for
Menabilly Barton, Fowey, are referring to 'the Turnip Oxen').[4]

[1] The account of crop innovations which follows is drawn from references
listed below; a good contemporary summary is to be found in O. Lawson Dick
(ed.), *Aubrey's Brief Lives* (Harmondsworth: Peregrine Books, 1962), especially
pp. 28–9.
[2] R. C. Gaut, *A History of Worcestershire Agriculture and Rural Evolution* (Worcester: The Worcester Press, 1939), p. 97; F. Harrison, *North Wraxhall, Co. Wilts*
(London: Macmillan, 1913), p. 155.
[3] K. J. Allison, 'The Sheep-Corn Husbandry of Norfolk in the Sixteenth and
Seventeenth Centuries', *Agricultural History Review*, v, No. 1 (1957), p. 27; Daniel
Defoe, *A Tour Through England and Wales* (London: Dent & Sons, 1928), p. 58.
[4] Rashleigh Farm Accounts, uncatalogued, Cornwall Record Office; J. Rowe,
Cornwall in the Age of the Industrial Revolution (Liverpool: University Press, 1953),
p. 221; on another western county, see E. L. Jones, 'Agricultural Conditions and
Changes in Herefordshire, 1660–1815', *Transactions of the Woolhope Club*, XXXVII
(1961), p. 40.

In the west, however, turnips were usually sown in small lots as supplementary feed for livestock, not as a full course in the rotation of the whole farm. Considering the high production costs and the unreliability of the turnip crop, and the year-round growth of grass in the south-west, there should be no surprise that it failed to sweep the board. But it was not absent.

Clover leys were sown during the seventeenth century up and down the country from the south coast to Sherwood Forest and across from East Anglia to the Welsh border. Clover was much sown in the west. For example, Andrew Yarrenton grew it at Astley, Worcestershire, and in 1662 wrote his *The Improvement improved . . . by clover.* He engaged agents to sell the seed and his explanatory tract in many towns in the west Midlands. Similarly, Dutch woollen merchants living at Topsham on the Exe imported clover seed, which they distributed to markets throughout the south-western peninsula during the second half of the seventeenth century.[1] In addition, the seventeenth century saw an immense spread of floated water meadows from their points of origin in Herefordshire, Dorset, and probably Shropshire during Elizabeth's reign.[2] By 1700, these irrigated meadows were widespread in the Wessex chalk-lands and the west Midlands, and were still extending.

From our vantage point these innovations may seem to have come in unhurriedly. As late as 1750, all of them, especially the turnip, still had much ground to conquer. Nevertheless, it is undeniable that they were by then widely established. Grafted on to an agriculture which was already being modified by the creeping consolidation of holdings, they forced open the bottle-neck of too little fodder with which to over-winter a large stock

---

[1] Charles Wilson, *Holland and Britain* (London: Collins, n.d.), p. 108.

[2] Rowland Vaughan, *Most Approved and Long Experienced Water Works* (London, 1610), no pagination; letter to Humphrey Weld from his tenants of Winfrith manor, 1598, Dorset Record Office, Weld Collection D10/E(103). A floated water meadow is one in which river water is conveyed for a series of short periods over adjacent, gently sloping meadow land by means of a complicated system of hatches and ditches. This is in contrast with the older and simpler system of catchwork meadows, watered by washing stream water over hillside grassland. The effects are irrigation, raising the temperature and thus facilitating grass growth, and fertilizing.

of farm animals. The fodder crops and the forced grass of the water meadows had the same kind of impact: by increasing the supply of feed they enabled more stock to be kept and better fed, giving more dung per acre. This was a crucial advance for a society which lacked efficient artificial fertilizers. Heavier applications of manure would raise the yields of both cereal and fodder crops, more feed would permit still heavier stocking, and the whole slowly expanding circle would unfold once more. Total output would rise unless offset by a net withdrawal of land from cultivation.

The insertion of grass leys into farming routines, which has been acclaimed as a major advance during the sixteenth and early seventeenth centuries, was most unlikely to produce a *comparable* effect on total output. Ley husbandry may improve soil texture but not soil fertility, since on balance the grazing beasts will take out what they put in. While some improvement in yields may have resulted, the biological constraints made any substantial rise in output per acre improbable. The achievement of the 1540–1640 period in this respect must be judged meagre, its increases of output probably more the result of the extension of cultivation. Despite the early examples of floated meadows and a few cropping innovations, and despite many more studies of the farming of individual counties during the 1540–1640 century than have been made of the subsequent hundred years, no major technical transition in agriculture has been identified during the earlier period. That period looks to have been one in which inflationary profits were redistributed from the labourer to the yeoman and to the land owner, to be spent on the 'Great Rebuilding' of farms and on the erection of London houses, rather than one in which productivity far overhauled the growth of population.

The true transformation of crop rotations was accomplished with the adoption on a significant scale in the latter half of the seventeenth century of the innovations in fodder cropping. Nitrogen-fixing by the legumes contributed directly to soil fertility; the improved permanent grass of the water meadows, washed by lime from the chalk streams, fed animals which were daily moved out to dung and thus to transfer nutrients and minerals to the arable fields. These changes were perhaps revolutionary in their effects although not in their pace.

Direct evidence of a resultant rise in total agricultural output is limited, but M. A. Havinden has provided us with some measures of the impressive increases which were secured in Oxfordshire – on the whole an open-field county which, although it grew the new crops, would not be expected to be in the van of the movement.[1] The figures, derived from large samples of probate inventory data, denote a marked rise in livestock populations, especially of sheep and especially on the light soils. They also show a shift in cereal cultivation in favour of the highest-priced cereal, wheat – a feature which is quite contrary to continental experience during the seventeenth- and early eighteenth-century depression. Unfortunately the evidence on total crop production is extremely slender, although the suggestion is of a rise.

TABLE I

		Limestone uplands of Oxfordshire	*Thames Valley (clays and loams)*
Size of median sheep flock	1580–1640	14 animals	24 animals
	1660–1730	60 animals	51 animals
		Percentages	*Percentages*
Proportion of cattle herds containing over 5 animals	1580–1640	33	39
	1660–1730	46	45
(N.B.: not offset by a fall in the number of herds)			
Wheat as a proportion of total crops	1590–1640	14	25
	1660–1730	27	32

There is evidence from elsewhere. The national sheep population responded to the expansion of feed supplies with a considerable expansion during the seventeenth and early eighteenth centuries, and this was of course especially significant for the manuring of the wide expanses of potential new ploughland on the light-soiled uplands. On the other hand, the national cattle population seems hardly to have responded to the

[1] 'Agricultural Progress in Open-Field Oxfordshire', *Agricultural History Review*, IX, No. 2 (1961), pp. 73–83.

stimulus of more and better feed during the first half of the eighteenth century, although it seems to have done so earlier.[1] The output of tallow, hides, and soap remained in the doldrums, while a supply of dairy products was obtained from Ireland. After 1707, the Scots sent more and more store cattle to England, and the Channel Islanders found that they could send growing cargoes of 'green hides' and of re-exported French calfskins to this country, as well as more and more Guernsey and Jersey cattle.[2] Finally, grain prices slowly sank, and a struggle to encourage exports by means of the corn bounty went on (with intermissions like the lean years of the 1690s) from the 1660s to the 1750s.

This may indicate that supply did tend to pull just ahead of demand, despite the withdrawal from arable production of some land in the clay vales. At first sight more striking still, the notching up of agricultural output took place despite difficulties for the producers of grain. There was a high turnover of small farmers on heavy arable lands, especially in central and eastern England, during the extreme scarcity of the 1690s and the low prices of the first years and second quarter of the eighteenth century. Arrears of rent were high on both heavy and light land during some years between 1702 and 1705, 1709 and 1712, and in the 1730s and 1740s.[3] During the last-mentioned decades, a fortuitous run of good harvests raised the supply of grain well above what the home market, the bounty on corn export, the distilling of gin, and the grassing down of the clays could clear. Both grain and livestock prices dropped. Yet the arable acreage continued to be extended and new farms to be created on the light-soiled uplands; fodder crops came more and more into use; and there was a noteworthy re-equipping of farms by landowners.

[1] There is much scattered evidence on the size of the sheep and cattle populations and the output of their products, the most convenient summary being Phyllis Deane and W. A. Cole, *British Economic Growth* (Cambridge: University Press, 1962), pp. 68–74.

[2] Southampton Civic Record Office, Petty Custom and Wharfage Books from 1723.

[3] See especially G. E. Mingay, *English Landed Society in the Eighteenth Century* (London: Routledge, 1963), pp. 54–5.

II

First, we have to account for the improvement in husbandry techniques, chiefly the development of rotations involving fodder crops, during the second half of the seventeenth century and the first half of the eighteenth century. At the general level this may not be so difficult. European work shows the extension of fodder crops to be a regular feature of periods of poor cereal prices, when, *ceteris paribus*, relative prices favour a switch to livestock and therefore necessitate extra animal feed-stuffs. The spread of the fodder plants as field crops would have been delayed during the late sixteenth century, when grain prices were relatively high. At that time, although many of the fodder plants were available, there was less incentive to sow them as field crops, so that in England they tended to remain localized and in use only as vegetables, whereas their field cultivation had already become established in the Low Countries during the depression of the late middle ages.[1] The mechanics of their subsequent colonization of England need to be more fully worked out, particularly as regards their widespread insertion into common-field regimes which were until recently dismissed as totally inflexible; but it is worth noting that many country gentlemen (including many Royalists from western counties) made acquaintance with the Low Countries during the seventeenth century.

Second, and this is perhaps the surprising and uniquely English feature, we have to consider a rise not only in livestock production but also in cereal production at a time of poor prices for grain. It is certainly unlikely that net cereal output actually fell, while livestock output rose so that aggregate agricultural output would have increased. Two complementary explanations will be suggested for this phenomenon. But even if all the agricultural changes of the period were merely shifts in the locale of production within the framework of a static output of grain, it would still be necessary to postulate how,

[1] B. H. Slicher van Bath, 'The Rise of Intensive Husbandry in the Low Countries', *Britain and the Netherlands*, 1 (London: Chatto and Windus, 1960), pp. 130–53.

when cereal prices were falling, production could be so much extended on the light soils of the former sheep downs. The second part of our explanatory scheme could provide such an explanation.

We may first lay stress on English agriculture's built-in mechanism for minimizing differences in the level of investment between spells of rising prices and spells of falling prices. There were two distinct sources of agricultural investment – landowner and tenant. The shifting in their respective shares of estate-maintenance expenditure was (as has been observed of later periods) almost rhythmic. During the 1730s and 1740s, landlords wrote off arrears of rent and re-shouldered burdens like the land tax which in somewhat better times they had begun to foist on to the tenantry. Freed from these charges, tenants were able to devote all available resources to productive ends. In addition, in order to compete for and to retain suitable tenants on their farms, landowners even felt obliged to subsidize productive outlays themselves. They provided tenants with grass seeds, rearranged farm layouts, repaired the existing farm buildings and put up new ones, and on the chalk uplands they undertook the heavy capital expenditures needed to float water meadows and to bring into cultivation commons and sheep downs.[1]

There may have been a shift towards investment in capital items by landowners: in buildings, hedges, and roads, where sheep down was being broken up for arable farms. The agricultural investment of the period, notably of the second quarter of the eighteenth century, was in part therefore the outcome of the estate system. The late seventeenth and early eighteenth centuries had seen the extension of the estates belonging to great landowning families already established in the counties. This was at the expense of the smaller squires, who had been badly hit by war taxation from 1692 to 1715 and (once the hungry nineties had passed) by low grain prices too. The great estates which had been built up were, in H. J. Habakkuk's

[1] E. L. Jones, 'Eighteenth-Century Changes in Hampshire Chalkland Farming', *Agricultural History Review*, VIII, No. 1 (1960), especially pp. 7–10; M. C. Naish, 'The Agricultural Landscape of the Hampshire Chalklands, 1700–1840' (unpublished M.A. thesis, London University, 1960), *passim*.

phrase, 'units of ownership not of production'.[1] Their owners did not engage directly in anything so demeaning as husbandry; their incomes were lucratively supplemented, and sometimes half supplied, from non-agricultural sources such as army posts and pensions. The physical capital of most estates had been run down during the wars; but when high interest rates dropped after 1720, enclosures and improvements became profitable again. The larger landowners made it clear that they were in the market for good tenants and that, since they could let at lower rents than the lesser gentry, they would stay in the market even when times became less favourable. During the second quarter of the century, therefore, landowners, notably the great lords, were prepared to subsidize agriculture. For social reasons, and because of their other resources, they were comparatively insensitive to poor financial returns. They accordingly cushioned their tenants against the full force of falling prices and thus raised the level of investment above what it otherwise might have been.

III

A complementary explanation of the considerable innovation in agricultural practice which went on right through the low-price periods of the late seventeenth and early eighteenth centuries is to be derived from the dominant distribution pattern of types of farming. We must first discount the two dichotomies customarily used to organize English agricultural history: the distinctions between open-field and enclosed counties, and between a progressive east and a backward west of England. Research has diminished the sharpness of these divisions and proved them inadequate to explain the course of technical change or the economic experience of agriculturists. Examples have already been cited which make it clear that the east–west division is unhelpful: it is based on inappropriate indices of the rate of technical change – that is, on the adoption of a root break or of the full-blown Norfolk rotation. The link between this dichotomy and the rate of technical change in agriculture was in any case never very explicit. It depended mainly on the

[1] Habakkuk, *The Economic History Review*, x, p. 5.

fact that East Anglia is nearer than the west country to Holland
– the relevance of which seems less striking on a consideration
of the actual spread of the new crops within England. Similarly, the divergence between open-field and enclosed areas has
been blurred: in Oxfordshire, for example, it has been shown
that the introduced fodder crops spread faster on the light soils
of the limestone uplands, even in the open fields, than in the
more enclosed clay vales like that of Thames.[1] In the case of
the open-field–enclosure dichotomy, the link with innovation
was supposedly through the 'slowest ship in the convoy' thesis,
whereby the most dilatory open-field farmer dictated a snail's
pace of adjustment in the system of communal husbandry.[2]
Modern work, showing that the new crops were early inserted
into many common-field routines, appears to indicate a different
power structure, whereby the more pushing and articulate men
often secured their neighbours' consent to changes. Both the
east–west and open-field–enclosure distinctions do nevertheless refer to important factors influencing the detailed pattern
and timing of agricultural innovation, but in no all-embracing
or enormously revealing way.

A more fruitful division is offered by the scarp-and-vale
topography of lowland Britain. This cuts boldly across
county boundaries, dividing agriculture into two main groups
of farming systems: on one hand, those on the free-draining,
light soils of the chalk and limestone uplands, the lightest
loams, and some of the more fertile sand lands; and on the
other hand, those on the heavy loams and ill-drained clays. In
the former category are the Cotswolds, the Wessex chalklands,
the Norfolk 'good sands', and so forth; in the latter, the Midland clay triangle and the clay vales of other parts.[3]
The scope for innovating was not uniform across these two

[1] Havinden (cited in n. 1, p. 157), *passim*.
[2] Compare the categorical dismissal of the ability of open-field farmers to
utilize the new crops and the statements (culled from the biased 'improving'
literature) about the slowness of innovation, in Lord Ernle, *English Farming Past
and Present* (6th edn; London: Heinemann, 1961), pp. 122, 134.
[3] Many studies by historical geographers have attempted to measure agricultural differences between light-soiled uplands and heavy-soiled vales, and sometimes between finer units. Such work includes S. E. J. Best, *East Yorkshire: A*

divisions. Although varying from crop to crop, the potential value of the innovations was, in total, greater on the light soils which had previously been too infertile for permanent tillage but which were dry enough for stock (especially sheep) to be kept on the land during winter to feed off the fodder crops, thus returning manure for a following cereal crop. The light land of the Wessex chalk and the Cotswolds benefited, too, from the floating of their valley meadows. Once it became possible to keep their thin soils fertile, cereals could be grown more cheaply on them than on the heavy clays, where, in contrast, traction costs were high, the working season was curtailed, and the land was too wet for stock to be folded on forage crops during the winter months. Because roots grow better in the fine texture of light soils and are difficult to feed off (or even to lift from) heavy, ill-drained land, the turnip was especially slow to penetrate clay districts. On the clays, therefore, less advantage could be taken of the contemporary innovations. The available studies do indeed suggest that such areas were usually very tardy in taking up the new crops.[1]

As a result, during the late seventeenth and early eighteenth centuries, some of the clays went down to grass and specialized more than ever in fattening and dairying, whereas there was a marked extension of cultivation on the former sheep downs of southern England, and as far north as the sand lands of

---

Study in Agricultural Geography (London: Longmans, 1930); D. R. Mills, 'Enclosure in Kesteven', *Agricultural History Review*, VII, No. 2 (1959), pp. 82–97; J. A. Sheppard, 'East Yorkshire's Agricultural Labour Force in the Mid-Nineteenth Century', ibid., IX, No. 1 (1961), pp. 43–54; D. B. Grigg, 'Changing Regional Values during the Agricultural Revolution in South Lincolnshire', *Transactions of the Institute of British Geographers* (1962), pp. 91–103. But these writers have hardly generalized their findings or pursued the economic implications, while historians are usually content to work with administrative units which often blur agricultural distinctions.

[1] See, for example, G. H. Kenyon, 'Kirdford Inventories, 1611 to 1776, with Particular Reference to the Weald Clay Farming', *Sussex Archaeological Collections*, XCIII (1955), pp. 78–156; and C. W. Chalklin, 'The Rural Economy of a Kentish Wealden Parish, 1650–1750', *Agricultural History Review*, X, No. 1 (1962), pp. 29–45. The problems of the rates of assimilation of the new crops by different farming systems are discussed in E. L. Jones, *Transactions of Woolhope Club*, XXXVII, pp. 32, 38–42, and in his 'English Farming before and during the Nineteenth Century', *The Economic History Review*, 2nd series, XV, No. 1 (1962), pp. 145–7.

Sherwood Forest. During the third quarter of the eighteenth century this distinction was emphasized, according to contemporaries, when the output per acre on light soils rose, for example on the Cotswolds, to 'equal that of a like quantity of land in the vale, where the rents are double and treble the price and the land will not admit of proportionable improvements'.[1] In other cases, there was a reappraisal of rents in keeping with the altered values of the two kinds of land; for example, it was observed that 'the dry grounds in Hertfordshire, which formerly were lett for a trifling rent, are now lett at twenty shillings per acre, since the introduction of clover & turnips into their poor & barren hills; while the low lying stiff grounds pay only ten shillings, which is the rent they gave near a century ago'.[2]

Thus the centres of arable prosperity were shifting from the heavier lands to the lighter lands. As regards the overall economic condition of the Midlands and the heavy-clay vales, some compensation was probably found in two movements which may have tended to hide the problems of husbandmen on their arable open-field lands. First, cottage framework knitting was spreading into these areas, absorbing under-employed labour or hands ousted from farming as the vale countryside turned more to pastoral husbandry.[3]

Although the relative rates of population growth by land-use divisions have been assessed from nineteenth-century census data, next to nothing is known of their earlier history. Seemingly, there were greater opportunities and pressures towards additional settlement and non-agricultural employment in the vales and on the lowland heaths than on the light-soiled uplands. The conversion of the uplands to tillage and the establishment on them of isolated new farms may have needed some hands beyond those previously present but under-employed;

[1] Simon Moreau, *A Tour to Cheltenham Spa* (Bath, 1783), p. 62.

[2] J. H. Smith, *The Gordon's Mill Farming Club, 1758–1764* (Edinburgh: Oliver and Boyd, 1962), p. 149.

[3] J. D. Chambers, 'The Vale of Trent', *The Economic History Review*, Supplement 3 (1957), p. 13, n. 8; W. G. Hoskins, *The Midland Peasant* (London: Macmillan, 1957), p. 227; Joan Thirsk, 'Industries in the Countryside', in F. J. Fisher (ed.), *Essays in the Economic and Social History of Tudor and Stuart England* (London: Cambridge University Press, 1961), pp. 70–88.

but the new cereal culture could doubtless have been carried on without much of a permanent influx, since the work was seasonal and harvest hands, for instance, were obtainable from the vale and the clothing towns.

Second, the trends of animal production were more favourable to the heavier soils. Within the increase in the size of the national flock there was a noteworthy increase in the population of long-woolled sheep in the Midlands. In Defoe's day, Leicestershire was 'a vast magazine of wool'. That county, which in the first half of the seventeenth century had been notable for its tillage, had turned more and more to grass. Wool from Leicestershire, Northamptonshire, and Lincolnshire poured into Cirencester and Tetbury markets for the clothing trade of the west of England; more mutton was in demand as a cheapening loaf released spending power. This was the period which saw the rise of the gentlemen graziers, building William and Mary and Queen Anne houses in the Midland shires; but it was a time which offered unsatisfactory compensation for sinking grain prices to those small farmers in the open fields whose fortunes still depended centrally on the cereal markets.[1]

Although stated very baldly here, this distributional model helps to explain much of the adjustment which was taking place within agriculture. The existence of this broad twofold grouping of farming systems was noted by contemporaries and continues to be recognized by farmers and naturalists. The topographic distinction is often sharp. But a mechanism whereby this could influence the course of innovation and output during spells of low prices and incomes has not hitherto been spelled out. The classification used here does not of course exhaust the ecosystems of lowland Britain, while any simple dichotomy runs the risk of violating some part of the evidence.[2] Nevertheless,

[1] Defoe, II, p.89; W. G. Hoskins, *The Making of the English Landscape* (London: Hodder & Stoughton, 1955), p. 124.

[2] The third main division in terms of area, the lowland heath, may however be ignored here as consisting of sandy soils also termed 'light', but too infertile for cultivation except for a little temporary enclosure during periods of exceptionally high prices, such as the Napoleonic wars. See E. L. Jones and C. R. Tubbs, 'Vegetation of Sites of Previous Cultivation in the New Forest', *Nature*, cxcviii, No. 4,884 (June 1963), pp. 977–8.

M

the distinction seems to yield a useful categorization of farmers' economic fortunes and of the rates at which they assimilated new techniques. What the present discussion attempts to add is a brief account of the function of the dichotomy in terms of different physical constraints and costs of agricultural production.

Such an account offers a 'pie-slicing' thesis. Producers on light soils were able to take a disproportionately bigger slice of the pie (the market) at the expense of the higher-cost clay-land cereal producers. Their comparative advantage was reinforced by their proximity to the markets: East Anglia to London and the east-coast ports; the Wessex chalk to London, Bristol, and Southampton (whence grain was sent to Iberia); the Cotswolds and the Ryelands of Herefordshire to Bristol and Monmouth, whence grain was also exported to Iberia. The Midlands farmers had to dispatch their grain farther and over worse roads to reach any of these outlets. Higher production and transport costs thus placed them in an inferior competitive position even given stable grain prices.

During the gentle subsidence of cereal prices during the late seventeenth and early eighteenth centuries, therefore, light-land farmers found that by innovating they could profitably expand their output. By putting a bigger volume of produce on the market, even at reduced prices, they could at least maintain their incomes. Technically, they had more room to manoeuvre than did their clay-land competitors. Except in some years between 1702 and 1712 and during the 1730s and 1740s, there is no reason to think that the total profits of light-land farmers fell. But the increased output of grain from the light soils necessarily tightened the screw of low prices on the higher-cost, technically less flexible, clay-land farms. The rapid turnover of tenants, the selling out of owner-occupiers, and the conversions to pasture on the clays suggest that, despite more modification of their open-field farming than was accepted by the older writers, the clays were being outcompeted in the grain markets. There is some evidence that clover was adopted by farmers on the Chilterns, where the chalk is capped with clay-with-flints, precisely because they were obliged to improve their yields if they were to remain competitive with the grain from the freshly ploughed up downland of the Salisbury Plain area.[1]

During the sharper price falls of 1702–5, 1709–12, and the 1730s and 1740s, not all light-land farmers escaped. Arrears of rent mounted up on some estates in those districts. In the last of these spells there are signs that output went up and the new husbandry spread faster than ever in Norfolk. It may be suggested that this was the result of a perverse reaction to lower prices. Faced with falling prices but with the costs in arable farming incurred well ahead of selling, farmers would find their incomes squeezed. The light-land men were the most likely to react to this situation by increasing output. On the light lands, the fixed, inescapable costs imposed by high rents on long leases (instead of the annual agreements and low rents of the clay-land open-field farms) and by the hiring of a high proportion of the labour input were greater than on the small wheat-and-bean farms of the clays. Costs were therefore 'sticky', and although in the long run technical innovation would reduce them and maintain profit margins, in the short run there were certain to be adjustment difficulties. Variable costs could not be cut down fast enough. The burden was to some extent thrown on to the landlord in the form of high arrears of rents, and in the long run it was eased by cost-reducing, yield-raising innovation, most of all on the light lands. The possibilities of cutting unit costs of production by introducing the new fodder crops and associated husbandry regimes were greater on the light soils than on the clays. Thus the price–cost squeeze on the light soils was most intense (the clay-land owner-occupier may at times have retreated into subsistence) and the prospects of eventual repayment for innovation, in the form of higher rents or at least by abolished rent arrears, were brightest. Certainly higher rents were sometimes a condition of the landowner's outlay on capital items on light-land farms – as an illustration, forty pounds was 'allowed towards building a New Rickhouse 1738 as per Agreement on Farmer Morgans taking an advanced Rent' on a farm at

[1] John (cited in n. 1, on p. 153), p. 147.

Broughton, Hampshire.[1] And light-land farmers were willing to turn to the new crops specifically as a way out of their dilemma: for instance, in 1745 a farmer at Stoke Charity on the Hampshire chalk attempted to extricate himself from financial entanglements with his landlord by proposing to sow large acreages of 'Cinque Foyle' in future years.[2]

Combining our explanations, some of the agricultural development of the period may be attributed to the rhythms of the landlord–tenant system and to the growing social motives for the ownership of agricultural estates, and some of it to the disparate technical and cost situations of light-land and heavy-land farmers. Light-land farmers, during the prolonged, gentle deflation of cereal prices, were persuaded or obliged to exploit their opportunities of taking a larger share of the market. During the sharper falls in agricultural prices, they inclined more energetically to expand their output to protect their incomes. This response was what the nineteenth century was to call high farming. In the first half of the eighteenth century, agriculture was even less free to contract if faced with a fall in prices than during the nineteenth century, since in a pre-industrial society there were comparatively few attractive alternative occupations, although there was a gradual drift of labourers into framework knitting and, as Arthur John shows below, into certain towns. A land-use inversion between the uplands and the vales lasting fifty or one hundred years was not, in the circumstances, a particularly sluggish adjustment. It is possible that the rise in national cereal output to be expected from the breaking up of new land could be held in check by a much more limited grassing down of the clays; for, after an initial spurt of fertility, yields per acre on the light lands were usually lower than in the vales. But there does seem to have been some pressure of excessive production because of the inability of resources to flow freely out of clay-land agriculture.

[1] Jones, *Agricultural History Review*, VIII, No. 1, p. 9, quoting Nottingham University Archives, Manvers Collection, Rentals.

[2] Ibid., p. 9, citing Stoke Charity Papers, Hampshire Record Office: 18M54/Box E, pkt. A.

IV

What might the implications of this analysis be for the totals of agricultural investment and income? As regards investment, the scraps of evidence at hand do not point to striking changes in aggregate levels. Instead of producing more when his income was squeezed, the small clay-land owner-occupier may merely have worked harder himself to avoid buying inputs or hiring labour (he was, after all, likely to be under-employed much of the year), and to that extent cash spending on inputs may have fallen. But on larger holdings where labour-intensive fodder crops replaced a grain course or permanent pasture there was presumably a net increase in employment. On the light lands, farmers seem to have invested more vigorously in improved techniques in attempts to extricate themselves from the price–cost squeeze. And landowners certainly in many cases stepped up their agricultural investment during the 1730s and 1740s. The tentative conclusion (which is all that can be drawn) is that total investment, on balance, probably went up by some modest proportion.

When it comes to assessing changes in total agricultural income, we are making bricks quite without straw. I suggest as a working hypothesis that during the late seventeenth and early eighteenth centuries as a whole, when the small farmers of arable clay land were often embarrassed, any fall in their incomes may have been offset by the gains of the more successful innovators, predominantly light-land men. This perhaps implies the concentration of income in fewer hands, with implications for the ratio of basic to luxury goods purchased. During the 1730s and 1740s, total agricultural income may have dropped, for there were spells when on both heavy and light lands rents fell and farmers were in distress. Yet, as far as spending by agriculturists on the products of an incipient industrial economy is concerned, it has yet to be shown that this in itself had enormously depressing consequences. The period saw a sharper phase of the secular shift in resources and distributions in agriculture, whereby the clays tended to go down to grass and the light lands to be converted to tillage, with concomitant expenditures on new building, floating meadows, paring and burning the grass downs prior to their cultivation, and so forth. These undertakings were primarily located on the light lands, whereas during the third quarter of the eighteenth century, when grain prices were rising, landowner investment may have been lower on the light lands,[1] concentrating instead on Parliamentary enclosure (perhaps an attempt to create in the jumbled open fields of central England the physical setting of an improved agriculture which had earlier and more readily been provided on the empty sheep downs of the light soils) and on transplanting Norfolk-type rotations *en bloc* to less developed regions like Scotland. But the income generated by the undertakings of the second quarter of the century may have balanced any fall at that time in the purchase of consumer goods by the farm sector. In addition, most big landowners could bear their part in such enterprises from non-agricultural funds and without foregoing conspicuous forms of consumption. The checks and balances of landlord and tenant and of the two dominant groups of farming system, therefore, tended to circumscribe a fall in total investment or income.[2]

Any net decline in consumption in the farm sector might be expected to have been offset by the surplus real income created among the buyers of food, although the gain in income for the consumers of a cheaper loaf was spent partly on white bread as a replacement for rye bread, partly on more meat, partly on tea

[1] See Naish, *passim.*

[2] English experience contrasts sharply with that of Europe, where the fall in population and depression in agriculture were very severe. This is of particular consequence with respect to the Low Countries, which had formerly been ahead of England in agricultural techniques but which failed to respond so energetically (or perversely) to the fall in prices. In the reclaimed areas of Holland, the drainage network remained a fixed charge on agriculture when farm-product prices were falling. The status of landowning was lower than in England (seignorial rights could be acquired without buying land) and did not attract investment in the same way. And when returns from agriculture fell after 1650, the one hundred or so Amsterdam merchants who owned land in the Beemster, North Holland – the reclamation of which they had financed – quit their estates and retreated to the city. On the European experience, see B. H. Slicher van Bath, *The Agrarian History of Western Europe, A.D. 500–1850* (London: Arnold, 1963), pp. 206–20. I am also indebted to that author for a typescript of his lecture, 'Die Europaischen Agrarverhältnisse im 17. und der ersten Hälfte des 18. Jarhhunderts', and to Drs A. M. van der Woude for showing me the Beemster.

and sugar, partly on gin, and some of it surely was taken out in increased leisure. The second quarter century was not unreasonably described as a 'golden age' for the labouring man.

Within agricultural production, systems were being regrouped, however much subsequent periods of high grain prices might rejuvenate clay-land arable farming and thus, temporarily, put the clock back. But by comparison with later periods (though not with earlier ones) resources were still choked up in agriculture as a whole. This, together with the near stagnation of population growth, meant that the rise in purchasing power brought by cheaper food was not yet strong enough to throw down the final barriers against large-scale industrial expansion. This was to come in the third and fourth quarters of the century, when prices rose because a long run of inclement weather depressed yields and (rather later) when the growth of population extended the market. At that time the upsurges of investment and income in agriculture seem to have swamped any damage done to expansion elsewhere in the economy by higher food prices.

7 Agricultural Productivity and Economic Growth in England 1700–1760[1]

A. H. JOHN

[This article was first published in *The Journal of Economic History*, Vol. XXV (1965), and a postscript was added in March 1967.]

The rise in productivity described by Dr Jones, coupled with a static population, brought to an end the upward movement in the relative prices of farm products which had characterized the one hundred and forty years preceding the Restoration. With the passing of the lean years, there followed almost a century of comparative plenty, bringing an increasing flow of food and raw materials.

The most pronounced fall in prices occurred in grains; and within this category, wheat and barley were more affected than oats. In 1717–24, and again in the 1730s and 1740s, wheat prices – at least over southern England – were between 25 and 33 per cent lower than the average level for the decade 1660–69. The value of animal products, on the other hand, showed less change. The prices of butter and cheese supplied to St Bartholomew's and St Thomas's hospitals, London, although there are minor fluctuations, were remarkably stable between 1680 and 1740; and except for some short periods, notably in the 1730s, so also were those of meat and tallow. This is to some extent what might be expected from the fact that bread, meat, and dairy produce are complementary foods; a fall in the

[1] This is a revised version of a paper given at the Joint Conference of the Economic History Society and the British Agricultural History Society at Reading, 1964, where I was asked to elaborate the views I expressed in 'Aspects of English Economic Growth in the First Half of the 18th Century', *Economica*, May 1961.

price of bread, then the major element in the diets of most people, would tend to increase the demand for other and more expensive items. Wool prices moved about a great deal more. The earliest series available to me begin in 1716, when prices appear to have been high: a fall occurs between 1723 and 1725, followed by a recovery into the early 1730s, then a second fall until 1742. During the next decade, wool prices were extremely high, only to collapse again between the autumn of 1752 and 1758. The position may thus be roughly summarized as a long period of declining grain prices, broken only by bad harvests, and of relatively stable (and higher) prices for animal products, interrupted by short periods of glut or by occasional shortages caused by animal disease.

The first consequence of this situation arises from the cheapening of bread grains. Because these entered very largely into the diet of most groups in society, a fall in their prices lowered the cost of living and so raised *per capita* real incomes; and in some parts of the country this gain was enhanced by rising money wages. It is improbable that milling and baking margins rose sufficiently to offset these advantages, and some evidence for this is seen in prices of the quartern loaf determined by the London Assize of Bread. Pursuing this analysis further, buyers of grain or grain products benefited more than the producers, and those for whom bread comprised a very large element of expenditure more than others. There was, therefore, a shift of income in favour of persons other than farmers and also in favour of the poorer groups in society. In this way, income tended to move into the hands of people who, through habit and/or necessity, were more likely to spend than to hoard; and the gains were likely to be geographically widely diffused.

These beneficial effects of cheap bread have been widely recognized by economists and were a household concept among nineteenth-century economic journalists. According to the *Economist* of 10 April 1875, for example, 'We may safely say that there has been a clear gain to the nation of over a million a month in consequence of last year's good harvest; and the gain to the masses of consumers, reckoning the saving in price of home as well as foreign produce consumed, must be reckoned at a larger sum. Possibly this saving has something to do with the steady increase in the quantities of tea and sugar consumed, and anyone can see that it enables the masses to spend more on other articles than necessaries, and neutralizes a considerable fall in wages.'[1] This is essentially the accepted explanation of the rise in real incomes in the last quarter of the nineteenth century; yet the doctrine seems to have evoked far less support among historians of the earlier period, and this for two broad reasons.

Lower grain prices, it is argued, reduced the income of farmers and, through failure of many tenants to pay full rents, that of landowners. In this way, the purchasing power of a major section of the economy was curtailed and this counter-balanced the gains to others. Dr Jones has broadly decided against such an interpretation and has tentatively concluded that 'total investment, on balance, probably went up by some modest proportion in agriculture'. I agree with this view if only because it takes account of regional differences in prosperity arising in part from the diversity of systems of farming and in part from the effect of technical innovation. It is, how-ever, worth emphasizing the very considerable rise in the animal population on English farms, especially in the numbers of sheep. To the evidence which Dr Jones has adduced on this point, other examples can be added. According to one scholar, the size of sheep flocks on the Yorkshire wolds doubled be-tween 1700 and 1743;[2] at Castle Donnington in 1738, the 490 acres of 'Beast Pasture' carried 4,705 sheep in addition to cattle, and it was agreed to stint the former by half and the cattle by a quarter;[3] while at the mid-century, Lincolnshire farmers claimed that they 'had of late years been at great ex-pense and trouble in improving the breed of sheep'.[4] This evi-dence certainly suggests that large groups of farmers were in-creasing their capital stock and that the greater traffic in lambs,

---

[1] *Economist*, 10 April 1875, p. 423.
[2] A. H. Harris, *The Rural Landscape of the East Riding of Yorkshire, 1700–1850* (London: Oxford University Press, 1961), p. 32.
[3] Great Britain, *Journal of the House of Commons*, XXIII (1737–41), p. 56.
[4] Ibid., XXVI (1750–54), p. 410.

as well as in lean and fat stock, made a substantial contribution to the growth of inland trade. Thus, while there may have been short runs of years when large sectors of farming found times difficult, over the period as a whole there seems no reason to believe that the gains of innovation were at the expense of the farming community.

The second objection rests on the belief that a significant part of increased real incomes was taken in the form of leisure rather than in increased consumption. There were doubtless many who had a high leisure preference, but it is equally true that these were most frequently to be found among the poorer and least-skilled sections of the community. But even here, there were factors which limited the economic effects of this tendency. In the first place, the age structure of the population meant that a substantial part of the labour force comprised either apprentices or indoor servants, and for these the chances of idling were more limited than for the outdoor worker. In 1696, for example, there were in the parish of Clayworth, Nottinghamshire, sixty-one indoor servants – half of them male – compared with twenty-four outdoor labourers.[1] It seems that it was only out of what can be called overtime earnings that apprentices could buy clothes and other items which appealed to the youth of the time. Secondly, preference for leisure was countered by sharp increases in wages during the seasonal rushes of work which were so marked a feature of pre-industrial economies. There was a considerable difference between summer and winter wage rates in agriculture; London tailors were paid 25 per cent more during March and June than during the rest of the year;[2] London shipwrights received double wages when required to work on Sundays.[3] In this way, when work was required to be done, leisure was made more expensive and so less attractive. Thirdly, there is evidence of a good deal of migration, both seasonal and permanent, to areas of growing activity, suggesting that expanding sectors, whether in

---

[1] H. Gill and E. L. Guilford, *The Rector's Book, Clayworth, Notts.* (Nottingham, 1910), pp. 84–7.

[2] Great Britain, *Journal of the House of Commons*, XXVI (1750–54), p. 377.

[3] J. C. Fox (ed.), 'The Official Diary of Lieutenant General Adam Williamson', *Camden Society*, 3rd series, XXII (1912), p. 102.

agriculture or industry, obtained at least part of their additional labour requirements. It is hardly likely, therefore, that the existence of a high leisure preference was powerful enough to be anything more than a limiting factor on the increased demand liberated by cheap food.

For these reasons, neither objection to the dynamic effects of increased agricultural productivity upon the domestic market is very convincing. And, in fact, there is much positive evidence for the growing consumption of what the *Economist* called 'other articles than necessaries'. Tea, sugar, tobacco – even gin – can be cited in support of this contention; so also can the widening range of manufactures. Printed calicoes, so it was claimed at the beginning of the century, were so generally worn by female servants that gentlemen distinguished their 'wives from their chambermaids' with difficulty.[1] Irish linen imports – 'chiefly for the wear of the common people'[2] – rose from 299,992 yards in 1700 to 6,400,000 yards in 1740,[3] and although retained imports of German linens grew more slowly, they reached 23,500,000 yards in 1738–39 and 24,740,000 in 1747–48.[4] Despite these large supplies, the domestic market was sufficiently buoyant to permit a notable growth of English linen and 'cotton' production during the first half of the eighteenth century. Petitions to Parliament and evidence given to Parliamentary committees are virtually unanimous on this expansion, while trade figures and other evidence show that exports played a minor role before 1740. Development during the second quarter of the century was marked. Not only was there a substantial growth of Manchester, but during the thirties the price of Scottish linen yarns rose by 12 per cent, partly because of exports to England 'to be wrought up into Cottons'.[5] Imports of Irish yarn were 20 'trusses' more in

---

[1] P. J. Thomas, 'The Beginnings of Calico Printing in England', *The English Historical Review*, xxxix (April 1924), p. 207.

[2] British Museum, Add., 21134, f. 2, quoted in L. M. Cullen, 'Anglo-Irish Trade, 1660–1800' (unpublished thesis, University of London, 1959), p. 91.

[3] Ibid., p. 86.

[4] Great Britain, Parliamentary Papers (*Reports from Committees of the House of Commons*, 1738–65, Vol. II), p. 301. (Hereafter cited as *Reports.*)

[5] Ibid., p. 312.

1750 than in 1746, 'occasioned', according to Samuel Touchet, 'by new branches for home consumption'.[1] Exports also consumed a small proportion of the English linen output before 1740, partly because the cloth was too coarse compared with the products of the great European industry. Foreign shipments certainly rise after this date, to some extent at least because of the need to clothe British soldiers abroad and to provide sailcloth for the British fleets.

Again, it was conceded by those who clamoured for protection against imports of American pig iron, that iron was increasingly being used in the 'common concerns of life'.[2] The rise of bar-iron imports from an average of 16,000 tons annually in 1710–19 to 25,000 tons in the thirties, owed something to exports but much more to the growth of the home market. Consider the development of the furniture trade and some of its more important implications. Quite apart from the demand for woodworkers and timber, 'the manufacture of articles of cabinet brass foundry lay at the root of the brass trade in Birmingham', according to Timmins – and this was destined to become one of the major industries of that great metal fabricating centre.[3] Furniture upholstery had always been an important factor in the growth of both silks and 'cottons', but so great was the fashion by 1750 that a third of the Manchester check weavers were engaged on fabrics for this purpose.[4]

One further example may be cited. Between 1715 and 1745, exports of pottery and glassware rose by about 25 per cent. There was an enormous increase in foreign sales in the post-war boom of 1748–52, followed by an equally sharp fall. What proportion of the increasing exports before 1744 came from Staffordshire is not known, but whatever its rise it could hardly have been responsible for the tenfold increase which is reputed to have occurred in the number of kilns making stoneware

[1] *Reports*, p. 290.
[2] Great Britain, *Journal of the House of Commons*, XXIII (1737–41), p. 110.
[3] S. Timmins (ed.), *Birmingham and the Midland Hardware District* (London, 1866), p. 275.
[4] *Reports*, p. 291.

between 1700 and 1750.[1] Here, if anywhere, can be seen
the consequence of cheap living and some indication of the
social depth of demand. For it was possible in the thirties and
forties to buy cups and saucers at 1½*d.* a set and beer-drinking
mugs at the same price.[2] By the mid-century, too, the demonstration effect of porcelain in the houses of the rich encouraged
Ralph Wood of Burslem and other potters to make 'clay
figures in great variety, cheap enough to find a place in the
houses of farmers and cottagers'.[3] The improvements of Elers,
Astbury, and others during the first half of the century led to
the use of Dorset and Devon clays and Chiltern flints, as well
as to a greater consumption of salt, lead, and coal; and both
made greater demands on transport. The period, too, saw the
introduction of the lathe and water-driven grinding mill into
pottery manufacture. It was in this small but growing centre
of industrialism that Brindley was trained as a millwright before
making his name as a builder of canals.

This evidence is sufficient to support the case that many of
the growth points of the economy stemmed from a buoyant
home market. This does not, of course, exclude the operations
of other factors such as foreign trade or import substitution.
But the argument does assert the vital significance of the demand released by increased agricultural productivity. And this
in turn meant a greater demand for building, transport, and
items of simple capital equipment.

Given the technical and financial resources of early
eighteenth-century England, increases in real income as a
consequence of a rise in agricultural productivity, far from
slowing down growth, had their own special contribution to
make to it. The buoyancy of the domestic market, compared
with conditions abroad, provided a favourable environment for
the introduction of new kinds of goods and the improvement of techniques which encouraged import substitution.
Cheap crockery, japanned wares, lace, Sheffield plate, the ex-

[1] For a summary of developments in the pottery industry, see A. and N. Clow,
The Chemical Revolution (London: Batchworth Press, 1952), pp. 306–8.

[2] R. E. Leader, *The History of the Company of Cutlers in Hallamshire in the County
of York* (Sheffield, 1905–6), II, p. 186.

[3] Bernard Rackham, *Early Staffordshire Pottery* (London: Faber, 1951), p. 37.

pansion of the copper and brass industries, the making of cheap mixed fabrics and their printing illustrate these points. Side by side with new products went qualitative changes in furniture and other articles. 'One pair of some sorts of shoes now made,' it was said, 'is better than two or three pairs made formerly. The work is different and that which was done 40 years ago would now be condemned.'[1] These changes permanently affected the structure of demand by increasing its social depth, thus changing levels of expectation among a widening range of people. F. J. Fisher has shown that this was already under way in the seventeenth century,[2] but a further fifty years of cheap food deepened its impact. The growing responsiveness of the home market encouraged manufacturers to be inventive and to direct production towards cheapness, as fashion ceased to be the sole prerogative of the rich. Nor should the effect of these influences be considered simply on class lines: no group, for example, was more exposed to them than indoor servants, who formed a large element of the working force. The line of causation runs from growth to trade, since many of the products developed on the home market later helped to expand foreign trade.

The increasing volume of agricultural output, coinciding as it did with the disruption of Danzig grain supplies, also had an effect upon England's external economic position. The total quantities of corn exported rose from 2·8 million quarters in the decade 1700–9 to over 6 million in the forties and fifties and maintained this level during the early years of the sixties.[3] According to Mrs E. B. Schumpeter, unprocessed agricultural products accounted for 4·6 per cent of English manufacture exports in terms of official values in 1700, 11·8 per cent in 1725, and 22·2 per cent in the peak year 1750.[4] These last figures exaggerate the overall importance of agricultural products in the structure of trade, because both 1725 and 1750

[1] Great Britain, *Journal of the House of Commons*, xxiii (1737–41), p. 181.
[2] 'The Sixteenth and Seventeenth Centuries: The Dark Ages in English Economic History', *Economica*, New Series, xxiv (February 1957).
[3] J. Marshall, *A Digest of All Accounts* (London, 1833), ii, p. 88.
[4] R. E. Boody, 'Trade Statistics and Cycles in England, 1697–1825' (unpublished thesis, Radcliffe College, 1934).

were years of dearth in important parts of Europe; but there can be no doubt about the upward trend in such exports. This development meant more work at home and, by providing a bulk outward cargo, the more efficient use of British shipping. Above all, it gave an extra command over foreign currency at a time when European markets for British manufactures were sluggish. According to the Procureur-Général of the Breton Parliament, for example, France alone paid 10·5 million *livres* for British grain in 1748–50.[1] Money earned in this way could be used by means of the European money market to offset debts incurred with other countries.

It may be observed in passing that, if export figures are to be used as an indicator of industrial activity in its narrow sense, they should be figures which are net of unprocessed farm produce. Some approximation in this respect can be obtained from the totals given by Mrs Schumpeter in No. 12 of her tables.[2] These suggest that after a post-war boom in 1714–17 there ensued a fall in industrial exports which lasted until the end of the twenties. Recovery occurred in the next decades, when exports reached (and slightly surpassed) the levels attained in the earlier post-war boom, sinking somewhat in the war which followed, to rise sharply after 1748. Two comments may be made here. Although there was no marked increase in industrial exports between 1714 and 1748, there are reasons for thinking that England's current account in foreign trade showed a surplus. Grain shipments, re-exports, invisible items, and favourable terms of trade all contributed to maintain the inward flow of imports. The recovery in the 1730s was largely due to improved foreign sales of woollen cloth, which is one reason for the high level of activity in the West Riding. One recent work on this area in fact suggests 1729–51 (with 1698–1709 and 1769–72) as one of the major periods of growth of the Yorkshire industry before the last decades of the century.[3] Secondly, the high level of foreign trade in 1748–52 was not

[1] G. S. Keith, *Tracts on the Corn Laws of Great Britain* (London, 1792), p. 220.
[2] E. B. Schumpeter, *English Overseas Trade Statistics, 1697–1808* (Oxford: Oxford University Press, 1960), pp. 35–8.
[3] R. G. Wilson, 'The Merchants of Leeds' (unpublished thesis, University of Leeds, 1964).

limited to England and her possessions overseas but seems to have formed part of a spasm of growth which affected the commerce of Western Europe.[1] The development of internal trade which followed from these changes inevitably affected distribution and transport. One gets the impression that there were few large villages – let alone towns – without a shop or two by the mid-eighteenth century; and this, with other developments, led to an increased number of middle-men. There was, too, a growing demand for transport facilities, which in some towns was already involving the now familiar process of demolition and rebuilding. This was not simply a matter of a growing volume of products to be carried but also an increase in long-distance haulage as the domestic market expanded and industry changed its location. Cotton, for example, imported at London needed to be transported to Lancashire; millions of yards of mixed fabrics were carried back to the capital to be printed and then distributed over the country. The fact that the demand for transport tended to press upon supply is reflected in such evidence as we have about charges. Water carriage from London to Abingdon was stated to be 10*s*. a ton in 1719,[2] 15*s*. in 1729, and 18*s*. in 1739,[3] while the cost of land carriage between Birmingham, Leicester, Sheffield, and London is said to have doubled between 1700 and 1729.[4] Further research might well reveal the emergence of large firms in the business of inland transport during these years.

Such pressure helps to explain the growing amount of legislation on transport facilities. Gross numbers of turnpike and river improvement acts are indifferent indicators of investment activity for a variety of reasons. The timing of the actual investment is uncertain, and many of the measures were

[1] The pattern suggested by the available French statistics, for example (annual averages of imports and exports in million *livres*), in 1733–35, 277·5; 1736–39, 361; 1740–46, 430·1; 1749–56, 616·7; and 1756–63, 323·5. E. Levasseur, *Histoire du Commerce de la France* (Paris: Librarie Nouvelle de Droit et de Jurisprudence, 1911), I, p. 512.

[2] Great Britain, *Journal of the House of Commons*, XXI (1727–32), p. 417.

[3] T. S. Willan, *River Navigation in England, 1600–1750* (London: Oxford University Press, 1936), p. 119.

[4] Great Britain, *Journal of the House of Commons*, XXI (1727–32), p. 486.

N

concerned with renewals or changes of powers. In the case of turnpike legislation, there is an additional difficulty in that many of the early bills deal with road systems and not, as later, with relatively short stretches of highway. Nevertheless, the volume of legislation can safely be regarded as a measure of the interest in the problem, and in this respect the second quarter of the century is something of a turning point. There were 37 turnpike acts between 1700 and 1719; 64 in the decade which followed; 41 in 1730–39; and 55 in 1740–49. Between 1700 and 1750 there were some 46 river improvement acts, four-fifths of which fall between 1720 and 1740. Nor were attempts to improve matters limited to the provision of better roads and waterways. Horses increasingly replaced men in the hauling of barges, enabling them to be pulled in groups rather than singly. On the Great Ouze, at least, the size of lighters had been trebled by the early forties, to match the larger coasting vessels then in use on this side of the country.[1]

But problems of transport might well have become even more pressing had not horses and horse-keep been cheap. These are major cost items whose significance has not been properly appreciated. 'The excessive price of barley,' wrote a merchant from Cadiz in September 1765, 'has put a stop to all land carriage in Spain'.[2] Nothing as drastic as this happened in England, but the upward movement of agricultural prices after 1750 is important in explaining the greater investment in roads and canals. 'Whereas the carriers from this town to London,' it was announced in Birmingham, 'cannot carry so much by one third of the weight as they aforetime have done upon the account of the badness of the roads, and badness of hay, and likewise such a rise upon Horsecorn, that the carriage will not defray their expenses, except there be an advance; which will be general withall from Monday, 17th instant of October, 1763.'[3] More expensive land transport encouraged the search

---

[1] Great Britain, *Journal of the House of Commons*, xxv (1745–50), p. 787.
[2] Great Britain, Public Record Office, C/109/1. William Dalrymple to Miles Nightingale. Letter dated 10 September 1765.
[3] J. A. Langford, *A Century of Birmingham Life* (Birmingham, 1868), I, p. 114. See also Edward Hughes, *North Country Life in the Eighteenth Century* (London: Oxford University Press, 1952), p. 255.

for alternatives, and not merely in the form of water transport. Expensive horses and horse-keep are regarded as being instrumental in timing the appearance of successful steam locomotion on the Northumberland coalfield during the Napoleonic war.[1] Because of the wide areas over which raw materials were distributed, these factors may well have encouraged the adoption of machinery in spinning to a greater extent than in weaving; and certainly they help to explain the integration of farming with industry in most of the big concerns which emerged in the cotton and iron industries towards the end of the century.

Developments in transport, distribution, and industry must have increased the demand for labour and so exercised some influence on the upward trend of wage rates which characterized areas of growth during these years. Mrs Gilboy's figures are well-known: day wages in Lancashire rose from 8*d*. in 1700 to 12*d*. in 1750 and in London from 20*d*. to 24*d*.[2] Increases similar to those in Lancashire must have occurred across the Pennines, where lightermen on the River Don earned 14*d*., 16*d*., or 18*d*. daily in 1739.[3] It was upon the skilled workman – the key figure of contemporary industry – that, in particular, the greatest pressure fell. Continuous statistics are scanty, but the fragments existing for London suggest that clothworkers, tailors, bakers, and watermen, with the building craftsmen, were some of the groups getting higher pay by the end of the twenties. William Smith, master shoemaker, stated in 1737 that the wages of journeymen in his trade had advanced 'although there are a greater number of hands than formerly'. He paid 22*d*. for work he would formerly have had done for 15*d*. or 16*d*.[4] The person who wrote in 1734 that 'wages are vastly high' was thus accurately reflecting the current position.[5]

[1] L. T. C. Rolt, *George and Robert Stephenson* (London: Longmans, 1960), pp. 43–4.

[2] Quoted in T. S. Ashton, *An Economic History of England: the Eighteenth Century* (London: Methuen, 1955), p. 232.

[3] Great Britain, *Journal of the House of Commons*, XXIII (1737–41), p. 494.

[4] Ibid., p. 180.

[5] Great Britain, Public Record Office, C/103/131. Alexander Hume to Thomas Hall. Letter dated 9 August 1734.

In turn, the demand for labour in the industrial and transport sectors involved some redistribution of the labour force between farm and non-farm work; and this was facilitated, at a time of relatively stable population, by the rise in agricultural productivity. This shift was achieved in a variety of ways. There may well have been an increase in the volume of seasonal migrations into some industrial areas, as in the case of labourers into Newcastle upon Tyne to load coal during the shipping months.[1] Expensive adult labour probably meant an increased demand for female and child labour, whether as apprentices or not. As the Nottingham stockingers explained to Parliament, they employed 'persons not free' of the Framework Knitters Company, 'Women and Children, in common with their Neighbours; and if that were not the Practice, it would be very injurious to Trade as Hose are made as low priced as 1½*d*. a Pair, in which Branch of Trade no Person will work who has served an Apprenticeship of Seven Years.'[2] To some extent, at least, this involved the extension of part-time industrial activities in the countryside. Finally, the industrial demand for labour was met by permanent migration from the countryside to the town. London, of course, exercised the greatest pull; but other industrial centres like Birmingham, Sheffield, and Manchester also attracted their quota. Of the '29 recruits signed on by Captain John Robins in Wolverhampton' to defend the town against the Pretender, almost two-thirds had been born elsewhere, though all but two were locksmiths, filecutters, or chainmakers.[3] Much the same pattern is seen at Sheffield, where the number of apprentices rose from 50 in 1700, to 153 in 1735, to 400 in 1750;[4] while according to Miss E. Meteyard, the growth of the North Staffordshire potteries was such between 1735 and 1760 that 'it was difficult for the agriculturalist of the surrounding country and the tradesmen of the adjacent villages to meet with workmen and boys for apprenticeships'.[5]

[1] Hughes, p. 252.
[2] Great Britain, *Journal of the House of Commons*, xxvi (1750–54), p. 781.
[3] D. B. M. Huffer, 'The Economic Development of Wolverhampton, 1750–1850' (unpublished thesis, University of London, 1958).
[4] G. I. H. Lloyd, *The Cutlery Trades* (London: Longmans, 1913), pp. 154–7.
[5] *Life of Josiah Wedgwood* (London: 1865–66), I, p. 153.

It is feasible that this pressure may have been reflected in the revived growth of population; but what it certainly did was to broaden the industrial base of the economy, so providing a greater reservoir of both skill and entrepreneurship.

In the case of some products, the higher costs caused by rising wage rates were passed on to the consumer. Hide leather, for example, was 9½*d.* a pound in London in the early twenties and 11*d.* by 1737, which with higher wages meant more expensive footwear.[1] London-made bricks had risen in price by 1725 as had lead by the early thirties, so that building had also become more costly.[2] But more important was the fact that an increasing range of goods was being made by relatively cheap labour in the west and north, outside the older settled areas of southern England. It is this, together with the greater use of coal, which led to a more rapid change in the location of industry in the first half of the century and at the same time laid more firmly the basis of a national market. The same principle explains in a measure the continued import of manufactured and semi-manufactured goods – linens and linen yarn from Scotland, Ireland, and the Continent, and bar-iron from the Baltic. But the growing skill of the workers in the north and west of the country was tantamount to an increase in the productivity of labour as a whole. As long as labour in these developing areas remained fairly cheap, labour-saving devices such as the fly shuttle, the gig mill, and the warping mill, although in use, were only slowly adopted. It was when costs and prices altered in a drastic way during the late fifties and sixties that the way was open for more radical changes.

Finally, rising real incomes encouraged the saving necessary for capital formation. Favourable terms of trade increased affluence, especially in the growing industrial centres, which coincided with a willingness of people to use these small accumulations productively. In this way, the financing of new looms, workshops, and transport improvements, together with the discounting of bills, was done by a web of lending

[1] Great Britain, *Journal of the House of Commons*, XXIII (1737–41), pp. 180–1.
[2] St Bartholomew's Hospital Records, London.

either directly to manufacturers or through channels established by social intercourse. In Lancashire, according to Wadsworth and Mann, 'Merchants and manufacturers . . . were able to draw on the savings of their neighbours by borrowing money at interest. This form of investment is met with at all points in commerce and industry.'[1] In Birmingham, said Hutton, 'About every tenth trader was a banker or retailer of cash. At the head of these was marshalled the whole train of drapers and grocers.'[2] In Yorkshire, a third of the capital in the Don Navigation Company, formed in 1732, was subscribed by clergymen, shopkeepers, and a carpenter, even though each share cost £55.[3] These local pools of capital were an important source of strength in the early stages of development. Banking was merely an institutional form of a long-established practice: and further research may well show that the significance of reinvested profits in the financing of British industry has been overemphasized to the detriment of the immense amount of lending in each of these local capital markets. What is clear, however, is that there was never any problem of transferring the gains of increased agricultural productivity to the industrial sector.

II

The changes described by Dr Jones are therefore of great significance in understanding economic growth in eighteenth-century England. In advancing this case, it has been argued that the years from 1725 to 1750 were not, on the whole, years of stagnation. It is, among other things, necessary to establish this in order to get the rise in exports during the fifties into perspective. For if the second quarter of the century was broadly one of activity, then it is not improbable that the surge in foreign trade after 1748 was, to some extent, achieved by a transfer of output from the home to the foreign market and that, consequently, export figures in the fifties exaggerate in

---

[1] A. P. Wadsworth and J. de L. Mann, *The Cotton Trade and Industrial Lancashire, 1600–1780* (Manchester: University of Manchester, 1931), p. 249.

[2] W. Hutton, *The History of Birmingham* (London, 1834), p. 201.

[3] Leader, II, p. 171.

some measure the growth in total production, as, for reasons already given, they underestimate it in earlier decades.

Pieces of evidence exist which, if not conclusive, are consistent with such an interpretation. The inter-war years, and especially 1749 to 1751 (inclusive), saw a remarkable rise in import prices. Plantation cotton, which had cost 8*d.*–9*d.* in the thirties and 11*d.*–12*d.* in 1742–43, reached 24*d.* in 1750–52 and was still 18*d.* a pound in 1754. The prices of Levant cotton also roughly doubled between 1735 and 1750. Imported German linen yarn (6 pounds a bushel) had increased from 10½*d.* a pound in 1739 to 12*d.* in 1747–50,[1] and that from Ireland to an even greater extent. The average price paid by the East India Company for Swedish bar-iron during the War of the Austrian Succession was approximately £12 a ton; in 1748–55, £13 7*s.*; and in the four years 1756–59, £16 8*s.*[2] The value of Muscovado sugar dropped slightly with the return of peace in 1748 but recovered in and after 1753;[3] while imported Bolonia silk rose 30 per cent in price in 1749.[4] Most dramatic of all was the change in the value of gum Senegal, a small but essential import. This rose from 31*s.* a hundredweight in 1743 to 55*s.* in September 1749, 117*s.* 6*d.* in 1750, and to over 200*s.* in the early months of 1753.[5] Because the prices of manufactured articles are unlikely to have increased as quickly as raw materials, terms of trade must have become markedly adverse. Part of the additional cost of imports was met by the exceptionally heavy grain shipments up to 1751; re-exports may have made a contribution although, as far as can be judged, their volume was steady; but manufactured exports increased considerably. Even so, 'the rates of exchange moved sharply against Britain immediately the war was over in April 1748. They were exceptionally low from the Autumn of 1752

---

[1] British Museum, Add. 38342, ff. 232–6; Wadsworth and Mann, p. 155; *Reports*, pp. 289–316.

[2] Great Britain, Commonwealth Relations Office, *East India Company Records. General Ledgers.*

[3] R. B. Sheridan, 'The Sugar Trade of the British West Indies, 1660–1756' (unpublished thesis, University of London, 1951), Appendix 1.

[4] Great Britain, *Journal of the House of Commons*, xxv (1745–50), pp. 996–7.

[5] Ibid., xxvi (1750–54), p. 442.

to the Spring of 1754,'[1] aggravated as the position was by the repatriation of some Dutch investments in England and by falls in exports both in 1752 and 1754. 'England,' according to one observer, 'being obliged to pay abroad what balances were against her, specie became so scarce in 1753 and 1754 that at the bankers in London you could scarcely obtain a payment of one hundred pounds in lawful gold coin of the country.'[2] This position must in some measure have been communicated to the provinces; London building certainly seems to have been reduced in 1754. England's external financial position was thus clearly less comfortable than it had been during the preceding quarter of a century.

Domestic consumption held up until 1751, 'when there was a halt in the production of most consumer goods'.[3] From then until the harvest of 1758 was garnered up, the food position at home because steadily worse. A series of bad harvests, beginning in 1751 in the north and west and culminating in the generally disastrous years of 1756 and 1757, as well as the effects of a long period of cattle disease, progressively pushed up food prices and caused sporadic but widespread rioting. At the same time, accelerating population growth was beginning to undermine the strong position which labour had earlier enjoyed. When foreign trade began to increase again in 1756, one contemporary commented, 'A War with France, Trade dead at home, Money scarce, the Poor in great Want':[4] and two years later, Lancashire weavers argued soberly that their real wages were substantially below what they had been twenty years earlier.[5] It was not until 1759 that, with cheap food and a boom in exports, many wage earners were able to press successfully for higher wages, and the domestic market regained in buoyancy.[6] But it was a temporary reprieve. Some-

[1] T. S. Ashton, *Economic Fluctuations in England, 1700–1800* (Oxford: Clarendon Press, 1959), p. 124, n. 43.
[2] J. H. Clapham, *The Bank of England* (Cambridge [Engl.]: University Press, 1944), I, p. 236.
[3] Ashton, *Economic Fluctuations*, p. 148.
[4] T. Short, *A Comparative History of the Increase and Decrease of Mankind in England* (London, 1767), p. 107.
[5] Wadsworth and Mann, pp. 361–9.
[6] Ashton, *Economic Fluctuations*, p. 150.

thing was lost when exports fell in 1762 and more when the harvests again became poor later in the decade.

That the fifties witnessed much economic expansion is clear; but whether the sharp division between the second and third quarters of the century suggested by export figures really existed is far less certain.

POSTSCRIPT

The reprinting of this essay provides me with an opportunity of commenting upon the criticisms of Dr M. W. Flinn in his paper entitled 'Agricultural Productivity and Economic Growth: a Comment' published in the *Journal of Economic History*, Vol. XXVI, March 1966. On the basis of Exeter wheat prices, Dr Flinn argues broadly that the fall was not significant enough to have had an effect on the internal demand for manufactures, especially since some of the 'released' purchasing power might well have been spent on more bread and other forms of foodstuffs. On more general grounds, he questions the validity of the long-run decline in grain prices because 'our knowledge of grain prices is often more restricted than we are prepared to admit'.

As far as the last point is concerned, it is true that historians working in this period could do with more price material; but he greatly exaggerates the lack of evidence. This is certainly more pronounced for the second half of the seventeenth century, although Houghton has a good collection of grain prices for the years 1690–1700. There is, on the other hand, a very considerable amount of material for the first half of the eighteenth century. By far the best evidence for London and some of the other centres in southern England is to be found in J. E. T. Thorold Rogers, *A History of Agriculture and Prices in England*, Vol. 5; and there is much information in the growing number of provincial newspapers during the century, some of which seems to have been extracted by the late Lord Beveridge and his assistants. Further, wheat prices in many of the ports of continental Europe are given in J. Marshall, *A Digest of all the Accounts*. The publication of the Eton,

Winchester, and Exeter figures in B. R. Mitchell and P. Deane, *Abstract of British Historical Statistics*, adds little to what has long been conveniently available.

On the first and major issue, Dr Flinn concedes that 'real income rose most significantly (certainly in the north of England and Scotland) in the first half of the century' and 'that money incomes were also rising in this period'. Nor does he appear to reject the considerable evidence that has been gathered on the growing output and consumption of manufactures during these years. What he denies is the causal relationship between these phenomena and the price of food. If this relationship is ruled out it is difficult to see what other hypothesis can be substituted. Overseas trade made little contribution. The volume of manufactured exports remains virtually stationary between 1708 and 1735. It begins to increase again after this date but in a marked way only after 1748. Favourable terms of trade between 1715 and 1735 certainly helped real wages but this contribution was, of necessity, limited. There were some strategic industrial innovations and a great number of minor ones. But the slight evidence on the prices of manufactures does not suggest a fall sufficient to generate a 'significant' rise in real incomes. The same general considerations apply to the volume of investment. By denying the importance of cheap food, Dr Flinn is forced to accept this kind of explanation which, in fact, jeopardizes his concept of the 'Industrial Revolution' as a post-1783 phenomenon.

Considerations such as these, in my opinion, inevitably suggest a causal relationship between the cost of food, the rise in industrial output, and the demand for labour. Whatever qualifications Dr Flinn may introduce into the explanation of his Exeter wheat prices, they still show what can be fairly called a downward trend. But it is important to realize that it is a mistake, as Dr Flinn seems to envisage, to expect an equal fall in bread-grain prices over the entire country. Imperfect means of transport, differing weather conditions, the pace at which better farming methods were adopted meant the persistence of regional grain prices throughout the early eighteenth century. An attempt was made to show this elsewhere, and a

division between 'an agriculturally active south-eastern region
and a more sluggish western and northern England' was suggested.[1] As far as south-eastern England is concerned, the long
upward trend in grain prices during and after the last quarter
of the sixteenth century reached its peak in the 1660s, and it is
difficult to interpret the next ninety years other than as a 'long-
run decline'. The farinaceous index compiled by Professor
Phelps Brown and Miss Hopkins shows the following decennial
averages:[2]

1630–39	783·0	1700–09	619·7
1640–49	749·5	1710–19	768·4
1650–59	712·0	1720–29	659·7
1660–69	795·2	1730–39	543·8
1670–79	746·8	1740–49	568·7
1680–89	660·2	1750–59	677·3
1690–99	772·0		

The fall in bread-grain prices in southern England was clearly
marked in the 1680s; and the succeeding years were unquestionably characterized by easier living conditions than before
1660 even if broken up by years of dearth.

The long-term fall in bread-grain prices in south-eastern and
parts of south-western England was sufficient in my opinion to
'release' purchasing power for the purchase of manufactures.
The significance of the fall in this area, and particularly the
south-eastern region, lies in the fact that it was by far the
richest part of the nation. London alone may well have
accounted for something of the order of a quarter of the total
national income. The growth of Midland and northern industry was, in great measure, a response to the internal demand released in this area, supported by that elsewhere.[3]
As money wages rose in the Midland and northern regions,
the result of expanding industry, so real incomes began to
rise, even if food prices fell less than in more favoured areas.
This, in turn, reinforced the upward trend.

[1] A. H. John, 'The Course of Agricultural Change', in *Studies in the Industrial Revolution*, L. S. Pressnell (ed.) (London, 1960), p. 141.
[2] I am grateful to Professor E. H. Phelps Brown for permission to use these figures.
[3] A. H. John, 'Aspects of English Economic Growth in the First Half of the Eighteenth Century', *Economica*, May 1967, Section V.

The argument that the demand for manufactures was greatly affected by the use of 'released' purchasing power in the substitution of wheat for coarser bread grains, or for buying other kinds of food, is dubious. Wheaten bread was already well established in southern England by 1700, especially in London; while the poorer groups in the rural areas gained something from ampler gleanings because of better harvests. In Lancashire, for example, the taste for oat and barley bread remained largely unchanged despite a substantial rise in money wages. The greater consumption of meat, milk, butter, cheese – even gin – swelled the incomes of those who produced, distributed, and serviced such products. The manufacture of pots for the carriage of butter, for instance, helped the growth of the Staffordshire potteries. Such larger incomes would almost certainly have been reflected in greater purchases of manufactures. Farmers engaged in animal husbandry also gained from the rise in productivity which resulted from the rapid spread of clover in the grazing areas of southern and parts of central England. Those near Monmouth in the 1690s, for instance, had 'fallen into the vein of clover, and those which kept no kine before now keep some 12, some 20, and they take care that they have two or three pieces of clover under one another, for it holds but three years at most'.[1] The ample evidence that exists on the rise of the number of animals kept on farms during the late seventeenth and early eighteenth centuries, especially sheep, show that this is no exceptional case.

The fall in bread-grain prices was the result partly of long-runs of good weather, partly the impact of better methods of farming. The breakthrough in the development of farming techniques occurred in the second half of the seventeenth century and the newer methods were widely adopted in a piecemeal fashion over southern England by 1700. There is no reason to believe that innovations in agriculture are any less important than those in other sectors of the economy, especially in the early stages of economic development – a fact borne

---

[1] Bodleian MS. Aubrey 2, f. 152 quoted in 'Edward Lluyd and some of his Correspondents', *Transactions of the Honourable Society of Cymmrodorion*, 1965, Part I, p. 82, n. 1.

out by the experience of a variety of countries. As a consequence, it is illogical to note improvements in farming and to omit their dynamic consequences. Sustained growth has in most countries been preceded and accompanied by increasing productivity in agriculture. England was no exception to this almost general rule. The centrality of agricultural change and a dynamic home market to British economic growth needs to be recognized.

Select Bibliography

The following works, additional to those reprinted, are ones which deal extensively with the relations between agriculture and economic change in eighteenth-century England, or some major aspect of this, or express an important point of view on the subject. More general works by development economists are not included, but a good introduction to these may be found in a book of readings by Carl Eicher and Lawrence Witt, *Agriculture in Economic Development* (New York, 1964).

ASHTON. T. S. *The Industrial Revolution 1760–1830* (O.U.P., 1948).
Economic Fluctuations in England 1700–1800 (Oxford, 1959).

CHAMBERS, J. D. 'The Vale of Trent 1670–1800', *The Economic History Review, Supplement III* (1957).

'The Rural Domestic Industries during the period of transition to the Factory System, with special reference to the Midland Counties of England', *Communications*, Second International Conference of Economic History, Aix-en-Provence (1962).

CHAMBERS, J. D., and MINGAY, G. E. *The Agricultural Revolution 1750–1880* (London, 1966).

COLEMAN, D. C. 'Labour in the English Economy of the Seventeenth Century', *The Economic History Review*, 2nd series, VIII (1956).

DEANE, PHYLLIS, and COLE, W. A. *British Economic Growth 1688–1959* (Cambridge University Press, 1962).

DEANE, PHYLLIS. *The First Industrial Revolution* (Cambridge University Press, 1965).

FLINN, M. W. *The Origins of the Industrial Revolution* (London, 1966).

HABAKKUK, H. J. 'Economic Functions of Landowners in the Seventeenth and Eighteenth Centuries', *Explorations in Entrepreneurial History*, VI (1952).

'The English Land Market in the Eighteenth Century', in J. S. Bromley and E. H. Kossman, *Britain and the Netherlands* (London, 1960).

'Historical Experience of Economic Development', in E. A. G. Robinson (ed.), *Problems in Economic Development* (London, 1965).

JOHN, A. H. 'Aspects of English Economic Growth in the First Half of the Eighteenth Century', in E. M. Carus-Wilson (ed.), *Essays in Economic History*, II (1962).

LANDES, DAVID S. 'Technological Change and Industrial Development in Western Europe, 1750–1914', in H. J. Habakkuk and M. Postan (eds.), *The Cambridge Economic History of Europe*, VI (Cambridge University Press, 1965).

MINGAY, G. E. 'The Size of Farms in the Eighteenth Century', *The Economic History Review*, 2nd series, XIV (1961–62).

'The "Agricultural Revolution" in English History: a reconsideration', *Agricultural History*, 37 (1963).

English Landed Society in the Eighteenth Century (London, 1963).

POSTAN, M. M. 'Agricultural Problems of Under-developed Countries in the Light of European Agrarian History', *Communications*, Second International Conference of Economic History, Aix-en-Provence (1962).

PRESSNELL, L. S. *Country Banking in the Industrial Revolution* (Oxford, 1956).

THOMPSON, F. M. L. 'The Social Distribution of Landed Property in England since the Sixteenth Century', *The Economic History Review*, 2nd series, XIX (1966).

WILSON, CHARLES. *England's Apprenticeship 1603–1763* (London, 1965).

YOUNGSON, A. J. *Possibilities of Economic Progress* (Cambridge, 1959).